Design Works

Revised and Expanded Edition

DESIGN WORKS

A Guide to Creating and
Sustaining Value through
Business Design

Revised and Expanded Edition

Heather M.A. Fraser

University of Toronto Press
Toronto   Buffalo   London

© Heather M.A. Fraser 2019
Rotman-UTP Publishing
University of Toronto Press
Toronto   Buffalo   London
utorontopress.com
Printed in the U.S.A.

ISBN 978-1-4875-2290-2

♾ Printed on acid-free paper.

Library and Archives Canada Cataloguing in Publication

Fraser, Heather M.A., 1957–, author
Design works : a guide to creating and sustaining value through
business design / Heather M.A. Fraser. – Revised and expanded edition.

Includes bibliographical references and index.
ISBN 978-1-4875-2290-2 (softcover)

1. Organizational change. 2. Business planning. I. Title.
HD58.8.F73 2019   658.4'06   C2018-905717-3

University of Toronto Press acknowledges the financial assistance to its
publishing program of the Canada Council for the Arts and the Ontario Arts
Council, an agency of the Government of Ontario.

Dedicated to the memory of my parents,
Elizabeth and Herbert.

CONTENTS

INTRODUCTION

When I wrote the first edition of this book in 2012, enterprises around the world were wrestling with how to awaken their capacity to innovate. A lot has transpired since then. Increasingly, innovation is no longer seen as a stream of activity but rather the nature of business itself. To thrive and survive, an enterprise must be continually searching for new ways to create and sustain value to the market and capture value to fuel the enterprise.

To help unlock enterprise potential, many enterprises have evolved their ideology and practices. Design thinking has become all the rage, and innovation labs and incubators have popped up everywhere. Yet, despite these well-intended efforts to ignite innovation, some fundamentals are often missing in building an enterprise's capacity to continually innovate and to more seamlessly integrate "business" and "design":

▶ Embedding design thinking takes more than a few short boot camps and playbooks that oversimplify the complexities of turning ideas into business.
▶ New ideas must be explicitly linked to the enterprise strategy and integrated into the running of an enterprise.
▶ Integration of data analysis and validation is key to building a business case. Numbers matter when it comes to making a business investment. Fact-based *reasons to believe* build confidence in the innovation pathway.
▶ Innovation is a shared quest. It calls for engagement throughout the enterprise and of leadership at all levels.
▶ Innovation is much more than an application of methods. It calls for the right mindset and regulation of thinking modes.

These are the critical factors that have inspired this second edition. This book is intended to bring Business Design into the current context and reflect work in this discipline since the first edition and a broader view of how to create value, based on my thirty-nine-year career and the learning of others. My precept is that business is a very creative act, and that everyone in an organization can and should contribute to creating and delivering new value. I continue to believe that there is an opportunity to *inject more "design" into business and more "business" into design.*

Background

My personal background includes a decade at Procter & Gamble, where I listened to consumers, made prototypes to get executive input to product and marketing ideas early on, and crafted bulletproof business plans. Working across disciplines at P&G was always rewarding, because people across all functions in that company had something insightful and clever to contribute. Wondering what it would be like to be creative *all* the time, I decided to jump the fence and go into advertising and design.

In the next fifteen years, I learned a lot about the magic of imagination and the value of making ideas tangible. I also learned that strategy is often inspired by a novel idea. While I initially resisted that notion because I was a strategist, I came to appreciate the truth in that notion. As humans, we naturally begin with insights and ideas, not strategies, though we absolutely need to have a clear strategy to optimize our way forward.

I then met Roger Martin, the visionary dean of the Rotman School of Business with an ambition to transform business education. He offered me the opportunity to bring those two worlds together and contribute to an experiment in business education, centered on the notion of Business Design. The idea behind Business Design: to integrate the best practices of business with design-inspired mindsets and methods to help organizations tackle their innovation challenges. In collaboration with David Kelley (co-founder of innovation consultancy IDEO and Stanford's d.school) and Patrick Whitney (dean of the Institute of Design, Illinois Institute of Technology), we set off to design a fresh approach to education and business innovation. Our approach would focus on how to best meet customer needs, generate breakthrough solutions for customers, and translate those big ideas into focused and actionable business strategies that would greatly increase the chances of innovation success. This was the inspiration for the 3 Gears of Business Design: Empathy and Deep

Human Understanding, Concept Visualization, and Strategic Business Design, as you will read about in chapter 1.

In 2005, Roger brought an exciting opportunity to this group. One of the world's most admired companies believed that design thinking could play a key role in unlocking innovation, defining more competitive strategies, and ultimately delivering greater value to the market and the enterprise. That company was my alma mater, Procter & Gamble. A.G. Lafley, P&G's CEO at the time, wanted to propel P&G's level of innovation and growth into the future by pushing the value of design beyond its current application in product and packaging. To lead this quest, he appointed Claudia Kotchka, a P&G business leader with a strong track record for results and a passion for design as the company's first vice-president of Design Innovation and Strategy. Our integrated approach was first put to the test with the Global Hair Care Team in December 2005 and subsequently refined and rolled out to the enterprise globally to fortify P&G's reputation as one of the most innovative companies in the world. Part 1 of this book ends with an interview with Claudia on her tips to lead such a massive global enterprise transformation.

Concurrent with scaling the P&G program, we launched a full-scale initiative to advance the practice of Business Design and formed a strategy innovation lab called DesignWorks at Rotman. Our ambition was to turn this design-inspired approach into a methodology that could be applied in a deliberate, rigorous manner to full-scale innovation projects. Over the next seven years, we engaged in a combination of teaching, research, experimentation, and practice activities aimed at advancing the discipline.

We worked with top industry executives and business teams across a variety of sectors and companies, including P&G, Nestlé, Pfizer, Medtronic, Whirlpool, Frito-Lay and SAP, as well as public institutions and government teams. We applied Business Design to many sectors and countries, including extensive work in Singapore. There our program entailed a broad-scale program for business executives commissioned by the Singapore government agency, SPRING, an organization dedicated to developing a productive, innovative, and competitive small-to-medium-enterprise sector to create meaningful jobs for Singaporeans. We developed and delivered a comprehensive "teach the teachers" certification program to transfer Business Design knowledge and skills to the faculty of Singapore Polytechnic. Their ambition was to play an important role in Singapore's national agenda to embed design broadly into their workforce.[1] They have achieved remarkable results, as told in chapter 7 of this book.

All of these activities enabled us to build out our methodologies and test the value of Business Design with many different organizations and types of challenges. This work culminated in the first edition of the book, which captured the learning from those years at Rotman and the mounting evidence that Business Design

▶ is a learnable innovation discipline that can transform the way enterprise teams create new value, shape strategies, and mobilize support;

▶ has the potential to bring out the creative side of everyone without compromising the rigor required to make a meaningful market impact;

▶ helps get to bigger ideas faster by engaging teams in a common ambition, with the buy-in and know-how required to make important things happen; and

▶ brings a valuable balance to conventional business planning by expanding opportunities and devising breakthrough business strategies.

To test this premise outside the academic realm, I established a practice in 2012 called Vuka Innovation, to put Business Design to work, do research into what helps and hinders enterprise-wide innovation, and advance the discipline of Business Design. Some of that work is shared in this second edition to further demonstrate how Business Design can help create and sustain new value.

Common Enterprise Challenges

Some of the challenges that enterprises face have not changed, as I often hear.[2]

"We are not different enough. The changes we are making are incremental and not truly innovative."

"We are spending time and money on a lot of initiatives, but we wonder if we are investing in the right things – those that really matter to our customer."

"We've been stumped by the same challenge for years. We can't seem to make any meaningful headway. We need a new approach."

"We operate in a mature, saturated industry. It's hard to find ways to drive growth."

"How can we maximize the impact of design in a risk-averse, data-driven organization?"

"How can we create a stronger appetite to experiment and learn in the market?"

"We can't afford to always outsource the innovation process. How do we engage our enterprise to participate in this process to gain first-hand market insight?"

If any of these resonate with you, I am hoping that the practice of Business Design as presented in this book can give you some practical principles, frameworks, and tools to tackle these issues, from insights and ideation through to strategy and activation. This edition reflects the insights, observations, questions, and feedback from a wide range of enterprises and moves beyond the contents of the first edition to address more deeply how to create positive change in business culture. It shares the key principles, frameworks, and tools that innovation pioneers have found most valuable in their ambitions to transform and advance their businesses, building on the work we did at Rotman through 2012 and the work we (at Vuka Innovation) and others have done since.

How This Book Works

Part one of this book is about the practice of Business Design – what it is, how it is done, and what it can yield. This practice is anchored in the 3 Gears of Business Design, a framework for thinking about how to design new solutions and strategies for success. I begin with an Overview of Business Design and move through Preparing for Your Quest and Contextualizing Your Challenge, followed by chapters on each of the 3 Gears. I conclude part one with a chapter on Transformation, sharing learning from others on how to embed these innovative practices into your enterprise culture.

Each chapter in part one (after the Overview of Business Design) begins with a story to illustrate the application of Business Design, followed by a brief overview of the goals, activities, and outcomes for that phase of development and principles to guide you through those activities. Each chapter ends with an inspiring interview with people who bring these principles to life.

Part two is your Tool Kit and includes the methods and tips that others have found most valuable. Each tool includes brief instructions and examples from a variety of projects. These tools can enrich your discovery and development processes and unlock the ingenuity of your enterprise teams.

This book is designed to serve as an ongoing reference, not a one-time read. Its value will be determined by what you do with it. Here are some things you might do as you read this book:

Reflect on your current state. What's your biggest challenge? How ahead of the game are you in creating your future? What is your success rate with big, breakthrough ideas? What holds you back from getting big ideas to market? What factors – structural, operational or cultural – are slowing you down?

Have a disruptive project in mind. Think about that challenge and define it more specifically. This may be an unfulfilled ambition or major challenge that you haven't been able to tackle for some reason within your current way of working. With a real-world challenge in mind, this book will enable you to imagine how a Business Design approach can help you tackle a challenge that is important to you.

Apply these methods and reflect. Don't be afraid to experiment with methods. If you discover that one method brings a fresh perspective to your development efforts, inject it into ongoing projects. This is the best way to see immediate value in your newly discovered skills. Every time you put Business Design into practice, ask yourself what was different from how you normally work and how it enhanced your capacity to innovate. At the same time, reflect on what makes intuitive sense. There's a lot of common sense at the root of Business Design.

Appreciate the deeper value of Business Design. This approach can enrich your ability to generate new insights and ideas. It can also help you get to bigger ideas faster. Spending time on the more critical elements of innovation (customer needs, game-changing ideas, and strategies to realize new value) can save you time and money. Business Design is a natural way to create and capture new value.

Take the time to do it right and commit to action. Business Design is not about one big "Aha!"; it is about generating both immediate and long-term impact. Making meaningful market impact requires time, commitment, and perseverance. As you work through the process, you will discover new insights, ideas, and "quick wins" that will allow you to activate your new learning. At every step, ask yourself, *What value have we brought so far? How can we act on it **now**?*

Teach, propagate, and celebrate. Success inspires success. If you like where the practice of Business Design takes you, you can move toward expanding the practice. With some evidence of value, you can begin to strategically roll out Business Design in a systematic way and boost your own expertise in the process.

Business Design is a journey of new discoveries and learning that can transform the way you work and make your work more meaningful. I'm hoping you'll gain inspiration from the stories in this book and also acquire practical ideas on how to enhance your innovation journey within your enterprise.

A Word on Words

Every discipline has its own nomenclature, which is often dismissed as jargon. There a few words used frequently in this book that I have chosen for specific reasons. Here are some of these terms and a guide to how you should think of them:

Value: The most important notion in Business Design and intended in the broadest terms to mean anything of relative worth, merit, or importance – financial or otherwise.

Enterprise: Any organization that aims to create value – public, private, or not-for-profit. It reflects the spirit of any organization that is ready to undertake projects of importance.

Stakeholders: Your end customers (consumers, customers, clients, or guests) as well as important enablers and influencers. In a comprehensive solution, many of these stakeholders will play a role in your success.

Frameworks: Not to be confused with methods or tools, frameworks help anchor, prompt, or organize your thinking.

Methods: Used to refer to a methodology, a way of getting things done. This word is used interchangeably with "tools."

Outcomes: I have focused on "outcomes" rather than "results" because results, in business, are often thought of in financial terms and take time to realize. Outcomes, however, should be more immediate and tangible.

Part One

The Practice of Business Design

The discipline of Business Design is inspired by the many organizations that have created new value and have demonstrated a track record of sustained success. This section presents what Business Design is and how you can put these tried and true principles and practices to work for you in a deliberate and consistent way. The goal of Business Design is to catalyze and accelerate your development on a path to create new value for the market and for your enterprise.

1

OVERVIEW OF BUSINESS DESIGN

CREATING, DELIVERING, & SUSTAINING VALUE

The principles of great Business Design are evident in many successful business ventures. Applying these proven principles deliberately and consistently can help increase your odds of turning your insights and ideas into great business. Here is one such example that brings to life the underlying principles of Business Design.

In 1992, I facilitated an innovation session in Nestlé's global training center in Vevey, Switzerland. When I went to help myself to a cup of coffee, what I found was unexpected – a rather unique and extraordinary coffee machine that made an incredible cup of espresso. All it required of me was the place-ment of one small, easy-to-use coffee capsule into the machine and the push of a button!

Fast-forward sixteen years later to 2008. While visiting the Champs Élysées in Paris, I came upon a magnificent Nespresso Boutique selling the same coffee system I had discovered more than a decade earlier in a conference room. Nestlé had leveraged that coffee system into something much more. Not only did the Nespresso Boutique experience prompt me to become a loyal customer of the company, it also drove me to know more about how they had expanded this idea into such a remarkable business. What had Nestlé done to create such momentum and turn Nespresso into such a phenomenal market success?

Let's first consider the market in which Nespresso chose to compete. Coffee is one of the most popular beverages worldwide. The consumption of coffee worldwide currently exceeds 500 billion cups a year. Annual consumption has steadily climbed in volume with the proliferation of cafés, coffee franchises, and specialty coffee beverages.[3] As consumption has escalated, so has competition. Many companies are jockeying for position to be the one to provide you with your special coffee occasion.

What if a magical café encounter could be experienced at home? To the coffee connoisseur, having your own stylish espresso bar at home and being able to make a perfect cup of coffee at the touch of a button without any mess is true indulgence. This is where Nespresso delivered a new and game-changing experience to its customers.

Your Nespresso experience begins at the moment of its discovery. Entering a Nespresso Boutique for the first time is a delight to anyone with an appreciation for coffee and stylish design. Beautiful and inviting, you might first wonder if you're entering a café or a chic art gallery. Brightly colored, high-tech, pre-filled coffee capsules are artistically displayed along the café's walls alongside exhibits of sleekly designed coffee machines and accessories. Your experience is further enhanced by a Coffee Ambassador who assists you with coffee selection, as well as an espresso bar where you can taste various options.

If you are one of the many who purchase a Nespresso system, your life changes immediately. Not only can you enjoy your favorite coffee any time you like in the comfort of your home, but you also receive many perks as a Nespresso Club member. Members receive special offers and superior customer service either over the phone or through the online Nespresso Boutique. The company also effectively communicates their commitment to the environment through its capsule-recycling program. And if you travel often, you will be pleased to discover that many luxury hotels provide Nespresso machines in their rooms.

Nespresso's success started with a vision to create the ultimate coffee experience for coffee lovers around the globe in a unique, innovative way through a new proprietary coffee system. Through exquisite design, high-quality manufacturing, and dedicated customer service, Nespresso brought new value to the coffee market. These pursuits were combined with sophisticated retail concepts and well-choreographed fulfillment centers to further enhance value and customer experience.

How did they effectively turn their ideas into a powerful business? For one, the company collaborated with some of the best design and manufacturing companies in the world, like Alessi, Krups, and Magimix. Nespresso also conceptualized a distinct route-to-market approach to link their retail boutiques, fulfillment, and customer-service goals. And the company demonstrated its commitment to environmental and social responsibilities through its Ecolaboration initiative, which supports capsule recycling and agricultural programs. These add up to a distinct and effective business strategy.

With this strategy, Nespresso has grown from one boutique in 2000 to more than 700 worldwide in 2017, and it operates in seventy-six countries with more than 13,500 employees, 50 per cent of whom are in direct contact with customers. It has established more than 100,000 recycling points and home collection in eighteen countries. With more than 6.5 million Facebook fans and an ever-expanding club membership, Nespresso has built sales to more than $4 billion annually.[4] Nespresso has successfully leveraged its brand loyalty, continually expanded its product line and accessories, and built strong hotel alliances. By all accounts, these are impressive results!

Nespresso's remarkable success puts them on the roster of exceptional companies like Apple, Disney, Procter & Gamble, Netflix, LinkedIn, Nike, IKEA, Fidelity, Four Seasons, Virgin, and many others that have enjoyed long runs of success in competitive industries. In studying these companies, one can appreciate that there are many things these companies do well. One can also see that there are three things they all do exceptionally well:

1. Demonstrate a deep, holistic understanding of their customers and their needs;
2. Continually explore and deliver new offerings and experiences that uniquely fulfill these needs; and
3. Engage in a distinct combination of activities that leverage their enterprise activities and capabilities in a way that is difficult for others to replicate.

This is the inspiration behind the central framework of Business Design – the 3 Gears. Initially developed in 2005 to help Procter & Gamble, the concept of the 3 Gears of Business Design has been used to drive value creation for more than a decade with enterprises of all types around the world.

The 3 Gears of Business Design

The 3 Gears of Business Design leverage the learning from successful innovators and address three critical questions: *What do people need? How might we better meet those needs? What is our strategy to deliver and scale this idea?*

Here's an overview of the 3 Gears of Business Design (Figure 1) to help you understand how each one can enhance opportunities for innovation success.[5]

Fig. 1 **The 3 Gears of Business Design**

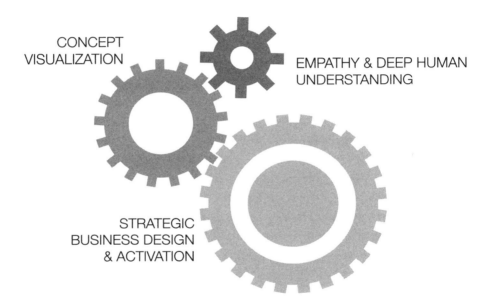

Gear 1: Empathy & Deep Human Understanding – What do people need?

Great Business Design calls for a deep understanding of people, especially customers. This requires more than market research and customer-satisfaction surveys; it calls for an empathetic, holistic appreciation for people's needs. When needs are unfulfilled, customers are not completely satisfied. That represents a tremendous opportunity for creating new value.

Gear 1 of Business Design entails understanding individuals at a much deeper level than you may be accustomed to. It calls for understanding individuals beyond their consumption behaviors and preferences. It is also valuable to appreciate the broader human context – the various roles and relationships within the human ecosystem. It is important to ask, *Who matters and what do they need?*

This process also inspires and motivates teams, as I have heard through my work that *"Connecting with people on a deeper and more authentic level gives meaning and purpose to our work."*[6] Daily activities naturally assume greater meaning with a stronger sense of human-centered purpose.

Empathy and deep human understanding in Gear 1 will inevitably shift your perspective and help identify new opportunities to create value. Many times, you may find the initial problem was not adequately defined or was too narrowly framed. Gear 1 helps **reframe** human-centered opportunities and provides an inspiring springboard for exploration in Gear 2.

Gear 2: Concept Visualization – How might we better meet those needs?

Truly disruptive ideas deliver new experiences that better meet the needs of your customers and other stakeholders. That calls for an open exploration of new possibilities that are outside your current paradigms. Going beyond the familiar and comfortable will lead to bigger, more holistic solutions that have the potential to create greater value for the market.

Gear 2 of Business Design encourages exploration of bolder ideas and the design of experiences that will better meet human needs. Through this process, you will be able to expand your perspective, create meaningful new value, and refine your ideas into a distinct vision for success before committing precious resources and investments to a particular pursuit. While innovation requires you to take risks and be courageous, the potential for positive results and unimaginable outcomes are well worth the journey.

Through the concept visualization process of Gear 2, you will **refresh** your vision of how you might bring novel solutions and better experiences to the lives of your stakeholders. Defining valuable, high-potential solutions in concrete terms will prepare you to devise your strategy and activation plan in Gear 3 of Business Design.

Gear 3: Strategic Business Design & Activation – What is our strategy to deliver & scale this idea?

Gear 3 is the essential step in turning ideas into business. Boosting the odds of innovation success and return on investment requires a clear strategy, a solid business case, and properly designed systems to activate and ultimately deliver new ideas at scale.

Gear 3 of Business Design helps you strategically focus your energy and resources to best realize your vision and goals. This aspect of Business Design identifies opportunities to monetize your idea, reveals specific capabilities that must be developed, and informs the design of management systems to support new ideas making their way to the market. Through these efforts, your vision will become more viable and valuable, and ensure that every important stakeholder wins. And as a result, the entire enterprise gains increasing potential for competitive advantage in the marketplace.

Gear 3 of Business Design aims to answer important strategic questions that will turn your ideas into business and enhance your competitive advantage. Strategy is the answer to these five interrelated questions, defined by Roger Martin, former dean at Rotman School of Management, and presented in *Playing to Win: How Strategy Really Works:*[7]

What is your winning aspiration? The purpose of your enterprise, your motivating aspiration.

Where will you play? A playing field where you can achieve that aspiration.

How will you win? The way you will win on the chosen playing field.

What capabilities must be in place? The set and configuration of capabilities required to win in the chosen way.

What management systems are required? The systems and measures that enable the capabilities and support the choices.

Gear 3 provides you with clarity on how to activate your new vision and create new value by making explicit choices. This process will help you **refocus** your resources in the most effective way. When used in combination with the other gears of Business Design, an enterprise's potential for success in innovation is greatly enhanced.

Business Design is a highly iterative process that requires a deep understanding of people, the exploration of new possibilities, and the ingenuity to turn new ideas into business. Those who suggest innovation success can be achieved through boardroom strategy exercises are missing the importance of connecting with stakeholders on a human level, engaging others in idea creation, and forming a cohesive vision and strategy to get there. Likewise, those who see innovation as unbridled creativity fail to appreciate the responsibility and commitment needed to deliver on enterprise goals. Great Business Design recognizes that both creativity and analytical rigor are critical to innovation and enterprise success.

Important Mindsets, Methods, & Thinking Modes

Mounting evidence now supports the notion that the application of design-inspired methods can foster innovative thinking and improve your success. However, simply mastering specific methodologies is not enough. While the methods are important, so is your mindset and how you regulate your mode of thinking (Figure 2).[8]

Skillful designers have a way of performing their work and relating to the world. Through education, experience, and practice, they determine best practices that historically have not been taught in business schools or incorporated into enterprise practices. For the innovative leaders at Nespresso, intuition was the initial guide, but the organization was also able to become more deliberate in its strategy and value creation over time. That's what led to its incredible success, and that's why Business Design is an exercise in agility – emotionally, tactically, and cognitively.

Fig. 2 **Mindsets, Methods, and Thinking**

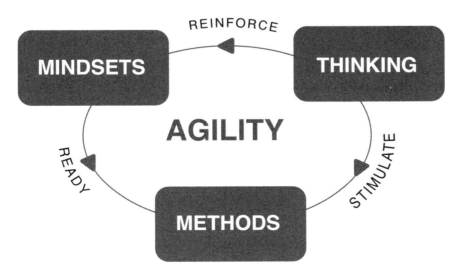

As in other design disciplines, your ability to excel in Business Design is dependent on the right mindset and the ability to use appropriate methods along the way. These methods will unlock your best thinking and tap into your intuition, imagination, and ability to create original value – to the market and the enterprise. Practiced on an ongoing basis, Business Design will become an increasingly intuitive way to enhance productivity. The following section is an overview of the mindset, methods, and thinking modes of Business Design.

Mindset Matters

Having the right mindset from both an individual and team perspective can be a source of energy and inspiration in the journey of discovery, creation, and decision-making. However, the wrong mindset can hinder collaboration and stall progress. Your mindset affects how you relate to others and your intrinsic motivation in tackling the challenges at hand, your capacity for learning, and team productivity.

Mindset facilitates the ability to see and create new value. It empowers the people within an enterprise to exercise creativity along with the boldness required to introduce innovations to the market.

An abundance of research exists that links mindset to performance. The three key mindsets that are critical to the effective practice of Business Design in my experience are empathy, positivity, and courage.

► **Empathy:** Understanding how others see the world is fundamental to creating new value. At the same time, empathy enhances the ability to collaborate and work with others, and nurtures a greater sense of purpose and meaning in daily activities. An empathetic mindset elevates inspiration, motivation, and creativity.

► **Positivity:** Nothing kills a creative, pioneering spirit like negativity. Critical thinking is important, but a positive can-do attitude and a commitment to seeing challenges and problems as unique opportunities for innovation are also key. Positivity is contagious and helps build team conviction and resilience in the pursuit of a shared vision.

► **Courage:** Any pursuit that is new and has uncertain outcomes requires courage. Courage is rooted in a commitment to *doing the right thing*. In Business Design, that is anchored in putting people's needs front and center, exploring and validating new ways to deliver value, and making sound decisions on how to move ideas forward.

Methods as a Way of Doing Business

With the right mindset, methods provide a practical way of exploring new options, building robust solutions, making key decisions, and taking bold action. Design-inspired methods help us tap into insights, intuition, imagination, and innate ingenuity through deliberate tasks. Methods also help accelerate the development process through a thoughtful and deliberate approach to framing the questions you must answer and the methods you deploy. This design-inspired discipline will optimize your innovation pathway.

There are two ways in which methods can push your thinking: to open up and explore new possibilities (divergent methods) and synthesize and effectively make decisions (convergent methods) (see Figure 3). From a Business Design perspective, every stage of innovation requires both.

Divergent methods are all about exploring *options.* They enable you to expand your perspective of the market, discover new unmet needs, and generate new solutions. Divergent methods also allow you to consider strategic ways to configure your business model to deliver your vision.

Convergent methods help you to assess and focus your scope of consideration by synthesizing core needs, soliciting feedback on early ideas, and forcing strategic choices. In each phase of development, there comes a turning point where you must begin to synthesize and make *decisions.*

While there are literally thousands of design-inspired methods in the public domain today, they generally fall into these categories:

▶ **Multidisciplinary collaboration:** Capitalizing on diverse perspectives and types of expertise. This leads to richer, more robust, and more well-considered outcomes.
▶ **Need-finding:** Developing a deeper understanding of the people that matter, complementing quantitative analysis with more ethnographic methods such as observation and listening to user stories. This leads to new discoveries that can be synthesized into what matters most to the people you serve.
▶ **Visualization:** Helping others to *see* relationships, new user experiences, and even new strategies in visual ways, instead of relying on documents and verbal descriptions. This helps ensure everyone is on the same page.

Fig. 3 **Divergence and Convergence Process**[9]

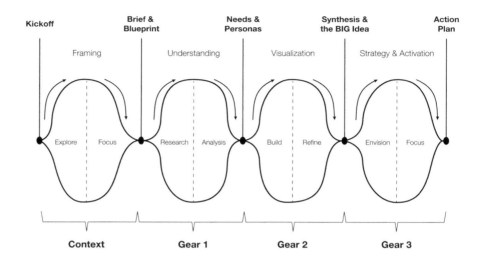

▶ **Iterative prototyping:** Translating abstract concepts into the concrete prototypes in rough form early on (before the big bucks get spent). Making is a catalyst for thinking, dialogue, learning, and solution improvement.

▶ **Co-creation and feedback:** Inviting users and other stakeholders into the development process to gain valuable feedback and advance both solutions and strategic models. This accelerates learning on how to ensure that ideas deliver the most value.

▶ **Systems mapping:** Making connections, visualizing relationships, and synthesizing the way people, solutions, and enterprise systems all connect. This helps create a more cohesive picture.

▶ **Storytelling:** Capturing the richness and complexities of big ideas though compelling stories. This helps others to feel the impact of the vision in a holistic and human manner.

▶ **Experimentation:** Trying new things and testing uncertainties with the intent to learn and advance development. This helps to improve ideas and mitigate risk as you advance and scale ideas.

Most people associate these methods with coming up with a big idea. In Business Design, these design-inspired methods are equally valuable in designing a great business. Designing a strategy to bring new ideas to life is a high-octane exercise in stakeholder need-finding, systems mapping, iterative prototyping, collaboration, and storytelling. These methods are useful at every stage of development.

During my ten years at Procter & Gamble, and throughout my fifteen-year career in brand design and communications, I witnessed all of these methods put into practice in a more intuitive way. Consistently, those who use these methods – and understand when to diverge and converge – make progress more quickly, gain more widespread support, and ultimately achieve better results.

Regulating Three Modes of Thinking

How you regulate your thinking mode affects your ability to complete specific tasks and your ability to collaborate with others. Fortunately, your mode of thinking is not static, and you can choose how you "think" at different times by developing greater mindfulness, discipline, and mental agility. Mastering how you regulate your thinking is just as important as mastery of mindset and methodologies.

A tool I have used in teaching Business Design was developed by One Smart World, to help people better appreciate their own personal thinking preferences.[10] Many of my students cite this profiling tool as critical in helping them work more effectively on teams and tackle some of the more difficult project tasks required. In essence, this tool highlights three key modes of thinking:

▶ **Understanding:** In each gear of the Business Design process, there will be times to push the pause button to deepen understanding. A lack of understanding can lead to reckless behaviors. And while it is an essential component in Gear 1, it remains important throughout the Business Design process. Whether you are considering people, ideas, choices, or actions, understanding is needed for optimal results.

▶ **Generating:** This mode of thinking offers the opportunity to unleash your insights and capacity for creativity. Like understanding, it is important at every stage of Business Design. Generating hypotheses and prototypes that answer questions, *What might people really need? How might we address that need? How might we configure our business to meet this goal?* These questions help generate a more diverse array of options to consider.

▶ **Synthesizing and deciding:** While divergence is critical, there are natural points in the Business Design process at which you will need to synthesize and make choices. *Which opportunity gaps in the market are we going to pursue? Which components of the idea offer the greatest value? What strategy will you employ to achieve your vision? How will this strategy be activated? This mode of thinking is particularly important in the realization of your innovation goals.*

Most people tend to prefer one mode of thinking over another; for example, one might love generating ideas but not making decisions. Recognizing that each of us has different preferences, you can leverage team diversity in thinking preferences according to the task at hand. At the same time, it is important to be able to switch gears, depending on the task. By having a high degree of mindfulness and discipline in each of these cognitive modes individually and collectively, you will enhance your productivity and capacity to innovate.

Business Design & Enterprise Transformation

As businesses are continually changing, your competitive advantage will be determined not only by the strategy you design for future success, but also the principles and practices that shape your innovation culture. An important aspect of any enterprise is its capacity to either seize new opportunities to grow or pivot at the right time. This capacity must transcend every level of the enterprise. The practice of Business Design can help enhance your collective capacity to adapt and grow within an ever-shifting business and social climate. Here are five key ways by which Business Design can create value within the enterprise:

▶ Fostering deeper customer understanding and sensitivity within the enterprise;
▶ Giving enterprise members the license to explore bigger ideas;
▶ Stimulating collaboration, dialogue, and learning;
▶ Creating greater alignment through a clear and focused strategy; and
▶ Establishing new structures and systems to support and sustain innovation.

The practice of Business Design is valuable at every level of your organization. As an *individual*, you will be better equipped to lead by harnessing the power of teams and navigating the course of progress in an inspired and confident manner. As a *team*, you will have a greater sense of alignment and ability to create and act on opportunities in a productive and accelerated fashion. As an *enterprise*, the practice of Business Design will help enhance your ability to continually seize new opportunities and maintain competitive advantage. And at the highest level, Business Design principles and practices have the potential create and sustain an innovation *economy*. (See Figure 4.) Singapore is a country that exemplifies how design can inspire an economic transformation, as you will read in chapter 7 of this book.

Fig. 4 **Business Design: A Platform for Innovation and Growth**

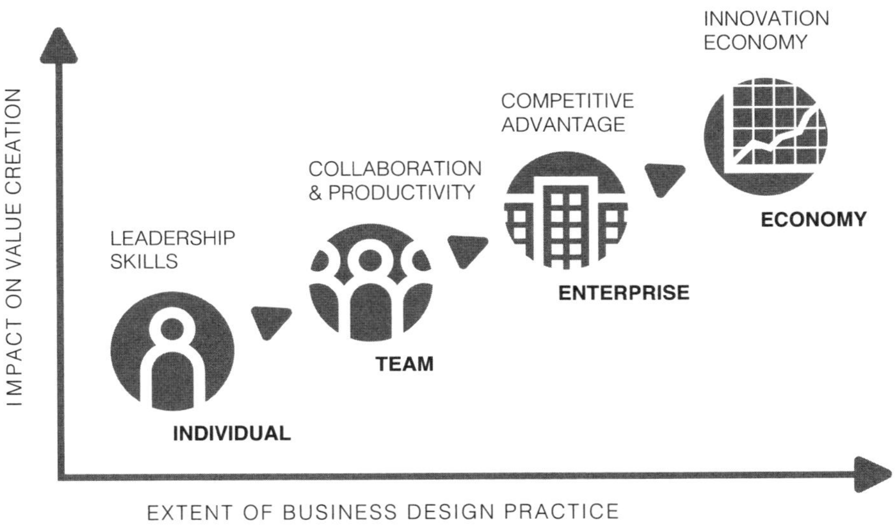

INNOVATION ECONOMY

COMPETITIVE ADVANTAGE

COLLABORATION & PRODUCTIVITY

ECONOMY

LEADERSHIP SKILLS

ENTERPRISE

IMPACT ON VALUE CREATION

TEAM

INDIVIDUAL

EXTENT OF BUSINESS DESIGN PRACTICE

Setting You Up for the Rest of Part One

Now that you have a sense of the core concepts behind the practice of Business Design, the balance of part one walks you through the process, from the time you decide to take on a quest through to activation. The last chapter provides some learning on how to lead others through a broader enterprise transformation. While I'm sure you're eager to jump into Gear 1, there are two important steps to consider before that: Preparing for Your Quest (starting with a thoughtful plan) and Contextualizing Your Challenge (taking stock of the world around you and your current state). Experience shows that if you skip over these two important preludes to development, it will come back to bite you later.

Each of the chapters in part one of the book offers a consistent format in presenting your goal for each phase, key activities and outcomes, activation principles, and other important considerations. Here is how the rest of part one will unfold, with a brief summation of the content and purpose of each of these chapters:

Chapter 2: Preparing for Your Quest: This chapter covers how to frame your project in the context of your enterprise, design your project roadmap, identify the right people for the innovation journey, and establish the right conditions for success. *This will foster commitment to a shared ambition and set you up for a productive pursuit.*

Chapter 3: Contextualizing Your Challenge: By examining current market trends, industry players, stakeholder ecosystems, and enterprise capabilities and resources, you will identify market opportunities and ways to leverage your strengths going forward. *This will help you identify market-based opportunities and determine the key areas you wish to pursue.*

Chapter 4: Gear 1 – Empathy and Deep Human Understanding: Human-centered value creation is rooted in understanding the world through the eyes of every important stakeholder, including both your core customers as well as others in your external ecosystem who will be important to effectively delivering your solution to the marketplace. *This will help you to identify human-centered opportunities for value creation through the discovery, understanding, and validation of stakeholder needs.*

Chapter 5: Gear 2 – Concept Visualization: This chapter presents the value of exploring and prototyping ideas and concepts through collaboration, experimentation, and an attitude of continuous refinement. *This helps you to formulate a concrete vision for success, identify potential solutions for evaluation, and validate important game-changing ideas.*

Chapter 6: Gear 3 – Strategic Business Design and Activation: This chapter shows you how to translate your vision into a strategy and activate it. It's about setting a game plan, establishing priorities for developing and testing initiatives, and designing your organization for innovation success. It helps you identify collaborative partners and key capabilities for resource investment, monetize your idea, and formulate a strategy in which all stakeholders win. *You will define your unique proposition, create a comprehensive enterprise strategy, and gain clarity in your path forward.*

Chapter 7 focuses on the importance of leadership in both innovation projects and enterprise transformation. Part two is a Tool Kit of methods, frameworks, and tips to get you going and serve as an ongoing reference.

Things to Keep in Mind

Business Design methods, frameworks, and principles are valuable at any point in your innovation process and highly adaptable. Here are some things to keep in mind:

Business Design is not a rigid, linear process. The principles and practices of Business Design are a highly *iterative and integrated way of thinking and doing.* At all times, a true business designer acts as an advocate for the user, a protector of the idea, and a disciplined strategist who actively pursues a clear path toward future success.

Business Design provides practical principles and an expandable tool kit. You can integrate Business Design into your current enterprise activities and leverage it to boost your innovation and strategy practices. Business Design is not a mechanical process, nor is it about checking boxes or filling out templates. It is about turning fresh thinking and new ideas into a compelling business proposition.

Business Design is a flexible and adaptable practice. Ultimately, you will want to create a Business Design approach specific to your enterprise. This will include repeatable, scalable practices that best fit your culture and management systems.

Business Design is an ongoing exercise in agility. You can apply Business design principles and practices on a day-to-day basis with short-term challenges or use them within a complete process on long-term development projects, or even enterprise transformation. The more you apply these principles and practices, the more intuitive they will become. The more you practice, the more you will rewire your way of thinking, and this, in turn, will help nurture a culture of innovation and creativity.

You can start to apply Business Design at any time and in many ways. You can begin by implementing the basics of Business Design to deepen your stakeholder understanding, enhance your customer experience, or refresh and restate your strategy. I always advise organizations *"Start where you are!"* The more you anchor your efforts in the 3 Gears of Business Design and apply the basic principles and practices, the more you will build a culture of design-inspired innovation and agility.

As a prelude to the next chapter, Preparing for Your Quest, the following interview with Isadore Sharp, founder of Four Seasons, brings to life the underlying principles of Business Design. His inspiring perspective reveals how vision, shared purpose and values, ongoing exploration of new ways to create delight for guests, and building on a clear strategy all contribute to long-term enterprise success. His story underscores the human nature of business success and the importance of empathy, open-mindedness, and courage in building an enduring culture of respect, collaboration, and innovation. His full account of building Four Seasons is captured in his book Four Seasons: The Story of a Business Philosophy.[11]

Interview with Isadore Sharp
Founder, Four Seasons Hotels and Resorts

" At Four Seasons, the focus has always been and is still on the customer. Give people what they need and expect, and always exceed those expectations.

For a lot of the first things that we put together, other people who had more experience would say, "You're crazy. That's going to cost you money. People don't really need it." There were a lot of naysayers. People need to have the courage to come up with something that they believe might work. *Because it also might not.* And that happened along the way. It took me five years to get the first small little motor hotel built. Five years of naysayers. People laughed me out of the room and wouldn't give me the time of day. But it didn't deter me. I could see how it would work, even though they would point up all the reasons why it might not.

Being innovative calls on your ability to believe in yourself and in your own opinions, in spite of the fact that nobody else might agree with you. We decided to position ourselves in the industry by establishing our advantage through service. To be the best, we would have to have a workforce that was able to give the customers that special experience, making our service different. That had to be through the efforts of the people who met the customer, dealt with the customer, and talked with them, whether it was the salesperson, the doorman, or the housekeeper.

What makes our service special comes from a culture, and a culture can't be mandated. It has to grow from within. Could we create a competent, qualified workforce that would be better than our competitors based on an ethical credo? That, again, was laughed at. Some said, "This is foolishness. It's not a philosophy class we're running here." But we created a workforce based on an ethical credo – the Golden Rule. In practice over the many, many years, this credo became a part of our culture. Today we have over 35,000 employees who believe in this. And, yes, it makes us better.

My son Greg once said *"The mind is like a parachute. It only works when it's open."* That's exactly what it's about – keeping an open mind and listening before you decide what could be the case. When you create an environment that allows people to express themselves, they come up with ideas. We encourage people to participate and speak up. If you think we're doing something that's not right, please speak up. And if you ask the question, "Why do we do this?" and we do not have a good answer, maybe we shouldn't be doing it.

I think that's how people grow together – when you have that openness and don't criticize people for having ideas and trying something that doesn't work. You give people the encouragement to use their common sense and give them an opportunity to think about their job and how to make it better. You will get enormous amounts of input.

We have many people who come up with the ideas. It could be anywhere. And they do. All we do is say, "Before you move on any idea, please make sure we just talk about it. Because maybe we've already thought about that, and maybe it's been discarded or maybe someone else has had a better way of dealing with it." So, nobody has the autonomy just to do what they think; they've got the autonomy to think and come up with ideas. This openness and transparency is the way the company grew.

People ask me "How can you rely upon all these people and give them complete authority to do what is needed to satisfy the customer?" I say that we're not giving them a blank sheet – we're getting people to use their common sense and be reasonable when they're thinking about something. Everybody who works usually has a much greater responsibility than their job, whatever their job might be. When they're dealing with their family, those are major, major decisions that they have to deal with. They have the ability to do that. Why wouldn't they have the ability to know how to react when a customer comes in and they're irate with something? Most people have the ability to use their common sense.

If people know you trust them, they will go to great lengths not to disappoint you. If you say, "It's up to you. What do you think you should do?" then people will, by nature, rise to that challenge. This is what you are writing about. You're writing about empathy. You're writing about philosophy. You're writing about choices and the soft parts of business – about getting people to think about a more well-rounded way of running a business.[12]

2

PREPARING FOR YOUR QUEST

DESIGNING THE CONDITIONS FOR SUCCESS

The first step in embarking on an important project is to appreciate the enterprise context and ensure that the right people are brought along the innovation journey with a thoughtful game plan and under the right conditions. Doing so will enable you to collectively design a productive path forward. Here is story about using the 3 Gears of Business Design as the framework for strategic planning, demonstrating the importance of engaging the right individuals and giving full ownership to the development team to move their plan ahead.[13]

The Nestlé Confectionery Story: Sweet Success

The Challenge

In 2008, the Nestlé Confectionery team faced a challenge: How could they reconcile selling chocolate bars in a company that is committed to health and wellness? Reconciling a broader corporate ambition with a diverse portfolio is not uncommon in large companies. In the case of Nestlé Confectionery, the vice-president of Marketing at the time, Elizabeth Frank, saw this strategic tension as an opportunity to innovate.

It would require the engagement of the team members with the insight, imagination, and ingenuity to reframe the challenge and create a cohesive vision for the future. A project road map was designed to enable the team to really challenge their current paradigm and embrace their collective devotion to the happiness that good chocolate brings to everyday life. Their shared ambition was to determine how they were going to make confectionery as "good for you" as every other product produced by Nestlé.

Elizabeth, with the support of Sandra Martinez, then division president, assembled a cross-disciplinary team from marketing, operations, product development, finance, and sales for a three-day strategic planning session, in which the Nestlé leadership team engaged in a full run-through of the Business Design process. The session was designed to examine the current strategy for Nestlé Confectionery within the context of Nestlé's overarching corporate ambition, reframe Nestlé Confectionery's long-term business strategy, and align the team behind a new vision to reignite growth.

The Breakthroughs

With a diversified team anchored in a clear process, the breakthroughs came in several ways. They all culminated in a strategic reframe based on a new vision for the business and a series of initiatives from products to marketing campaigns.

The first breakthrough came in Gear 1, when we brought in consumers to share their stories about looking after their family's health and wellness. The Nestlé team was touched by the insights they discovered in these stories. There were smiles and even tears during these encounters. The surprise? Consumers believed wholeheartedly that "chocolate *is* good food" and part of their every-day wellbeing. That also inspired the Nestlé team to think longer term, take a more visionary stance, and implement a pragmatic and staged approach to building their business in a relevant and meaningful manner over time.

The next round of breakthroughs came in Gear 2, when the team was given the license to transform this renewed inspiration into new possibilities and co-create the future. Drawing from their collective insight, intuition, imagination, and expertise, they designed three fresh and distinct prototypes. They prototyped and role-played their preliminary ideas for consumers, to get early feedback. As an example, for one concept, they presented how their idea fit into the life of a teenager. They turned one room into a three-scene set, where drawings of high school lockers covered one of the walls for the first scene, a rough mock-up of a convenience store occupied another area to play out the next scene, and a kid's bedroom with a computer constructed out of old cardboard boxes completed the envisioned experience, all at a materials cost of seventeen dollars. Real teenagers appreciated their creativity and openness, and gave valuable feedback on how to make the Nestlé team's idea even better.

In Gear 3, the strategic breakthrough naturally surfaced from their development work. They rearticulated their strategy and designed a five-year plan to activate their new vision for the business. By reconnecting with consumers and exploring bigger propositions to address wellness in more holistic terms, the team was able to reframe their strategy, which enabled them to refocus their efforts on a stream of business initiatives that emerged from their shared vision. Passion, laughter, creativity, and determination filled the studio; the team came away ready, willing. and able to make their vision a reality.

"This approach to Business Design helped build team alignment early on around a common understanding of the consumer and a shared path forward. The outputs of this workshop approach were critical and salient and absolutely drove business results."[14]

ELIZABETH FRANK,
VICE-PRESIDENT, MARKETING (2008),
NESTLÉ CONFECTIONERY (CANADA)

The Outcome

The team collectively redefined the meaning of wellness within the context of Confectionery. They created a clear and cohesive strategy for enhancing the consumer sense of wellbeing and supporting responsible and meaningful indulgence. Initiatives included using all-natural ingredients, providing smaller-sized portions, offering products with health benefits (such as dark chocolate), and recommitting to Shared Value (a program for fair trade and sustainable environmental practices). Other important initiatives included investment in socially relevant programs like the Smarties Show Your Colors initiative aimed at inspiring kids to support social causes.

The team captured their strategic vision in a compelling presentation to the top decision-makers in the Nestlé global headquarters in Vevey, Switzerland. Inspired by the team's story, which wove in consumer insights and ideas from their development work, Nestlé Canada Confectionery helped shape the new global Confectionery strategy. In Canada, this new strategy drove double-digit growth for three successive years. As the Canadian CEO said after the first year, *"They've been on fire ever since! The results are outstanding."*

This story underscores the importance of understanding the current realities of the business, linking your quest to the corporate ambition, and engaging a team that would feel ownership of the outcomes. With the right process road map and design-inspired tools, the Nestlé Confectionery team was able to unlock their innate creativity and passion for driving remarkable business results in a purposeful way.

Your Goal in Preparing for Your Quest

Design a plan that will optimize your chances of success. Whether your aim is to boost a line of business or transform an entire enterprise, up-front planning is often the most critical determinant of your success.

The balance of this chapter highlights key activities, outcomes, and development principles; provides tips on the role of data analysis and validation; examines the mindsets, methods, and thinking modes that are most critical; and finishes with an inspired interview that brings important principles to life. Related tools are included in Part 2: Tool Kit.

Activities & Outcomes

Figure 5 shows some of the activities you will undertake in preparing for your quest and some of the most valuable outcomes that will get you off to a strong start:

Project Brief: A clear statement of your project ambitions in relation to enterprise goals, with a high-level case for future value.

Project Blueprint: A detailed plan for methodologies, key deliverables, timing, and resources required. It will demonstrate rigor, build confidence, and get you to your desired outcomes.

Fig. 5 **Activities and Outcomes in Preparing for Your Quest**

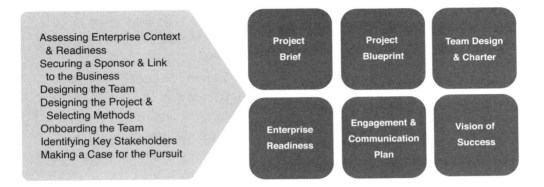

ACTIVITIES:

Assessing Enterprise Context
  & Readiness
Securing a Sponsor & Link
  to the Business
Designing the Team
Designing the Project &
  Selecting Methods
Onboarding the Team
Identifying Key Stakeholders
Making a Case for the Pursuit

OUTCOMES:

Project Brief · Project Blueprint · Team Design & Charter · Enterprise Readiness · Engagement & Communication Plan · Vision of Success

Team Design and Charter: A plan for who will be engaged, key roles and responsibilities, and the critical conditions for success.

Enterprise Readiness: A measured assessment of how prepared your organization is to deliver new solutions, especially in the case of an enterprise transformation.

Engagement and Communication Plan: A plan for how you will engage and communicate with key stakeholders (internal and external) throughout the project.

Vision of Success: A clear picture of how this effort will impact the business, the end customer, and the people of the enterprise.

Divergent activities include exploring the market, using methods that can help unlock fresh thinking, considering people who might contribute, and creating a shared vision for success. **Convergent** activities entail making decisions on what you are setting out to do, how you will achieve that, and who will be involved along the way.

Key Principles: Create the Conditions for Success

There are many successes that point to the importance of getting off on the right foot. When you are on an important mission, you don't want to be derailed because you didn't create the conditions for success from the start. Here are a few principles to consider:

Link your quest to the enterprise strategy. Doing so will establish relevance for your quest. There are countless examples of innovation teams going off on a tangent. Someone might have a clever idea only to find that it isn't aligned with the bigger enterprise picture. In the case of Nestlé Confectionery, chocolate was an important component of the corporate portfolio during this project. At the same time, it was clear that there was tension between chocolate and wellness. Being explicit about how your intentions fit within the enterprise vision up front will demonstrate strategic relevance and align your quest with the greater goal of building the business. Your efforts will more likely be supported by senior decision-makers and the organization at large.

Demonstrate business value. Innovation initiatives that just set out to explore are often the first to get shut down when there is a budget cut. It's helpful to make a business case for investing time and money in your quest. Assessing the state of your business can build confidence in your current path and elevate the urgency of exploring new paths. Future business value can be framed in two ways. *First*, there might be a huge opportunity to tap into a new target or category that would boost the business in a seismic way. *Second*, it might be that you are headed for a crisis if you don't address it now, as was the sentiment at the time of the Nestlé Confectionery project. In both scenarios, teams should make a business case for investing in a quest that would drive future business success.

There are several activities in framing the context that will help you better identify market opportunities. It is also valuable to solicit the perspectives of senior executives to capture a comprehensive, high-level picture. At the onset of your quest, important high-level questions to ask yourselves might include:

How are we faring in the market and in the eyes of our most important stakeholders?

How are our results trending?

What's keeping us up at night as we look to the future?

In framing your opportunity, it's helpful to put some numbers around it and set your sights high on the potential gains for your business. With a clear picture of the current state and your business proposition, you will be able to articulate a clear launch point for development. This is time to crystallize your ambitions in a clear and compelling project brief.

Secure executive or business-leader support. Incorporating the insights and ambitions of a senior leader will not only help frame your quest, it will also heighten the visibility of and support for it. If you are not on the executive team, you'll want to have someone in a leadership position to act as your executive advocate and provide air cover when you need it. Their endorsement gives license to expand thinking beyond today's business and helps position efforts in the context of other enterprise initiatives. They will be an invaluable sounding board as your developments unfold. The bigger the enterprise, the more valuable it is to secure support at the outset, rather than midstream in project development.

Create a team with a diversity of skills, perspectives, and cognitive styles. A diverse team will bring richness to the process and open your enterprise to possibilities and solutions that may be far from obvious. The intent is to harness the most valuable perspectives, insights, and know-how and to build commitment to delivering on the outcomes. It is easy to start with the intact team, which is used to working together. That's a good starting point. Considerations for setting up a diverse team are provided in the Tool Kit in part two of this book and include diversity in functional expertise, skills, geography, and generational and cultural perspectives.

"Who you select to be on the team builds alignment very early on around a common understanding and a shared plan forward. We had the people that I knew would see the roadblocks in the room to articulate whether they thought we were competitively differentiated or not. We created this safe place to build that alignment."

ELIZABETH FRANK

The freshest and most surprising solutions are often inspired and created through a blending of perspectives. While you want to right size your team, you will also want to ensure you have enough fresh blood in the innovation process.

Design a rigorous process and clear project blueprint. A well thought-through road map will not only guide your development efforts; it will also build confidence. The plan should include a core framework, key methods, timing, and outcomes at each stage, all captured in a clearly articulated and visualized project blueprint.

Anchoring your pursuits in the 3 Gears and trusting the process that you have designed will guide your development efforts. While certain core principles and frameworks apply to every Business Design initiative, no two projects are the same in terms of how they are played out. That means plotting out not only the broader steps and activities, but also the details of each step of research and development, and who will do what, and when. This early phase planning will ensure that resources are deployed effectively and efficiently, and keep the team on track as it explores new and unknown territories.

A clearly defined road map will give everyone confidence that no matter how complex the project, there is a process that will guide multiple players to a unified and productive outcome. While you never know at the outset exactly where the development process will take you, you will likely be pleasantly surprised and delighted by the outcomes!

Onboard and solidify the team with a team charter. Team buy-in to the road map is critical. Everyone has to commit to the process and respective roles, and be open to the outcomes at every stage. While everyone will have important and unique roles, there are some things for which everyone must be on the same page. A charter will help you get past the friction and enable you to capitalize on the fusion. It will also ensure that you deliver quality in an efficient manner. Here are some tips to consider as you formulate your charter:

- ▶ **Establish a common purpose and mandate.** This means complete alignment on a shared ambition for the project.
- ▶ **Anchor the team in shared values, codes of conduct, and commitment.** When the project gets rocky, the common values and commitment that comes from a team built on openness, respect, and collaboration for the greater good will prevail.
- ▶ **Identify roles.** Everyone will bring unique strengths to the project. Aligning roles with individual expertise will give everyone an important place in the process.
- ▶ **Be explicit about deliverables and accountability.** In designing the process, you will articulate the outcomes and deliverables in concrete terms at key

points for both the team and for individuals. You are mutually dependent in your pursuits.

▶ **Foster a sense of team spirit.** Because you're going to work hard and will likely be stretched beyond your comfort zone, support for each other and a sense of team spirit will go a long way. It can mean the difference between an energizing and rewarding project, and one that is just hard work and recurring tension.

Envision success from the start. Imagine your "destination" by asking, *What does success look like?* This might take the form of a collage of images, a future-case narrative of your journey and outcome, or a collection of drawings that capture your dreams for the project and the enterprise. It is often most meaningful if your vision captures emotions – how you want everyone to *feel* at the end of the project or project phase. While you don't know what the solution will look like yet, a general picture of success often helps people express and visualize their aspirations and pulls the team forward.

Plan for appropriate engagement and communications. Having a clear narrative and designing an effective communication plan from the start is invaluable, both for the team and anyone else who has a vested interest in what you're up to. Effectively engaging and communicating with others about your discoveries and progress builds stakeholder and enterprise confidence and momentum.

Clear, continuous, and transparent communication within the team will provide a good sense of where you are at all times. A cohesive team can raise red flags and help each other, or course correct if things are not going as anticipated. It is also helpful to establish a means of remote or virtual communication so every team member will always be able to log in and know where things stand.

Keeping both your executive sponsor and team members' management apprised of your plans helps to reinforce the value of every team member's contribution and inspire confidence in your progress. Acknowledging participation and securing permission to tap into expanded resources is critical in an environment where people need to account for their time and priorities.

Beyond the team, anticipate who else should be kept abreast of your developments – whether the organization at large or important external stakeholders. Bringing others along, for updates or engagement in the development process, demonstrates how you are creating new value along the way in terms of new insights or new ideas.

Be prepared to pivot. While it is important to have a clear plan, it is equally important to revisit your plan and assumptions at key points. Be ready to adapt to new information and evolve your game plan to maximize opportunity and optimize your path. Adaptation might be spurred by a problem reframe, a new entrant in the market, or a new development that warrants time for a pause and adjustment to the game plan.

State the conditions for success. In a sense, this is your "contract" with both the team and the enterprise. It's an explicit way of saying, *These are the conditions under which we will be most successful.* While these conditions are often nuanced and unique to every organization, you might consider being explicit about having the license to explore outside the current business model, the time to do the job right, the resources to develop the most robust solutions, and the engagement and support of key people.

All of these principles and considerations require an eye on both the big picture and the detailed tasks of your quest, foresight on how your quest might play out, and disciplined planning on every level: business, people, and tactics. These principles will increase the odds that your efforts are productive and eventually pay off.

Building a Business Case:
Data Analysis & Validation

As in every gear of Business Design, it is important to gather data to build a compelling business case and to leverage data and useful measurement tools where appropriate.

From a *business* standpoint, you can use your most salient data on the market and the enterprise business in framing your project brief. These are the critical facts that help you establish a business case for your quest.

At an *enterprise* level, it can be valuable to get a true picture of your enterprise readiness. In a case where "innovation" is not fully baked into your enterprise practices, systems, structures, and culture, it is often helpful to appreciate the way people work to deliver and capture value. Even though everyone loves the *idea* of innovation, there are ingrained practices, structures, and systems that have shaped the culture; these can often set up barriers to step-change progress. While most CEOs claim innovation as a top priority, many are less certain that their organization is ready to deliver truly breakthrough ideas.

The notion of readiness is critical to navigating success. Capturing the true picture of enterprise readiness reveals potential cultural and systemic blocks. This kind of profiling can diagnose the current innovation readiness of the enterprise, highlighting the structural, systemic or cultural factors that can either accelerate or impede innovation. For example, we use our Vuka Innovation Readiness Survey[15] to measure how clear and effective a current strategy is perceived to be, to what extent design-inspired principles and practices are currently being applied, how structures and systems support or constrain innovation, and what cultural factors influence the enterprise state of readiness to deliver and sustain readiness. Results of an enterprise-wide survey will inform you on how to build alignment on purpose and strategy, what mindsets and capabilities needed to be fortified, what systems and structures might need to be redesigned, and what cultural factors need to be addressed.

Important Mindsets, Methods, & Thinking Modes

Mindset Matters: No matter how great your challenge, the most important mindset at the onset is a big dose of *positivity*, along with a collective commitment to the game plan. While naysayers will have their opportunity to challenge the quest up front and poke holes along the way, it is important to keep an open mind to new possibilities from the start. It takes a lot of *empathy* to understand what motivates others in the enterprise and *courage* to create a burning platform and lead the charge.

Most Critical Methods: Without a doubt, the spirit of *collaboration* is set from the start. It's defined by how you design and form a team and engage various stakeholders. Innovation involves a lot of people working together toward a common ambition. That also requires some up-front *need-finding* from important internal stakeholders.

Regulating Thinking Modes: Preparing for an important quest starts with *understanding* the current state and what's at stake for whom. If you run off with an insight or idea before taking stock of the business, enterprise ambitions, and internal stakeholders, you will likely hit a lot of barriers along the way. Your plan requires a holistic understanding of the business and people across the enterprise. That will set you up to make *decisions* and swing into action.

The importance of engaging others in your quest is further brought to life in the following interview with Cathy Cummings of the Canadian Bar Association, who, in collaboration with Vuka Innovation and Happico, led the organization through a journey to define the purpose and service proposition of this important professional association.[16] This quest was undertaken in the context of the technology changes and generational transitioning that are disrupting the ways in which lawyers create and capture value. Engaging thousands of lawyers in this strategic rethink project brought the community along every step of the way and led to a deeper collective understanding of member needs, new ways to deliver value, and a clear strategy for the future.

Interview with Cathy Cummings
Project Director, Canadian Bar Association Re-Think Project

"The challenge going in for the Canadian Bar Association (CBA) was our complicated structure. I need to have input to any decision-making – including the strategic direction for the whole organization – from its 37,000 members, 1,500 engaged volunteers, 200 staff, and the governing board of directors. There are fifteen offices in total – one in every province and territory, the national office in Ottawa, and the Canadian Corporate Counsel Association office in Toronto.

How do you come up with a strategic direction that is going to work for everybody but also make them feel like they are an important part of the process? That, I think, was our biggest challenge going in, and I think this process helps solve that problem by engaging so many of the different groups from the outset.

We engaged everyone so that in the end everybody's voice was heard. Everybody, from the board to the senior staff, came with their own perspective and viewpoint on what issues needed to be addressed. To frame our challenge, we sent questions out to the offices, who provided a lot of information. We then got the board together to make sense of it so that there were some common, concrete starting points. By working on the foundation together, we were able to build alignment and get everybody on the same page.

Hearing the voices of our members was critical. An important outcome of the work we did was understanding our most important stakeholder – the member. Today, whenever we talk about either innovating or discontinuing any products and services, we start with the needs of our members. There are certainly people within the organization who continually bring those universal needs to the forefront. The seventy-seven who were interviewed were a fantastically diverse group, from young women to middle-aged managing partners, from the territories to Toronto, and from in-house to public-sector and private practitioners. We were really cutting across every aspect of our membership, and I feel quite strongly that the validity of that information should be a guiding force for the CBA going forward.

The qualitative research was hugely important. It gives us confidence in the validity of the information and inspires us because it is expressed in real-world phrases and brought to life in personas that resonate. The in-person meetings we did really resonated with people, from older members with whom our stated needs and strategies didn't resonate, to a young woman who urged us to consider the needs of the future and of a far more diverse cohort. We learned that there are a lot of different people to be heard and that the key is not to leave anyone behind.

One moment in particular stands out in this regard. We were lucky to conduct a session with twelve young lawyers who were neither engaged volunteers nor board members, nor in any way aware of the project or where we were going with it. We invited them to participate in exploring what the future might be – they brought a lot of energy to the task! They were so creative and innovative, and there were a lot of common themes in the forty-eight ideas that came out of it. We then synthesized those down to nine concepts, took them across the country into a series of roundtables where everyone had a chance to respond to them and offer ideas on how to make them even better.

In addition to the cross-country roundtables, we put those same nine concepts up on a virtual platform. Along with the in-person meetings, building a virtual community to extend engagement had some of the most powerful results. We started with a panel of 350, but we ultimately had thousands of people engaged in the platform. We know that those were unique visitors and not just the same people going on and on again. The virtual community happened in a limited time frame, and people were fantastically engaged in providing the feedback that would make those concepts better. We had people from every province and territory. Reaching out to members who wouldn't be able to come to a physical meeting in an urban center was hugely powerful. It enabled those that cared to be part of the discussion. And high levels of engagement did not go unnoticed by some of the skeptics, which built more support for the platform.

Then there was the board. This process made them ask some very difficult and fundamental questions, the most important of which was, *Who were we going to serve, and who they were not going to serve?* We set up the room that day with highly visual reminders of what we had gone through and what the research had shown us, who the personas were, what the universal needs – that all fed into a great strategic outcome for that day.

There was a lot of agreement when the small groups got back together to discuss our strategic choices to be made. For example, we agreed to focus on young lawyers and what we should be doing in that space. We also agreed that our mandate was to serve people within Canada, and that the judges were an important part of our community. There were a lot of things that were I think crystal clear to everybody. I don't think there was a lot of debate about what strategic direction we should be taking because it's the path that led us there.

As for that strategy, from a staff perspective, everyone refers back to it all the time. We use it in everything that we do. We use it for all of our reporting across the whole organization both on a staff level and on a governance level. So, for example, anytime we do a board report or when I write my executive director's report, I reiterate the five strategic pillars and I talk about how we have moved in those terms and how we have integrated that strategy through the whole organization. We have also enjoyed a much higher number of members applying the strategy to day-to-day decisions.

I see the process as being a departure from what I would call a traditional strategic planning session. Incorporating design thinking with strategy and using some different methodological approaches made for a much more powerful universal strategy across the CBA.[17] **"**

LIST OF TOOLS & TIPS

The following tools and tips are provided in part two to help explore, assess, and focus your thinking.

3

CONTEXTUALIZING YOUR CHALLENGE

TAKING STOCK OF THE BIG PICTURE

Before jumping right into the 3 Gears, it is important to take stock of the market context and your current enterprise activities. This will help frame market-based opportunities, assess your current distinctiveness and strengths, and inform your need-finding research plan for Gear 1. Here is a story about an organization that was well prepared for their quest, using all the principles in chapter 2. As they set out on a journey of strategic transformation, their work in this phase was critical to opening the lens on market trends and dynamics and aligning the team on enterprise opportunities for the future.[18]

Accreditation Canada: Transforming Healthcare through Standards

The Challenge

Accreditation Canada (AC) has a long history that began with ensuring that hospitals met high standards in practice as certified through an accreditation process. Over the years, AC had extended this practice to virtually every patient touch point in the healthcare system and had developed a codified process for standards development, assessment, and accreditation. Their stronghold in the Canadian market and more recent growth in international markets through Accreditation Canada International (ACI) positioned them as a critical lynchpin in healthcare systems. However, the healthcare landscape has been dramatically shifting in recent years, with increased focus on patient outcomes, healthcare-system productivity, integration of patient touch points across the system, and the application of emerging technology solutions. This called for a radical strategic transformation that would maximize the value AC could bring to healthcare systems in the future. In 2016, Leslee Thompson was hired as the CEO of Accreditation Canada and International to lead that vital transformation.

Such an enterprise-wide transformation requires broad engagement and enterprise readiness to harness the wisdom and ingenuity of the organization. In preparing for their quest, they followed all the principles outlined in chapter 2. To tackle the challenge, they established the FUEL development team of twenty-eight executives and emerging leaders, along with a plan to engage the board and the whole organization at every step of development.

A comprehensive strategy development road map was designed. A vision of success and conditions for success were made explicit. An all-employee and board innovation readiness survey was run to diagnose their current state of readiness – revealing strengths to leverage and opportunities to build a more innovative, future-forward culture. This thoughtful up-front planning set them up for a productive journey to define a future-focused strategy that would not just ensure the enterprise's survival but also fuel its growth in a step-change way.

The first step for the FUEL team was to establish a comprehensive picture of the market and take stock of the existing capabilities of the enterprise. That began with a work session using Business Design tools to capture the team's insights on critical trends, the landscape of players, the stakeholder ecosystem, and the enterprise's current strategy and operating systems. That was followed by fact-finding research and synthesis to validate the intuitive work from the work session.

The Breakthrough

This work led to some "Aha!" moments that reframed the *market-based challenge* for the enterprise and created alignment in the challenges and opportunities ahead. This reframing breakthrough came in several ways.

The first breakthrough came in the appreciation of how emerging trends would impact their transformation in seismic ways. For example, the increased focus on patient engagement and outcomes clearly pointed to putting the patient front-and-center and linking standards to outcomes. The complexities, fragmentation, and lack of integration across the system were driving up healthcare costs and impeding outcomes; that called for a health-systems approach to standards development. The role of emerging technologies was a game changer in the making, with digital communications, record-sharing, and dashboards shifting the way people interact and make decisions. That meant standards development would have to be a more dynamic and adaptive practice.

The second breakthrough came in zooming out to see the full landscape of players. Given the dire need for healthcare improvement, everyone was jumping into the health-standards game, not just those who were traditionally in the health-standards accreditation business, but also governments, advocacy groups, government agencies, and other commercial-interest groups, and particularly technology-solution providers that were disrupting the way healthcare quality is managed. That clearly called for a precise and distinct strategy for AC/ACI to win within an ever-changing landscape of players.

The third breakthrough came in mapping the broader group of stakeholders. While the central "client" had historically been the accreditation coordinator and their institutional decision-makers, there were many other stakeholders who could add tremendous value to the development and assessment process: health-systems leaders, patients, policy makers, front-line providers, surveyors, quality-management providers, and industry partners. The critical roles and interrelationship of all these stakeholders informed our extensive research in Gear 1, which aimed to understand the needs of all these stakeholders across many jurisdictions and countries. Every one of them was integral to future success in terms of both patient outcomes and the enterprise.

The fourth breakthrough came in mapping the current activities and capabilities of the AC and ACI organizations. This revealed that even though the organizations had slightly different approaches to the market, they were mutually dependent. AC had mastered the development of standards for sites, and ACI had pioneered a health-systems approach. That led to a restructuring of the organization as a health standards organization (as you will read in chapter 6), with standards development, assessment, and accreditation services leveraging the combined knowledge, processes, and technology tools of these two streams of business.

Last, the team generated a long list of considerations for future strategic choices to make their options explicit. With an appreciation for the complexities of the context and the multitude of players, it was clear that they would need to make some precise choices in Gear 3 to focus their efforts on winning in the future.

The Outcome

This broad sweep of the market dynamics and rigorous analysis of the emerging forces, players, and important stakeholders brought the market-based opportunity into focus. After this phase, there were no blind spots. Everyone was fully aware of the space in which the enterprise was operating: the FUEL team, the board, and all employees. The challenge ahead was big, but the opportunity to impact patients' lives in a meaningful way was very motivating to everyone on the extended team.

This phase of work helped frame up the work for Gears 1 and 2, and eventually informed the strategic choices in Gear 3 in an important way, as told through the story about designing your strategy in chapter 6.

This story underscores the importance of zooming out and appreciating the context in which you are operating at the outset of your quest. That is the time to understand how to seize trends, consider who might be competitors or partners in the future, identify who you need to deeply understand, and appreciate that you have some distinct capabilities to leverage as you evolve to your desired future state.

"We have to be nimble. We see how quickly things are changing."

FUEL TEAM MEMBER

Business Design tools helped to quickly and efficiently download the tacit knowledge of this multi-functional team in a *single day* through a process of inclusive discovery. That picture was solidified through fact finding and synthesis to bring focus to what was on the horizon and frame how the enterprise might define its future role in the market. That was shared with the board and employees to give a clear line of sight to the quest and align everyone on both what they were up against and the strong base of capabilities they could leverage in their transformation.

Your Goal in Contextualizing Your Challenge

To fully grasp the context in which you are operating and appreciate your ingoing position. Doing so will eliminate blind spots, as well as help you frame up the market-based opportunity and plan your research for Gear 1.

The balance of this chapter highlights key activities, outcomes, and development principles; provides tips on the role of data analysis and validation;

Fig. 6 **Activities and Outcomes in Contextualizing Your Challenge**

examines the mindsets, methods, and thinking modes that are most critical; and finishes with an inspired interview that brings important principles to life. Related tools are included in part two: Tool Kit.

Activities & Outcomes

Figure 6 shows some of the activities you will undertake and some of the most valuable outcomes that will contextualize and frame your quest:

Key Trends: Synthesis of the trends that are most likely to occur and most likely to impact your success, to allow you to design for the future.

Landscape of Players: A comprehensive picture of who else is doing business in this space, to identify how they could either be a competitor or partner in the future.

Stakeholder Mapping: A comprehensive mapping of all the people who matter in your success and their relationships to one another, so you can design with the entire ecosystem in mind.

Current Enterprise: A visual synthesis of your current system of inter-related activities and capabilities, which will help you both assess your current distinctiveness and appreciate what you might uniquely leverage going forward.

Future Scenarios: A snapshot of what the future might look like, to contextualize what unique and meaningful role you might play in creating future value.

Choice Considerations: A comprehensive list of strategic considerations, to equip you to explicitly decide what to do and what not to do when you design your strategy in Gear 3.

Divergent activities include capturing all of the tacit knowledge of the team to generate a broad list of considerations. This will enable you to quickly get a comprehensive picture of forces, players, stakeholders, and strategic considerations. **Convergent** activities entail deciding what and who matters most – to your quest and the work you will do in subsequent phases.

Key Principles: Context Is Everything

Broadening your awareness of the context and eliminating blind spots will frame and prioritize important considerations. Here are some things to keep in mind:

Think broadly about trends that will maximize your opportunity. By prioritizing and dimensionalizing critical trends, you will be able to align your quest with those that are important to your future.

While you should start with a long list, you should decide which trends are most likely to occur and impact your success. As noted in the method of STEEP analysis in the Tools section, it's important to think broadly about the social, technological, economical, environmental, and political trends. Ascertaining these high-impact trends and putting numbers against them will help you begin to frame your business case. For AC/ACI, the focus on systems integration, patient engagement, and health outcomes would drive the enterprise's pursuits.

Consider all the players that are broadly doing business in this space. It is not uncommon to focus on your biggest, most direct competitors, along with your existing partners. It's important to ask: *Who else is interested in "doing business" in this space?* That question can lead to a long list of existing and emerging players, some of whom you might not be paying enough attention to, including organizations expanding into your space or emerging players that are disrupting the system in which you operate, such as technology-solution providers. In the case of AC/ACI, there were a lot of players in this space to take into consideration: other accreditation players, governments, and technology start-ups. In healthcare, there are a lot of players that see a huge opportunity to create value for the system, the people in it, and themselves. Growing segments attract many players. You might also find that one of your own "customers" thinks they should take over what you currently do for them. A good example of this is the retail trade – both a customer of product manufacturers and a competitor with their own house brands.

Identify all external stakeholders that might matter in your success. This is not about just thinking about your central stakeholder; it's about identifying *all* the people who matter to your future success, as further explained in chapter 4. Expanding your view of who matters will ensure that you have a comprehensive plan for need-finding in Gear 1, when you ask: *Whose voices must be heard?* With a diverse team, you can use your knowledge and experience to broaden the list.

For example, in the case of AC/ACI, members of the FUEL team all had important perspectives from their experience with healthcare leaders, patients, policy makers, providers, and surveyors. Every one of these stakeholders plays a role in their success. By being aware of them and considering their relationships to each other and their role in your future success, you will design a more comprehensive need-finding plan – which will also inspire a more inclusive offering and delivery model.

Capture your current enterprise activities and capabilities. Ask yourself: *Where do we spend our time and money now? What are we really good at?* This is best done by mapping out core activities and capabilities as an integrated system rather than making a simple list. As further presented in chapter 6 and in the Tool Kit section of this book, the power of your system is based on how these activities and capabilities fit together. This is also the time to be totally objective about what you do really well and come to a team consensus on where you currently put your efforts and excel.

For example, the AC/ACI "Aha!" was that the two operating units, AC and ACI, weren't doing business in *exactly* the same way. However, there were important links between them and distinct and complimentary capabilities in each. The combined activities of AC and ACI could be leveraged into new and more powerful ways of doing business, eventually leading to a new enterprise structure that better strategically defined the purpose and offerings of the enterprise and built on the capabilities of these two organizations.

It's important to appreciate what you have in play at the start, as you will come back to this in Gear 3, when you have your new vision in mind. Ask yourself: *What do we have that no one else can match?*

Do the same for your competitors and then assess your distinctiveness. Organizations often focus on what they do best and don't stop to compare their model to that of others. When working with teams that have mapped both their systems and those of others, there is always an "Aha!" moment. In the case of AC/ACI, one of its advantages is that it works with virtually every point of care in the healthcare system, making it uniquely positioned to "connect the dots" across the healthcare system.

Through this assessment, you might also discover a "hidden gem" in your systems. For example, in working with Frito-Lay, their direct-to-store delivery system can sometimes be considered a *constraint*; looking at it through a different lens, you can think of the skills and know-how behind that delivery system as a powerful *capability* that can be leveraged into a myriad of other applications. On the flip side, you might find that putting your system next to your competitors' leads to the frightening conclusion that you look pretty much the same. That's often the case in more mature markets, like consumer-packaged goods.

To assess your current distinctiveness and competitive advantage, ask yourself, *How different are we? Can we grow and sustain success with our current system of activities?*

Map your critical processes. In every business in which there is a scaled activity, there is an underlying process. Sometimes that is intuitive, but more often quite explicit in large enterprises. It is vitally important to understand and acknowledge your ingrained ways of doing business. That can reveal several things. *One*, it might be that you have been doing things in a systematic way without knowing it; that's a good thing to explicitly codify. *Two*, it might be that you have a system that constrains your efforts and rejects new ideas. *Three*, you might find that your processes have been built for another time and need a redesign or streamlining to make you more responsive and agile. Those are all good discoveries to have in hand up front.

Being explicit about your processes will make you more prepared to leverage, refine, or rethink your processes as you prepare to scale in Gear 3. In the case of AC/ACI, it found that its standards-development process was rigorous and precise, but too lengthy and cumbersome for doing business in an agile, ever-evolving way. Being more explicit about processes helps in understanding what needs to be preserved and also what might need to be re-engineered for the future.

Imagine what the future might look like. Based on where you see the market, players, and stakeholders heading, it is helpful to paint a picture of what the future might look like. While you don't yet know precisely what your distinct role will be, you now know that the future won't look much like the present! By projecting a few scenarios of how trends and players play out into the future, you will have a greater sense of urgency to design for the future *now*.

Consider all your possible strategic choice considerations up front. In chapter 1, I referred to a list of questions that need to be precisely answered in defining your enterprise strategy. At the outset of a quest, everyone has ideas about what those options might be. By getting everyone's ideas and assumptions on the table up front, you will make your options explicit. You might discover that you have a relatively narrow set of considerations – or that you are all over the place. In either case, this exercise will give you a starting point from which you can begin to pare down the list and get focused on where you will place your development efforts.

Synthesize your most critical factors for market success. Through a process of sensemaking in which you share all your discoveries from this phase, it will be clear that there are some factors that will be critical to your success. For example, for AC, connecting providers and patients across the continuum of care in the system, and moving in step with an increasingly real-time and digital approach to managing quality healthcare were critical. At this point, you should identify and carry forward the most critical factors from a market and enterprise standpoint. At the end of Gear 1, you will have a keen sense of the human-centered opportunities. Combining your discoveries from Contextualizing Your Challenge and Gear 1, you will be in a position to synthesize design criteria for Gear 2.

All these principles, considerations, and actions will lead you to a solid understanding of the market context and a better grasp on where you stand now. This will give you some early hints to where you might play and how you might win in the future.

Building a Business Case:
Data Analysis & Validation

Given that the outcomes of this phase should be fact-based, critical data like trend validation and market sizing will help you make some early choices on who to serve and which segment to pursue; this will feed into a compelling business case in Gear 3.

Important Mindsets, Methods, & Thinking Modes

Mindset Matters: There is always a lot of enthusiasm at the outset of a quest. The challenges and the stakes can often be amplified in this phase. What will be most important is to maintain a big dose of *positivity* and a collective commitment to creating the future together. When examining your current state and processes, exercise empathy, as people will naturally have a sense of pride and ownership in their contribution to the enterprise to date. Moreover, this phase also calls for an *open mind* to new market opportunities and new ways of doing business in the future.

Most Critical Methods: The spirit of *collaboration* continues to be a critical factor in this phase. It's the most productive way to get everyone's insights and perspectives on the table in short order. You will also exercise your *systems mapping* skills in this phase, as you begin to appreciate the ecosystem in which you operate – both externally and inside your enterprise.

Regulating Thinking Modes: While this is the time to fully *understand* the gravitas of your operating context and generate a long list of what you might consider, this is also very much a time for *critical thinking and decision-making* to focus your efforts going forward in the development process.

With an appreciation for the context in which you operate your current state, you should now be aligned on the opportunities ahead and ready to explore what people really need!

The process of contextualizing your challenge can be a rigorous analytical exercise, as it was for AC/ACI. In other cases, opportunities may arise as a result of mindfulness of important market signals that inspire new ways to help customers. The following interview with Ashwini Srikantiah of Fidelity Labs brings to life how sensitivity to unmet needs can spark new opportunities to explore, and how engaging a broad set of stakeholders in the need-finding and iterative prototyping process can lead to a significant breakthrough in value creation for the enterprise.

Interview with Ashwini Srikantiah

Vice President, Emerging Products, Fidelity

Student Debt Program at Fidelity Investments

" About three years ago we started looking into the big, gnarly problem of student debt in America. Historically, Fidelity has not been in the lending business – we are asset managers, not debt managers. But as asset managers, we look at the role lending plays in personal finance because loans are a big part of personal-wealth management.

We started our look at student debt with a mix of primary and secondary research, interviewing people who had student loans, and reading to understand the macro- and micro-economic context of the problem. We also did some really quick tests and experiments within our own community of employees at Fidelity.

The first big insight was that student loans have a huge impact on people's lives. They feel very differently about student debt than about other kinds of loans. For instance, they see their mortgage as equity building, future facing, and positive. But they see their student loan as a "ball and chain" that is holding them back.

The second insight was that people don't understand how student loans work. And they are often made to feel stupid when asking questions about it.

The third was that people did benefit from having some guidance about their personal student loan. Some were able to successfully refinance and save. But when others tried, they were rejected, making them feel even worse than when they started.

So we were onto something. We had uncovered a real unmet need. And it was happening across America: about 60 per cent of millennials, 40 per cent of gen Xers and 25 per cent of boomers have student debt.

We identified three key opportunity spaces: direct help for employees acutely overwhelmed by and undereducated about their student loans; employers who were becoming more and more interested in helping employees navigate their student loan problem as both a way to attract talent and to aid productivity; and people who could avoid the debt cycle to begin with by honestly discussing the financial impact of college choices.

Fidelity is now helping its own employees pay off their student loans by contributing $10,000 over the course of five years on a monthly basis direct to their student loan accounts. We've become leaders in the student-loans benefits space.

We launched an online planning and advice portal after a year and a half of design and product iteration and continued launching to incrementally larger groups, continually taking feedback and basically improving and evolving the product.

We collaborated with the marketing engine behind our workplace services team to really broadcast that out. Within just three weeks, we had over 50,000 people log in to the tool and start to use it to get personalized guidance.

In three years we've grown from three to over a hundred people across five different sites working day in and day out to bring this to life, making it one of the top ten growth initiatives of the firm.

We would not be enjoying this growth had we not been able to figure out internally how and where to position these efforts so that they ladder up to the broader strategic objectives of the firm. Figuring out who is leading efforts that are moving toward a similar end goal and working together with them was critical.

So was getting the client voice represented through primary research, both qualitative and quantitative, and then sharing that with key plan sponsors across our most strategic clients. Engaging their interest enabled us to really pull through this effort because a Pepsi or an IBM was excited about what we were doing. That lent huge credibility to our efforts.

Another was continuing to articulate the vision of a large opportunity and a larger product system while simultaneously starting very small and making progress on releasing one piece at a time.

Our success has meant that now, the majority of my job is stakeholder management, strategic alignment, and making sure that we continue to be connected with the right people across the organization.[19] **,,**

LIST OF TOOLS & TIPS

The following tools and tips are provided in part two to help explore, assess, and focus your thinking.

4

GEAR 1: EMPATHY & DEEP HUMAN UNDERSTANDING

REFRAMING THE OPPORTUNITY

Creating human-centered value starts with appreciating the broader human context of your pursuit and deeply understanding the needs of the people that matter. Here is a story that demonstrates how a deeper understanding of important stakeholders can reveal new opportunities and raise the bar on ambitions. This story shows how using Gear 1 can lead to a radical reframing of the opportunity, a more holistic solution system, and eventually a shift in strategy.[20]

The Healthcare Company Story: Seeing the Problem with Heart

The Challenge

About 40,000 Canadians die from sudden cardiac arrest every year.[21] A leading healthcare company had a solution for some of these Canadians – a heart-rhythm device that monitors and, if necessary, resets a patient's heart rhythm following sudden cardiac arrest. While the device is not appropriate for all patients, it could save the life of those for whom it is indicated.

The company believed there was an opportunity to better identify and capture device-qualified patients and thus save lives while expanding sales. To tackle this challenge, the company and a major teaching hospital in Canada commissioned a study to shed light on this important issue and explore North American practices in the management of conditions for which a device is indicated, with a focus on resolving the Canadian challenge. At the outset of the project, it was thought the business opportunity lay in improving the effectiveness of referrals to electrophysiologists (EPs), the specialists who perform the procedure to implant these life-saving devices, along with better patient education. At the completion of Gear 1, the scope of opportunity was broadened to include consideration of the systemic challenge.

The Breakthroughs

The first Gear 1 breakthrough was a reframe of the challenge that not only identified where the more significant problems lay, but also magnified the business opportunity. Mapping the broader patient journey revealed a more accurate picture of the patient flow and the relationship among all of the key professionals they encountered along the way in managing their heart health. These other stakeholders included general practitioners, Emergency Department staff, internal medicine, cardiologists, and nurses at every point along the path. Often nurses in general practitioners' offices, emergency departments, clinics, and specialist offices have the most face time with patients, giving them valuable insights into the patient experience.

Understanding the context more broadly revealed that the patient journey begins long before the EP becomes involved, and even long before the patient's referring physician is brought into the picture. Visualizing the patient flow from one professional stakeholder to another, and from one site to another (i.e., GP's office, Emergency Department, hospital, or clinic), revealed a complicated system of rework, with patients often returning to the same people and places or, in some cases, dropping out of the system altogether. This visualization became known as "the pinball machine" (as depicted in Figure 7). The directional arrows show how the patient bounced around from one person or place to another in the system, while the "exit" arrows indicate where they dropped out of the system.

Fig. 7 **Healthcare Pinball Machine**

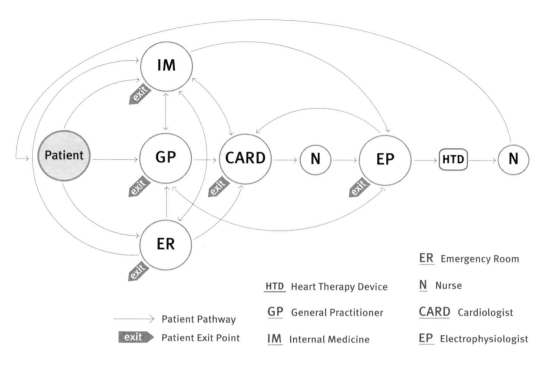

ER Emergency Room
HTD Heart Therapy Device
N Nurse
GP General Practitioner
CARD Cardiologist
IM Internal Medicine
EP Electrophysiologist

------> Patient Pathway
exit Patient Exit Point

As the arrows show, patients would land in Emergency and be referred to a cardiologist or perhaps back to their GP, who may or may not have been equipped to educate, diagnose, or refer the patient. Patients who made it to a cardiologist may or may not have proceeded to an EP, depending on their test results. And even if they were referred to an EP, they may have been sent back for repeated tests. These patients remained active in the system, but without timely or complete resolution of their clinical needs. Even worse, some patients, for a variety of reasons, were dropping out of the system completely, as indicated by the "exit" arrows. These patients were not being flagged for critical fast tracking and resolution of their potentially fatal condition. For the majority of patients, this experience led to higher anxiety, resignation, or ineffective resolution. For those at serious risk of a sudden cardiac arrest, not obtaining a device was particularly stressful.

Through further analysis, it was estimated that only 5 per cent of cardiac patients made it to an EP and only 10 per cent ever made it to a cardiologist, who often refers a patient to the EP.[22] That meant as many as 90 per cent of one particular group of cardiac patients were bouncing around in the system from their GP to other medical professionals. Many of these patients were ending up in Emergency and being discharged without any further referral or follow-up. That was putting lives at risk, eating up healthcare system dollars, and resulting in lost business for the company. *Given these facts, the original business challenge was then reframed to consider the entire patient pathway and broader referral system.*

The second breakthrough in Gear 1 came through a deeper understanding of all the stakeholders in the system. Deep understanding helped identify what the flow-limiting issues were and what stakeholder needs had to be considered in designing solutions to improve patient experience and outcomes. Through patient stories, we learned they were frustrated by the lack of information and empowerment they experienced. The stories from healthcare professionals revealed how each individual practitioner appeared to be technically competent, but all had a different set of protocols to follow. They did not have a clear referral pathway and did not really know if others adhered to the same test standards and protocols. The issues were thus complex and systemic; there was a pronounced need for broad and consistent education for both patients and professionals, simplified and shared protocols, and a clear path for patient referrals. *These insights pointed to specific areas of opportunity for more effective solutions.*

The Outcome

Key opportunities arose in the areas of targeted interventions, patient management and education, and defining referral systems and protocols. Most importantly, the outcomes of this project pointed to an important strategic shift – from selling to specialists to shaping a more effective healthcare system that would deliver better health outcomes and value.

While there were broader and longer-term systems-wide solutions to be deployed, Gear 1 alone provided a new framework for focusing efforts and developing solutions. First steps included expanding a fast-track procedure for patients who presented specific red flags in terms of symptoms and test results in the Emergency Department, along with marketing programs aimed at increasing general practitioner awareness. The learning was also shared broadly within the organization. One of the patient participants from this project was even invited to tell his story at a company event, and the company continued to support him in his patient-advocacy initiatives. This patient, and the compelling story of the company's new patient experience vision presented at the company's sales meeting, *humanized* the challenge for the broader company team.

This invaluable reframing and sensitivity to stakeholder needs set the team up to better meet the challenge of addressing a bigger opportunity than originally envisioned. To address this challenge, the company's team drew from the success of others, both locally and globally. It created new and specific tactical solutions to bridge the gaps in the system and help everyone work in a way that facilitates moving patients through a more efficient process. Longer term, it was clear there needed to be more extensive professional education, patient counseling aids, alignment on clearer and more consistent protocols, and a more clearly defined and effective referral network.

Since this project, the company has followed a steady path toward systems solutions aimed at value-based healthcare, taking into account the pathways of specific patient cohorts and activating solutions at the most critical points in their journey. More and more, healthcare systems in the world are focused on improving clinical outcomes, improving the patient journey, and creating a greater return on healthcare dollars. The pinball machine certainly frames up that opportunity clearly and has served as a helpful reference in mapping and pinpointing improvement opportunities.

"The output of the project has helped us reframe the issue and get focused on what really matters, which is ultimately the patient. This helped drive alignment within our organization and ultimately led to more focused efforts and improved long-term results."
TEAM LEADER

This story points to the value of both stepping back to see the problem more holistically and listening to important human stories that reveal points of pain and deep unmet needs (which will be further explored in this chapter). It also underscores the principle that if you do not fully understand the human system, you may be trying to solve the wrong problem. By understanding the needs of all key stakeholders in the system, you can build solutions to meet a broader set of needs and create stakeholder buy-in to new solutions. This undertaking requires empathy to see the picture through the eyes of others, backed by rigorous analysis and synthesis of data and a reframing of the business opportunity.

How many times do we fixate on a problem that we are sure we can solve and spend extensive time and resources on a singular point of tension, wondering, *"Why can't we make more meaningful progress?"* That's the time to zoom out to the big picture, and then dive into a deeper exploration of the underlying human systems and needs. This approach will inevitably reveal where the biggest opportunities lie. It will also help identify the issues that are holding back progress and, in this case, preventing full delivery on the ability to save more lives.

Better meeting the needs of your important stakeholders, especially the end user, is Job 1. By seeing the world through the eyes of others, you will develop a deeper understanding of the relationships, challenges, and needs of your important stakeholders. Gear 1 is the critical first step toward understanding both *who* matters in your broader human network and *what* matters to each of them. The activities of Gear 1 will help you to define relationships more explicitly, bringing greater clarity to the challenge at hand.

This deeper appreciation for the human factor will also help create a greater sense of empathy with your stakeholders and motivate you to generate ways to better meet their needs, which you will do in Gear 2. This first gear is always full of surprises and "Aha!" moments that reveal new opportunities to create value and tap into your problem-solving skills. Prepare to be surprised at how many people influence the course of actions, how their deeper needs are often not what they seem to be on the surface, and how this knowledge can not only reframe your opportunity but also provide the inspiration and platform for solution innovation as you tackle Gear 2.

Your Goal in Gear 1

To frame human-centered opportunities in three ways: fully appreciating the interdependencies of the human system, articulating unmet human needs, and defining design criteria for Gear 2. Framing opportunity in these ways will often lead to a substantial reframing and can have quite radical implications for both the magnitude and the precision of the opportunity.

The balance of this chapter highlights key activities, outcomes, and development principles; provides tips on the role of data analysis and validation, as well as the mindsets, methods, and thinking modes that are most critical; and finishes with an inspired interview that brings important principles to life. Related tools are included in part two: Tool Kit.

Gear 1: Activities & Outcomes

Figure 8 shows some of the activities you will undertake in understanding people more deeply and some of the most valuable outcomes that will guide your Gear 2 efforts and demonstrate ongoing value:

Articulation of Needs: What matters most to the people that matter in your success – unmet universal needs within and across stakeholder groups, defining opportunities to create new value.

Personas: Human depictions of archetypes that contextualize needs across diverse profiles – to keep important people "at the table" with you throughout development.

Current Journey: The end user's current experience – revealing the best and worst parts of their journey, with points of pain as specific opportunities to close gaps and enhance their experience.

Stakeholder Map: A more precise visualization of the human system – all of the people that matter to your success, their relationships to each other and the end user.

Design Criteria: Critical considerations to take into solution design in Gear 2 based on market context and human insights and needs.

Divergent activities in Gear 1 call for an open exploration of what matters to people and how you might fit into their lives. An open heart, open mind, and a healthy dose of curiosity will lead you to new insights. The **convergent** phase of Gear 2 calls for sense making, analysis, and fact finding that will validate your outcomes and bring focus to your work in Gear 2.

Key Principles: Appreciate the Human Factor

The benefits of developing a richer understanding of people as the basis for creating new value are evident in so many successes. Here are some important principles to keep in mind that will enhance the value of your outcomes from Gear 1:

Fig. 8 **Gear 1: Activities and Outcomes**

ACTIVITIES: **OUTCOMES:**

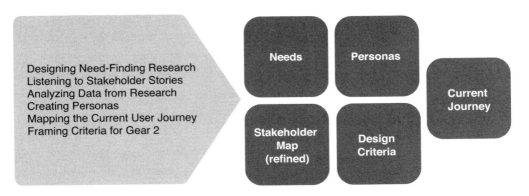

Designing Need-Finding Research
Listening to Stakeholder Stories
Analyzing Data from Research
Creating Personas
Mapping the Current User Journey
Framing Criteria for Gear 2

Needs

Personas

Current Journey

Stakeholder Map (refined)

Design Criteria

Appreciate all stakeholders and relationships within the human system.
Opening up the lens to understand the needs of *all* stakeholders and their
interrelationships will form the basis of an important connection between
human systems, solution systems, and business systems. This understanding will
be critical in making your business idea "stick." This was demonstrated in the
healthcare company case, in which mapping the patient journey in the context
of a broader stakeholder system revealed a more accurate picture of the business
opportunity. We sometimes focus on a single archetypical user and neglect the
others who are involved in enabling, delivering or influencing how a central idea
goes into play. Your initial stakeholder mapping and need-finding research will
help define the role of each stakeholder in your ultimate success. You might
consider these general categories of stakeholders:

▶ **The end user:** This is the central benefactor of the ultimate solution – they
make the final call on whether or not you are creating value. In the healthcare company story, the end user was the patient. In other cases, it might
be a consumer, a business customer, or employees.

▶ **Enablers:** They are critical to successful delivery of new solutions. They
facilitate an end user's decision-making and actions or act as a gatekeeper
in the decision-making process. By understanding their needs, you can
more effectively enroll them in adopting a new idea. In the healthcare
company story, all of the medical professionals as well as families and
friends were important enablers – they played a role in how solutions were

activated. As another example, understanding and better meeting a retailer's needs will enable you to work together to accelerate the sale of your product in their stores.

- ▶ **Influencers:** Though they may not be directly involved in delivering a solution, they shape users' and enablers' decisions and actions. In the healthcare case, the experts who defined clinical protocols were important because they shape the practices of those who cared directly for the patient. As another example, chefs and nutritionists might influence and shape the future of food and eating habits.

All of these stakeholders are important to consider in creating and delivering high-value solutions. As you move through Gear 1, you may discover others to integrate into your effort to understand the human factor. This will keep your offering relevant to everyone who matters to your success.

Design a thoughtful and rigorous research plan to establish credibility and build confidence. The key question that will be asked is, *Whose voices were heard and how confident are you in your conclusions?* While need-finding exploration is very inspiring to a development team, it also should be rigorous if it will serve as the basis for big decisions and investment down the road. It will also serve as a valuable ongoing reference in filtering new ideas. While some undertake research to stimulate inspiration and ideas, observing and listening to a handful of people won't serve as a valid foundation in your pursuits. It's important to comprehensively map who matters, design a sample that cuts across various stakeholder profiles, record (even transcribe) interviews, analyze them in a rigorous manner, and validate your findings. That will establish credibility in the research and confidence in the foundation of your work going forward. Some guidelines on research design are also provided in the Tool Kit.

Use people's needs as the basis for new value creation. At the root of many great brands and businesses is a deep understanding of human needs. For example, Four Seasons Hotels and Resorts is devoted to meeting the need for exceptional, personalized guest service on every level. Nespresso delivers on the coffee lover's need for moments of indulgence and pleasure through an exclusive, premium coffee experience. Virgin strives to deliver a better experience in every category they enter. These companies have grown their businesses over time by expanding the ways in which they meet customer needs through new products, services, and communications that enrich their experience. Some examples of how this played out in the healthcare project are included in the next point on storytelling as a method to discover unmet needs.

Moreover, the most revealing need-finding activities involve direct contact with people as opposed to just sifting through a stack of market research reports. While quantitative data will give you a good grasp of the numbers, it will likely not give you deeper insights into your stakeholder needs that will allow you to identify and seize new opportunities. The Tool Kit section of this book outlines several ways to explore and articulate these needs.

Listen to activity-based stories to discover new opportunities. While understanding how people choose and use your products and services will help you improve current offerings, it will tend to lead only to better versions of current solutions (e.g., a product improvement or line extension). By expanding your understanding to the *activities* relating to your current products and services, you will discover a broader array of untapped opportunities (Figure 9).[23]

In the case of the healthcare company, in-depth interviews with both medical practitioners and patients revealed new insights. We didn't ask either group what they knew about heart conditions or devices. Instead, we listened to practitioners recounting their best and worst stories about managing cardiac patients. These stories revealed the need for better patient management, more clearly defined referral networks, greater trust in colleagues and the system, a better grasp of protocols, and greater confidence in patient communications and counseling. These science-minded professionals revealed their more

Fig. 9 **Layers of Opportunity**

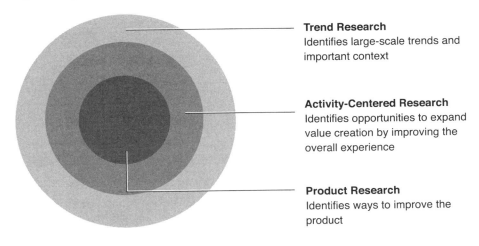

Trend Research
Identifies large-scale trends and important context

Activity-Centered Research
Identifies opportunities to expand value creation by improving the overall experience

Product Research
Identifies ways to improve the product

human side, which would not have been exposed had we asked about a heart condition or how a device might provide a solution.

We did the same with patients: we listened to their best and worst stories about living with their chronic heart condition. These patients were eager to understand what was happening to them and what they could do about it. They wanted the straight goods, without any confusing jargon. We heard stories about their experiences that went like this: *"The whole thing was scary. I didn't know what pills I had to take, where I had to go, who to see. Every doctor I saw wanted new tests done or wanted to know where I'd been … I'm seventy-eight years old. I can't keep track of these things. My nurse really guided me. Without her, I'd be lost."* These patients felt like a pinball in the system, and they didn't like it.

By listening to *activity-centered stories* with empathy and an open mind, and simply responding with *"Tell me more"* and wondering *"Why is that important to them?"* you will glean fresher insights than you ever would by drilling people with hundreds of questions. Guaranteed. These new discoveries will point you toward new opportunities and inspire a broader array of solutions.

Appreciate the "whole person." Humans are multidimensional in their needs. Considering the broader activity reveals more of a person's whole life and their needs on many levels – which leads to solutions that are not only relevant but also *meaningful.* That holistic approach calls for considering all types of needs, not just the practical and rational. Humans have many kinds of needs – functional, informational, relational, emotional, and identity based. Many enterprises are well versed on the functional needs for products and services, particularly within their current domain. Thinking more holistically about human needs will broaden your opportunities to better meet important needs and enhance people's experience.

The following framework (Figure 10), referred to in short as SPICE,[24] is based on analysis of interviews conducted across projects in my early days at Rotman DesignWorks. It helps to stimulate a more holistic consideration of people's needs and reveal other areas of opportunity beyond the design of a functionally better product or service. Consider the following:

▶ **Social:** *What do people need from their relationships with others?* In the case of the healthcare company, a doctor needs to have confidence and trust in his or her referral network.

Fig. 10 **SPICE Framework**

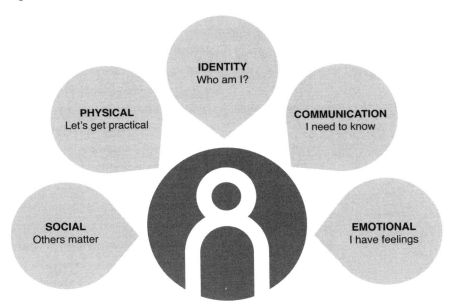

▶ **Physical:** *What do people need on a physical or functional level?* In the case of the healthcare company, the device itself is a life-saving solution.

▶ **Identity:** *What do people need to enhance their sense of self-worth or reinforce their personal identity?* In the case of the healthcare company, each patient needed to feel that their life mattered, while the practitioners needed to be seen as professionals who were doing the best for their patients. Needs like these are important to recognize and respect in the design of your solutions.

▶ **Communication:** *What kinds of information do people need and when and where do they need it?* In the case of the healthcare company, everyone could benefit from getting the right information at the right time. Patients needed to know what was happening to them and what to expect if they were to get a device; practitioners needed to know the latest in diagnosis and treatment protocols.

▶ **Emotional:** *What do people need psychologically and emotionally?* In the case of the healthcare company, patients needed to feel more empowered, and the practitioners needed to feel recognized for their contributions. These needs impact your design of the ideal experience, with the goal of helping people feel the way you would like them to feel as a result of your efforts.

Quantitative trend data can help to place these needs in context and give some dimension to broad opportunities, but they neither feed your sense of empathy nor reveal the deeper insights that activity-based need-finding will. All good research and opportunity framing involve a combination of qualitative need-finding and quantitative analysis, as will be noted later in this chapter.

Search for the truth and keep it real. That starts with turning off your "filter" when listening to stories. Transcriptions are a good way to remember and share the real story. When articulating needs, use first person and normal language, and leverage defining quotes. Create personas that are not idealistic; reveal their frustrations, anxieties, and points of pain. There is more on this in the Tool Kit section.

Cultivate shared empathy. Gear 1 is most powerful when everyone on the team, and your extended audience, shares a deep understanding of and empathy for the important people in the equation. Ideally, everyone on the team should have the opportunity for a meaningful, firsthand experience with those for whom they will design. It is valuable for everyone on the development team to connect with the people who matter; that includes involving financial officers, operations experts, marketing folks, sales personnel, and product development experts. As noted in chapter 1, *"Connecting with and understanding people in an authentic way gives meaning and purpose to our work."* If that firsthand experience is not practical, you can bring your findings to life through video clips and stories in a way that people are moved by the findings, as presented in the Tool Kit. That will also help to inspire empathy outside your development team.

Use your findings to define your criteria for solution design. While the needs will frame what people personally need to have an ideal experience, design criteria will provide important guidelines for building your solution. These criteria can be defined based on the needs of the market at large along with the insights and needs discovered in Gear 1. For example, solutions designed to improve cardiac-patient outcomes needed to connect all parties in the system. Ultimately, these criteria will not only help guide solution development, they will also inform your strategy in Gear 3.

Taking these steps to more deeply understand the needs and critical relationships within the broader system of people who matter will provide a solid foundation for value creation in Gear 2. It will also serve as a valuable reference in future development projects.

Building a Business Case: Data Analysis & Validation

Rigorous data analysis and validation of findings will fortify your business case. This will provide compelling *reasons to believe* that you are anchoring your development efforts in a solid foundation. With a deep and empathic understanding of the human factor in your quest, you will most likely have a different lens on the world and the opportunities before you. You should have a renewed sense of empathy and deeper understanding of the people in the system that matter.

At the same time, when important strategic choices and big capital investments are on the line, stories alone are often not enough. Facts and numbers can help to clinch your case. To further fortify your conviction, there are several ways you can build a fact-based picture of the critical implications of your discoveries. Here are some suggestions:

Turn your soft data into hard data. You can deconstruct a large bank of stories into deeper insights and convert them into thousands of data points through tagging and tabulation. One hundred interviews easily can turn up 10,000 data points. You can run those like any quantitative analysis, look for correlations by group, and ascertain the universal needs.

Run a simple survey. Once you have treated your data with objectivity and rigor, you can scale your user data by using a simple survey tool. It's simple, fast, cost-effective, and accessible to anyone using simple web-based technologies. You can ascertain both the importance of the need and current satisfaction to quantify the opportunity gap. There is more on this in the Tool section.

Re-tabulate your quantitative data. Given the open-ended nature of your Gear 1 exploratory, you likely have a fresh perspective and a new hypothesis on what's really going on in the market. Now's the time to dig into your research assets or tap into large-scale syndicated studies to rerun the data and test your hypothesis.

There are many other ways of building a data-based case for new opportunities. The key is to be efficient and resourceful, and ensure that your data-gathering design is methodically sound and the sources of data are credible. Business-minded people appreciate human stories. They also appreciate some hard facts.

Important Mindsets, Methods, & Thinking Modes

Mindset Matters: The most important mindset for Gear 1 is *empathy*; that will enable you to understand the human factor on a deep and authentic level. Your goal is to see the world through the eyes of others, and feel what they feel, to appreciate their deepest underlying needs. Putting aside your needs, opinions, and perspectives is critical. Too often, I have heard people watching consumers from behind a one-way mirror in focus groups make comments like, "She obviously doesn't know what she's talking about." That isn't empathy. Aim to put yourself wholly in the shoes of the other person.

To truly empathize, it is important to remember to turn off your filter when observing others and listening to their stories with *openness and mindfulness*. An open and unfiltered mindset will allow you to discover new opportunities to create value on a deeper and more meaningful level. Intuition, along with your natural curiosity, will guide you through the need-finding process. Instead of interpreting what they say, ask yourself, *Why is that important to them?* with the goal of understanding their deeper motivations.

That will fortify your *intrinsic motivation*; solving an unmet human need gives one a sense of purpose. Now is the time to set your extrinsic motivations aside (i.e., that next bonus or award). You are not collecting facts to support your case or preconceived notions; instead, you are listening for new insights that will inspire you to create new solutions.

Most Critical Methods: The most critical method in Gear 1 is *need-finding*, but you will also draw upon your *storytelling* and *systems mapping* skills in discovering and communicating new opportunities.

Regulating Your Thinking Modes: The most important cognitive mode for Gear 1 is *understanding*; that goes naturally with empathy, openness, and discovering a sense of purpose. Nonetheless, there will times in Gear 1 when you will have to *generate ideas* and hypotheses on the need behind new insights to discover deeper motivations and opportunities. And at the important convergent phase of the process, you will have to make sense of the data and *decide* on what matters most as you move onto the next phase of development.

One man who has always put people at the center of his dreams and believed that there are endless new possibilities to improve human lives is Earl Bakken, a life-long humanist, innovator and co-founder, chairman emeritus of the world's leading medical-device company, Medtronic Inc. Inspired in his childhood by the movie *Frankenstein* and the concept of using electricity to bring a being to life, he pursued his dreams and co-founded Medtronic in 1949 in a garage where his first wearable pacemaker was eventually built. His innovation pursuits extend beyond Medtronic, including the Heart-Brain Institute at the Cleveland Clinic, a holistic healing hospital in North Hawaii, and Earl's Garage, a program that inspires kids seven years and up with a sense of wonder, passion for learning, and capacity to create through minds-on, hands-on activities.

The following interview with Earl Bakken, co-founder of Medtronic, reveals the importance of dreams, intuition, prototypes, and collaboration – essential ingredients in innovation. It is an inspiring prelude to Gear 2 – imagining and visualizing new ways to make life better for people. In this interview, Earl Bakken refers to the North Hawaii Community Hospital (NHCH), a full-service acute-care hospital opened in 1996 as the first hospital in the United States designed completely around the philosophy of integrative medicine, and which serves as an innovative prototype for a patient-centric, holistic mind-body-spirit healing experience. Serving 30,000 patients in this community, NHCH was rated number one in Medicare's Patient Satisfaction Survey.[25] Earl Bakken has earned a long list of awards in innovation, entrepreneurship, leadership, science, and education; his story is recounted in his autobiography, One Man's Full Life.[26]

Interview with Earl Bakken
Co-founder and Chairman Emeritus, Medtronic Inc.

"I'm a big dreamer, and many of my dreams have come true. I find that during the time at night between going to bed and actually falling asleep, when my "mind" is free from thinking about all of the daily stuff (and my mind is free from my brain), "pieces" start coming together to form whole pictures and ideas – similar to a puzzle. I may have talked with different people about different issues or problems and, during that state of "almost sleep," my mind has the ability to organize connections that help solve issues or needs or problems. I keep a notepad next to my bed and an astronaut pen for writing upside down, and I often make scribbles of my ideas, which have to be deciphered in the morning.

It's important to try new things. There is the risk that you may not be exactly right at first, but you will see where you need to make adjustments in your aim as you advance toward your goal. The act of doing provides leaders with experience, the ultimate teacher. I refer to the wearable pacemaker prototype that I designed and we built in four weeks. We didn't intend for it to be used on a human, so we didn't make it look fancy. When Dr Lillehei (heart surgeon and early collaborator) didn't want to risk losing another child's life, he attached it to a child. When I saw that, I had such mixed emotions. Had we made it well enough for a child? While it saved the child's life, we also learned valuable lessons, like recessing the knobs so the children couldn't change the settings.

In helping to put together a community-health initiative here on Hawaii Island over the past twenty years, I have encouraged people to think out of the box. I try to connect the people I meet with each other so that assets can be combined and efforts can be supported.[27] "

LIST OF TOOLS & TIPS

The following tools and tips are provided in part two to help explore, assess, and focus your thinking.

5

GEAR 2: CONCEPT VISUALIZATION

REFRESHING YOUR FUTURE VISION

Envisioning new possibilities takes collective imagination. Here is a story about a team of dedicated healthcare professionals who were given the license to dream big in Gear 2.[28] Their collective vision planted the seeds of a comprehensive redesign of the patient experience in what was already a world-class hospital. While this example, like that in Gear 1, focuses on health care, one can imagine this as any service experience in which customer needs can be better met. No matter what business you are in, taking time to ask, "What if?" and engaging others in envisioning new possibilities will draw your enterprise forward.

The Princess Margaret Hospital Story: Turning Lost Time into Found Time

The Challenge

Managing cancer is a physically and emotionally draining journey that too many people have to endure. When your life is at risk, you and all those close to you are acutely aware of how every minute of every day passes. Faced with tough decisions and grueling treatments, the last thing patients need is an experience that can heighten their anxiety, diminish their self-worth, and turn their journey into lost time. The desired experience? One of hopeful healing.

That was the inspiration in 2008, when Princess Margaret Hospital (PMH) in Toronto decided to dream big and create a better healing journey. The redesign of the physical space of its chemotherapy treatment department offered an important opportunity to better meet the needs of patients and enhance their experience when undergoing cancer treatment. Normally, within the financial constraints of a public healthcare system, envisioning a hospital as a Four Seasons Hotel would be a stretch, but that didn't constrain this team of visionaries. The challenge was threefold: one, create a patient experience that would lead to better health outcomes; two, do so with an eye to being operationally efficient and responsible in a public healthcare system; and three, engage a broad base of stakeholders who could contribute to a renewed vision for patient care and help advance the cause at Princess Margaret Hospital. Creating a better experience and value for the end user, living up to financial responsibilities, and enlisting stakeholder support are often the pillars of success for any meaningful undertaking.

The Breakthrough

The Gear 2 breakthrough for PMH was a unified refresh of the patient experience, fueled by the medical staff's intrinsic motivation and devotion to world-class patient care. As with the healthcare company described in Gear 1, the process began with a broad scan of the current experience. In this case, mapping the patient journey both inside and outside the hospital visit gave participants a holistic picture of patient needs in the context of day-to-day living. Research revealed unmet needs around reducing anxiety, empowering patients, and turning what was felt to be "lost time" into "found time" in their journey of hopeful healing.

The solution came about by engaging a broad base of stakeholders, who conceived a new vision for patient care. Building on the identified patient needs, personas, and a deeper understanding of the patient journey, twenty staff at PMH, including oncologists, pharmacists, nurses, researchers, and administrators, participated in a group ideation session. We divided them into multidisciplinary groups and assigned each a patient persona and journey framework. We asked them to think of solutions that would improve the treatment experience for their personas. To encourage the broadest possible pool of ideas, participants had carte blanche to imagine new possibilities without constraints. For instance, we asked them to consider metaphors and analogies to other industries (e.g., hospitality, travel, the arts, health and wellness, virtual/online services, etc.) as inspiration for the ideal patient experience – turning the "lost time" patients feel waiting in a hospital into "found time" that could help them feel engaged and productive in their healing journey.

In a span of ninety minutes, staff generated more than 300 ideas, which included concierge services, cafes, first-class seating, Zen gardens, and relaxation pods. While many of the ideas seemed far-fetched, the groups realized that the intent behind them could potentially be preserved and translated into more feasible ideas. For example, one team drew analogies between patient treatments and flying on an airline. Some patients have "short-haul" treatments (e.g., less than sixty minutes), while others have long "transatlantic" treatments (e.g., more than four hours). The team drew inspiration from this and envisioned ways to enhance comfort (e.g., adjustable seating), entertainment (e.g., in-flight activities), and productivity (e.g., web access, work stations). This led the team to develop a patient experience around comforting treatment pods, access to inspirations and activities to keep patients engaged, and visions for a never-before-seen, ideal chemotherapy chair that could be designed one day. Some groups focused on technology-based solutions (e.g., websites, personal devices), while others developed the concept of a service-oriented support system.

We also asked the teams to *visualize* their ideas in their brainstorming. Instead of words on paper, we encouraged participants to draw, sketch, or map out their concepts. This exercise made the ideas more tangible, allowing for more robust discussion and concrete idea development. The brainstorming session led to several new possibilities for the new treatment facility and patient experience. The solutions did not rely solely on the treatment space but also on the purposeful delivery of patient-oriented services, activities, and information within the hospital, as well as services that could be accessed and delivered from home.

With so many exciting possibilities, this huge bank of ideas was synthesized into rough, conceptual prototypes of the ideal patient experience and presented back to hospital staff and patients in the form of visual storyboards. These storyboards were used to walk various stakeholders through an idealized yet realistic patient experience. Staff at all levels openly discussed the pros and cons of the prototypes and suggested improvements for each concept.

Fig. 11 **Envisioned Patient Journey**

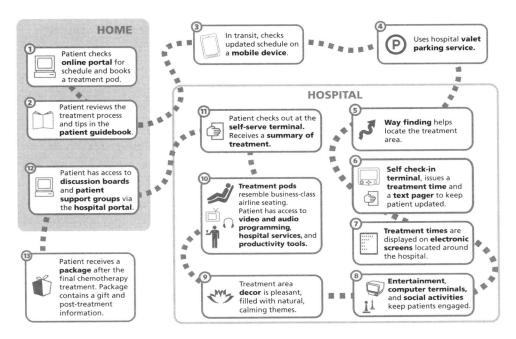

The prototypes were further refined and evaluated in an iterative fashion, until the ideal patient experience was fully formed (Figure 11). By visualizing the patient experience in a rough unfinished format, staff and patients were more open to contributing feedback. The active solicitation of feedback by hospital staff and patients gave all stakeholders a greater sense of ownership in the final outcome.

The Outcome

This case brings to life what open and imagination-rich collaboration can yield. Rather than simply representing change, this renewed vision signified meaningful and shared *progress*. This undertaking not only produced hundreds of inspired ideas, it also engaged dozens of important stakeholders in the creation of a comprehensive new patient experience and an institution-wide commitment to progress with purpose. From a management perspective, it underscored what really matters to patients and what does not. That led to an important re-prioritization of capital expenditures, a new vision for patient care, and operational efficiencies.

This new vision served as a lighthouse in a major donor campaign that raised funds for a transformational build-out. It formed the basis of a design brief for the architects who turned the ideas into space. It kept aspirations high for all parties, including donors, patients, and staff. The research and vision for this project has also continued to serve as an important reference for decisions since the project began three years ago. After ongoing iteration of ideas with broad engagement, the build-out of the new chemotherapy treatment center was completed in 2012.

This story demonstrates how collaboration can lead to bigger ideas, how engaging a broad group of stakeholders instills a sense of ownership and pride, and how this engagement leads to traction in advancing big ideas. It also shows how giving license to dream can lead to bigger, better realities that create transformational value.

Once you have framed the opportunity to create new value through Gear 1, you are ready to refresh your vision for the future and imagine new possibilities. This is not the time to focus on incrementally fixing or extending what you have in hand; this is your opportunity to step out of your current paradigm and dream!

"The project allowed us to bring people from across the hospital to design a new chemotherapy suite with the patient in mind – and with real patient feedback on their experience of care. Doctors, nurses, researchers, clerical staff, volunteers, management – many of whom have never worked together before were able to share ideas, build something tangible, and feel like they had a stake in the final outcome."

SARAH DOWNEY,
VICE-PRESIDENT, PRINCESS MARGARET HOSPITAL (2008–11),
UNIVERSITY HEALTH NETWORK, TORONTO, CANADA

Gear 2 is about collaborating to generate fresh ideas and new ways to deliver a better, more satisfying experience for the end user. As you create your new vision, you will cue off the unmet needs articulated in Gear 1, with no preconceived notions of what will work and not work. Don't worry about how you will do it. Every enterprise needs to reconcile dreams with operational realities, but that can wait for Gear 3.

Your Goal in Gear 2

To refresh your vision of the future, seeing possibilities for creating value through a new, high-value, seamlessly integrated experience for the end user.
After iterating through Gear 2, the development team should collectively feel excited and believe that "This is BIG! If we can deliver this, we would really change the game."

The balance of this chapter highlights key activities, outcomes, and development principles; provides tips on the role of data analysis and validation, as well as the mindsets, methods, and thinking modes that are most critical; and finishes with an inspired interview that brings important principles to life. Related tools are included in part two: Tool Kit.

Gear 2: Activities & Outcomes

Figure 12 shows some of the activities you will undertake, along with the most valuable outcomes of Gear 2 that will bring shape to your future vision. This will form the basis for translating your big ideas into sustainable value creation in Gear 3:

User Experience: A step-by-step multidimensional and seamlessly integrated user experience that shows how your vision will come to life through the eyes of the user – to ensure that every gap is closed and each critical component is defined.

Solution Components: Every new experience includes some critical components that have to be further developed through a proper design brief. This will inform your investments and partnerships in Gear 3.

Future Vision: A visionary story of what your role will be in creating unique value for the users of your product or service. It will serve as your "North Star."

Game Changers: Critical aspects of your vision that will add distinct value to people's lives.

Divergent activities include the collective exploration of an array of new possibilities. That calls for imagination and collaboration. It is a highly iterative process – nothing is ever close to perfection out of the gate. It can get messy, but it can be highly productive and fun if you put your imagination and team spirit ahead of your fears and ego. **Convergent** activities entail feedback and

Fig. 12 **Gear 2: Activities and Outcomes**

ACTIVITIES: **OUTCOMES:**

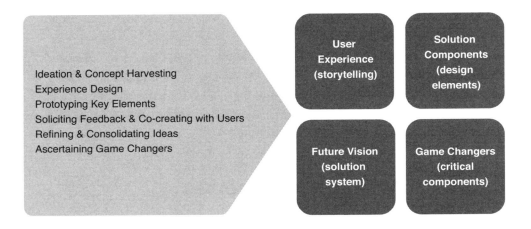

Ideation & Concept Harvesting
Experience Design
Prototyping Key Elements
Soliciting Feedback & Co-creating with Users
Refining & Consolidating Ideas
Ascertaining Game Changers

User Experience (storytelling)

Solution Components (design elements)

Future Vision (solution system)

Game Changers (critical components)

co-creation, and mining through your plethora of ideas, figuring out how they combine to form a bigger solution and ascertaining what creates the most value for your end user and other key stakeholders.

Key Principles: Dare to Dream

This is the time to suspend your current realities and focus entirely on creating the ultimate experience for your end user, and other key stakeholders. Step away from the business you are in today, how you currently operate, and the competition nipping at your heels. The only elements of your previous work that you will bring forward at this point are your collection of needs, personas, and design criteria. It is time to dream!

Here are some principles to keep in mind as you move through this phase.

Put your primary customer or stakeholder at the center of development.
Through every step of Gear 2, it is important to keep a user-centric focus. There will be lots of time in Gear 3 to figure out what it means to the enterprise. In the case of PMH, the patient remained front and center in the development process throughout Gear 2. While there are many stakeholders that matter in delivering the solution, the patient is their shared "customer." The end goal is to create a solution system that the end user (in this case the patient) will appreciate. That's every stakeholder's shared purpose. Doctors, nurses, and family members will

all play an important role in caring for a patient, so considering their needs in delivering new solutions will also be important.

Give yourself the license to dream big! This is the time to think big without restraint. For all of the mission-critical duties of their day-to-day work, the PMH team allowed themselves a few hours to dream – and dream big they did! Remembering that even the most far-fetched ideas have some inherent value will keep you from reconciling dreams with reality too early in the process. Visionaries like Steve Jobs of Apple, Richard Branson of Virgin, Isadore Sharp of Four Seasons, and Earl Bakken of Medtronic certainly allowed themselves to dream big.

"Dreams have a way of predicting and preceding reality."

EARL BAKKEN,
CO-FOUNDER, MEDTRONIC INC.

Always remember – everyone designs! Everyone has the capacity to envision new possibilities, no matter what their position in the organization. A healthy, open, and collaborative team dynamic will fuel creativity from every participant. Here are some key things to keep in mind as you tap into your collective imagination:

▶ **Harness the creativity of everyone on the team.** The more ideas you generate and consider, the more you will get past the obvious solutions. That is why you need everyone on the team engaged in the creative process.
▶ **There are no bad ideas.** In fact, bad ideas are often the catalyst to brilliant breakthroughs.
▶ **Set your ego aside.** In a shared quest, there is no room for personal agendas and egos. If you are willing to be wrong, you will be a more valuable contributor to success in the end.

This is a highly collaborative process; you will get the most robust solutions if you engage everyone who brings a unique perspective and expertise to the table. Encourage them to think outside of the box and let the creative juices flow!

Design the solution as a multidimensional experience. To ensure that you create a comprehensive and breakthrough experience, consider how better to meet needs through many dimensions. Oftentimes, an enterprise will focus on new products or better services, but those are only part of a winning experience.

Fig. 13 **POEMS Framework**

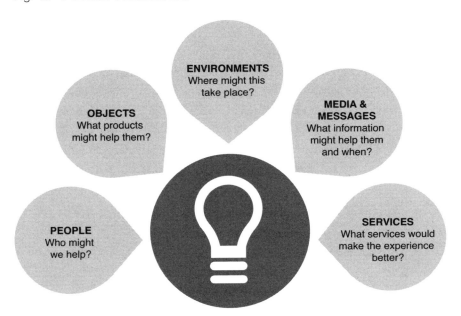

Think also about the needs defined more broadly by the activity and how those needs might be satisfied. The following POEMS framework (Figure 13) captures all the components of the solution that you could ultimately design:[29]

▶ **People:** *Who are the people that might help the end user?* In the case of PMH, what role could a nurse play counseling the patient?

▶ **Objects:** *Are there products or objects that could satisfy needs?* In the case of PMH, could a device help people access the information they need more readily than hanging around the nursing station with a crowd of other patients?

▶ **Environments:** *What places might be key to delivering the right solution in the right place?* In the case of PMH, would more natural light and nature create a greater sense of calm and clear wayfinding reduce anxiety?

▶ **Media and Messages:** *What information would be helpful and how best should it be delivered?* In the case of PMH, could patients access scheduling information online from home, rather than having to call the hospital and be put on hold?

▶ **Services:** *What kinds of support services would enhance the experience?* In the case of PMH, could wireless access, computers, and movies fill the void of lost time and help patients feel more engaged and productive?

In the exploration phase of solution development, each one of these dimensions is critical to designing a seamlessly integrated experience.

Explore LOTS of ideas. Exploring and visualizing lots of ideas in the early stages will keep you from getting stuck on perfecting one idea early on and give you lots of options to explore through the co-creation phase, when you seek feedback from users and other stakeholders. While the ideation phase can generate hundreds of ideas, you will want to consolidate them into bigger, more holistic concepts. I always suggest building out three different concepts to keep your considerations open for learning until you converge and consolidate. Through continuous iteration in low-cost, low-resolution prototypes and feedback, you will gain more insight into what resonates with your user or doesn't. You will move from a *volume* of possibilities through a feedback and assessment process that will focus your development on the ideas that create the most *value*. As you identify the most critical components of your idea, you will develop briefs to transform ideas into more concrete elements. This iterative development process will lead you to putting the elements with the most value into the market as you ramp up. Consider the following progression from volume of ideas to value of ideas (Figure 14):

Fig. 14 **Volume to Value**

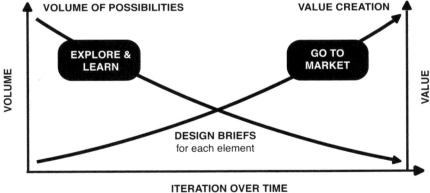

Visualize key components and show how they work within the experience. We often express ourselves in words, but words have different meanings to each person. Visualization is more universal. It entails drawing pictures and making prototypes to translate an *abstract* notion into a *concrete* idea and answer the question, *What might that look like?* That helps stimulate more productive dialogue within the team and with those whose feedback you solicit. Appreciation and thoughtful conversation around fragile new ideas will ensure that you are building off each other's thinking versus creating a lot of verbal noise.

Prototype in low resolution and resist perfection early on. High achievers often want things to be right as soon as possible. Early perfectionism will slow you down and hold back breakthrough thinking. Prototyping is a way to represent ideas in a more tangible form to get early feedback. Making mistakes and learning from early prototypes is all part of the creative process.

Most importantly, don't spend a lot of money on early prototypes. Instead, use your imagination to transform everyday items into rough-and-ready prototypes. You will be surprised at how they can stimulate thinking and dialogue. It is a better use of your money to explore lots of big ideas at a next-to-nothing cost than it is to spend a lot of money on expensive mock-ups early in the development process.

Engage end users and other stakeholders early and often. Co-creation calls for engaging others in the process and embracing feedback, even when it is not positive. Doing so will yield greater learning and lead to more robust ideas. I enjoyed working with David Kelley of Stanford University because he shows users his ideas, readies himself with pen and paper, and then says with enthusiasm, *"Tell me what you like, but also everything that's wrong with this idea so I can fix it for you."*[30] That's the true spirit of co-creation. In all of my work with low-resolution prototypes as a means of stimulating dialogue, I am always so amazed to see how imaginative the users are with rough-and-ready prototypes and how willing they are to help you make the idea better.

Visualizing new possibilities and soliciting early feedback is critical to productivity, learning, and progress in the design process. When feedback is reserved until the time a final and fully formed product is developed, it is more difficult to incorporate important and significant changes. Frequently, the request for feedback is really just a courtesy and formality, and if it results in changes, they tend to be incremental. By engaging users and other important stakeholders in the feedback process early and often, you can glean important insights before committing any significant investments or resources. This allows for important early course corrections.

In the case of PMH, we presented early prototypes to patients and asked, *What works here? What doesn't? What could be better?* Sharing prototypes with patients not only provided valuable feedback on the concepts themselves, it also stimulated dialogue that revealed even more insights into their points of pain and ways to alleviate them. The feeling that their entire lives were put on hold while they focused on treatment, combined with the long wait times in a Canadian hospital, made for a fairly bleak patient experience. While the hours spent in treatment or waiting for test results were never going to go away, the ability of patients to convert those seemingly wasted hours into something more meaningful would substantially improve their experience. For example, instead of staring at a blank wall or television screen, patients could have access to entertainment or workspaces that could help them feel more engaged and productive.

In that case, inspiration from patient stories and feedback helped the team realize how the hospital patient experience could become an enabler of intellectual, mental, spiritual, and social support, rather than only medical care. This led to subsequent concepts that would allow patients to continue, even enhance, their lives during their time in the hospital. Ideas included social and private recovery areas, work and education resources, engaging activities, inspirational cues, peaceful and natural designs, and comfortable furniture. Patients could also support other patients in their journey through a "chemo buddy" program to give them a sense of purpose and self-worth.

Iterate. Iterate. Iterate. You'll never get the solution perfect out of the gate. Consider the Dyson vacuum – more than 5,000 iterations until it was perfected![31] You'll need to explore, experiment, recast, and refine as part of the ongoing process of creating and learning. This is the messy part and can challenge those who want to complete the job too soon. The process of exploration and reconfiguring solutions in response to user feedback is all part of a productive development process – both in your internal lab and later on in the marketplace. As you move through the process of feedback and refinement, you will transition from volume of ideas to value of ideas, as noted earlier.

Ascertain the game changers and consolidate your vision. With lots of feedback and learning in hand, you can ascertain the game-changing aspects of your vision, either through rigorous synthesis of your learning to date or more quantitatively through scaled methods and surveys, as noted in the next section of this chapter. This will enable you to consolidate your vision and write a proper design brief, as plotted in Figure 14, the Volume to Value diagram.

In the case of PMH, the work from Gears 1 and 2 were used as the basis for an architectural brief. That's when design experts can begin to translate a vision into reality and continue the iterative process of design and build out.

Building a Business Case: Data Analysis & Validation

Your Gear 2 work should be based on a sound analysis and validation of needs. That's the most important starting point for imagining new possibilities. So any idea based on a good foundation of unmet needs should be considered. Throughout Gear 2, you will be brimming with a multitude of new ideas on how to solve people's dilemmas.

But you might be asking: *Which elements of our ideas create the most value? How do we know what to take forward?* Just as human stories are a powerful source of motivation, ideas can be quite compelling. But if important strategic choices and big capital investments are once again on the line, you might need more validation data to build your case.

To advance your ideas, here are some suggestions for scaled feedback and validation:

Capitalize on a large-scale gathering of stakeholders. If there is a gathering of important stakeholders, you can use this opportunity to conduct a large-scale feedback session. That lets you tap into valuable feedback and heightens stakeholder engagement. In the case of the Canadian Bar Association referred to in the interview in chapter 2, the team rolled out a series of in-person meetings across Canada from east to west to solicit input from local members across the country. For the project on healthcare standards, the organization seized the opportunity to solicit input from more than 300 accreditation surveyors at an annual meeting. This feedback helped further enhance solutions and ascertain the game-changing elements of the envisioned future.

Build a platform for high-volume feedback. If you really want to scale feedback, you can create a "virtual community" to invite others to weigh in on your ideas. For example, in the Canadian Bar Association project, after the in-person meetings, we opened up a virtual community platform that had the nine concepts uploaded in storyboard form and asked the broader member community in that geography to weigh in on what they liked and disliked about the concepts. The engagement and input of over 2,000 lawyers from coast to coast not only boosted engagement, it gave the development team important feedback on what association members found most, and least, valuable about the concepts.

Run small-scale, measurable experiments to test assumptions and hypotheses. Running measured experiments that isolate critical assumptions and risk factors can help improve solutions and mitigate risk. While you can certainly just "try this" in the early phases of iteration, it is helpful to take a more measured and "scientific" approach to experimentation as the stakes rise. A revelation I've heard expressed by development teams is that *"experimentation is not about just winging it; it's about gathering evidence that builds a sound case for investment in new ideas."*

There are many ways to build confidence in the potential of your ideas to meet unmet needs and to discover which elements create the most value. While there is power in the gestalt of big ideas, there is also merit in knowing which elements are creating the most value and how to mitigate risk.

Everyone loves a big idea. They also appreciate a thorough process of evaluation and validation to justify the time and investment big ideas often need to be realized.

Important Mindsets, Methods, & Thinking Modes

Mindset Matters: First and foremost, never let go of the *empathy* you established in Gear 1 – that's your ongoing jet fuel and is important to taking in feedback, particularly from the end user. In the creative process, *positivity* creates the best conditions for exploring new ideas. That means being both open to the ideas of others, open to new ideas that are not within the scope of your current business today, and open to feedback, no matter how brutal it might be, in the early phases of development. It's critical to have a can-do attitude that embraces the notion *If it's right for the user, we will find a way.* Even if it is outside your current business paradigm, but creates value for customers, maybe it is a business you *should* be in. There are a few things you must resist thinking or saying, because they will only diminish your outcomes. Here are some classic idea-killer comments:

"We're not in that business. We have no idea how to deliver that."

"That's totally absurd. If we do that, we'll all get fired."

"That's a lame idea, but I have a better one."

"Our salespeople would shoot us if we ever suggested that."

"We did that three years ago, and it failed."

By opening up the development process to a wide and diversified team and learning to constructively take in feedback, your ideas will become even more valuable. Plus, everyone will feel they have had an opportunity to put their own thumbprint on the future.

Most Critical Methods: Gear 2 is very much a *visualization* exercise: you take what's in your head and make it tangible – in pictures and prototypes. That's the most effective way to translate the abstract into something concrete that you can work with and share with others. It ensures that you all have the same "movie" – your team, your co-creators, and those you will need to bring on board. With concrete ideas to work with, the process of **co-creation** will help advance your ideas to a higher level of value.

Regulating Your Thinking Modes: This is the gear in which you hit the gas pedal on creativity and *generative thinking*, especially in the divergent phase of your work. During idea generation, prototyping, and feedback, it is also important to make an effort to **understand**: *What idea is being expressed? Why does the user like or not like that idea?* As you transition into the convergent phase, it is important to put on your critical-thinking hat and ask, *What creates the most value? What can we let go of?* There will be times when you have to make some **decisions** on that and move forward with your best solution.

Anchoring your innovation pursuits in the needs of people and designing experiences to surprise and delight create energy and momentum. At the same time, you have to leverage new ideas and organizational capabilities for strategic advantage. The following interview with visionary entrepreneur Sir Richard Branson highlights the remarkable ongoing journey of Virgin and the importance of integrating the principles of all 3 Gears of Business Design, from insight to ideas, to testing your way forward, to scaling up. Together these add up to ongoing business success. His story is a perfect prelude to the next chapter, on strategy and activation.

Interview with Sir Richard Branson

Founder and CEO, Virgin Group

" Virgin has made its name by breaking into new markets and offering great value, superior service, a fresh approach, and a bit of fun. When we assess new businesses, the first step is to submit every business idea to our "brand test." We are constantly presented with new and exciting opportunities that might make a lot of money, but if they fail the brand test, we move on. We also think that there is little point in entering a new market unless it provides the opportunity to really shake up an industry. Almost all our new ventures come about from our thinking up a product or service that we believe people really want. Looking back at the launches of Virgin Atlantic, Virgin Active, and Virgin Mobile, I'm reminded that we had a clear vision of what the customer wanted and how we would deliver it (with a sense of fun).

In the case of Virgin Atlantic, we offered great service, which meant that travelers received – among many other innovative services – extra touches such as onboard massages and seat-back TV screens. At Virgin Active, we focused on building large, family friendly health clubs with big gyms and swimming pools, and attentive staff. For Virgin Mobile, customers got a service that did not require signing up for onerous contracts and instead got flexible plans and a direct link to entertainment and music. This clarity of purpose and excellent customer care helped us to succeed.

You'll notice that making a profit hasn't entered the picture yet. It's rare for me or the team to consider only the money that can be made. I feel it's pointless to approach investing with the question, "How can I make lots of money? We must bring in the numbers guys and work out some business plans." The consultants will say your idea will work, while the accountants will prove that it cannot. No one will ever agree on exactly how to make money.

This brings me to a secret to lasting success: securing your customers' trust, which should be part and parcel of your differentiation and marketing. At Virgin, we do this by relying on openness and simplicity when we communicate with our customers. Since we'd created companies everyone on staff was proud of, we were all deeply concerned about quality and customer service, and our marketing focused on why the businesses were different and special.

Our ability to adapt quickly to changes has helped mitigate reverses. You must be quick to accept that something is not going well and either change tack or close the business. Although I believe in taking risks, I also believe in "protecting the downside." This means working out all the things that could go wrong and making sure that all those eventualities are covered. We have come close to failure many times. Most entrepreneurs skirt close to it. I nearly failed when Virgin was in its infancy, I nearly failed in the early 1980s, and, of course, I have nearly died more than once trying to achieve world records for boating or ballooning. But through a combination of luck and planning, both Virgin and I are still here. As an entrepreneur, you learn quickly that there's no such thing as a failure.

A successful business isn't the product or service it sells, its supply chain, or its corporate culture: it is a group of people bound together by a common purpose and vision. In Virgin's case, we fly the same planes as our competitors, and our gyms offer much of the same equipment as other gyms. What separates our businesses from the competition? Our employees. The best-designed business plan will come to nothing if it is not carried out by an enthusiastic and passionate staff. This is especially true when things go slightly wrong; a friendly and proactive team can often win people round, averting a potential disaster or even turning it to your benefit.

We at Virgin pride ourselves on trying to find the fun in our businesses, by which I mean that we try to ensure that both our staff and customers feel a real sense of warmth and affection. I have led from the front on this – dressing up in costumes, trying all manner of stunts (not all going 100 per cent right!), and generally showing that I do not take myself too seriously. My approach will not work for all businesses, but keeping a sense of perspective and not allowing management to be seen as aloof will help keep your staff onside. To foster employees' sense of warm, personal interest in customers' needs, it's crucial to ensure that they enjoy what they do and are proud of the company. This is vital to building lasting success and ensuring your service has an edge over the competition.[32]

LIST OF TOOLS & TIPS

The following tools and tips are provided in part two to help explore, assess, and focus your thinking.

6

GEAR 3: STRATEGIC BUSINESS DESIGN & ACTIVATION

FORMULATING A STRATEGY TO WIN

Translating an ambitious vision into a distinct and compelling business strategy is a critical aspect of Business Design. What follows is the continuation of the story told in chapter 3 about the Accreditation Canada team, which used Business Design to work through all the development steps in their journey of strategic transformation. This story illustrates how Business Design leads to a distinct and compelling strategy, as well as a plan to turn insights and ideas into future value.[33]

Health Standards: A Strategy to Create New Value

The Challenge

As presented in chapter 3, Accreditation Canada (AC) had played a pivotal role in ensuring that virtually every patient touch point in the healthcare system met high standards in practice through a codified process for standards development and assessment. In more recent years, Accreditation Canada International (ACI) had gained traction by leveraging the know-how of AC and applying it to international health systems. At the same time, the landscape was dramatically shifting, which called for a radical strategic transformation that would maximize the value the enterprise could bring to healthcare systems in the future. The enterprise needed to align its future strategy with emerging trends, consider the many established and emerging players in this dynamic arena, recognize a broader set of stakeholders, and strategically leverage the combined capabilities of AC and ACI operating units. The overarching ambition: connect the players and practices across the healthcare system to improve patient outcomes.

Gear 1 entailed story-based interviews with more than 150 patients, providers at all levels, health-systems leaders, policy makers, partners, and influencers around the world. This process revealed several universal needs, including centering standards on the most critical factors that helped all parties by "making it easier to do the right thing" and linking standards and decision-making to better outcomes. Design criteria based on learning from context and Gear 1 required that all standards initiatives in the future would need to do the following:

Put the person (and their health) at the center.

Actively consider and engage the right stakeholders in the right way.

Cultivate trust and accountability.

Connect people, actions, and information across the healthcare ecosystem.

Provide useful information that improves understanding and sharpens focus.

Enable the right actions by the right people at the right time.

Transparently communicate the link to better outcome.

Adapt to specific needs and situations to continually optimize outcomes.

That's a tall order, but one this team was fully committed to. Through a process of exploration, visualization, feedback, and refinement, the twenty-eight-member FUEL development team created a visionary stance on the role of the enterprise in the future, including concepts that were expressed through the eyes of patients, providers, and policy makers to ensure all parties would win through the enterprise's future efforts. This vision included key design components on the people, processes, technology platforms, products, and services that would be required to deliver on their vision.

The Breakthrough

The envisioning process in Gear 2 formed an important basis for deciding which activities the enterprise would invest time and money into, identifying the capabilities required to deliver on their vision, and making precise strategic choices. These choices were further reinforced through extensive engagement of employees and the board, as well as external stakeholders. What emerged was clear alignment on the game changers that would make this enterprise an important player in bringing a global perspective to supporting the integration of health ecosystems and driving quality and safety improvements.

By making the enterprise vision explicit and *tangible*, it was clear how it would serve the market in the future, what could be leveraged in current activities and capabilities, and which capabilities needed to be amplified or built through internal investment and partnerships. The engagement process was critical in building alignment and giving a voice to all of the stakeholders who play a role in improving patient outcomes.

The breakthroughs in Gear 3 came in several ways. *First*, this process inspired a more explicit dedication to standards development, with the historical "accreditation" practice as an important dimension of their work. This led to the establishment of a new overarching entity – the Health Standards Organization (HSO), launched in January 2017.

Second, the value proposition came into focus: *HSO builds global health services standards and innovative assessment programs so people in their local jurisdictions can save and improve lives.* That put patient outcomes at the center of their quest.

Third, the strategic focus shifted from sites to systems and extended to key stakeholders across healthcare systems. Products and Services focused on standards development, assessment programs (including accreditation), and activation tools and services. Channels expanded to include online, newly formed collaboration centers, and critical strategic partners.

Fourth, the capabilities that would be required, based on a concrete vision, were clear. Those capabilities defined investments in talent, processes, technology, and organizational structures. From that, management systems were defined to support the execution of the new strategy.

The Outcome

Every one of the five critical strategic questions outlined in chapter 1 were thoughtfully and precisely answered through this inclusive and iterative process. With a powerful vision and strategy for the future, a five-year business plan was built, activation priorities and investments were spelled out, and conditions for success were articulated, with unanimous board endorsement.

Along with establishing Health Standards Organization in January 2017, a Patient Engagement Office was established. A new structure and roles were established, along with strategically aligned KPIs. Development initiatives were activated to complement the continued delivery and enhancement of standards-centered products and services in the immediate term. New strategic alliances have been formed, with a shared aspiration of *"unleashing the power and potential of people around the world who share our passion for achieving health services for all."*

Transformation is a tall order and calls for changing ways of working and continually thinking about how to advance strategically and tactically. This requires agility and a learning mindset. With a clear and distinct strategy, and a measured path forward, HSO demonstrates how an enterprise can productively focus collective efforts on creating transformational new value over time. This story demonstrates that an inclusive, rigorous, and ambitious Business Design effort can bring clarity and alignment, tackle a formidable challenge, and create new opportunities for meaningful change.

> *"Transformation is not for the faint of heart. We have a purpose-driven enterprise full of smart people dedicated to doing what is right for patients and helping our customers and partners succeed. The journey is just beginning!"*
>
> LESLEE THOMPSON, CEO

A precise and distinct strategy channels your efforts and investments, and accelerates progress. This important step is often one of the missing links in many innovation projects and is one of the reasons so many innovation initiatives fail to deliver a return on investment, as noted earlier. Gear 3 is about defining a strategy to deliver on your vision and *win*.

For many, Gear 3 is the most fun gear of all. It requires as much creativity and exploration as Gear 2, combined with a rigorous analysis of how alternative models will play out financially and competitively. It is the ultimate design challenge for business-minded innovators. What makes strategy a design effort is that you will use all your design methods and skills to create your enterprise strategy – visualization, ideation, prototyping, systems mapping, iteration, co-creation, and storytelling. That's what makes the third gear both creatively and analytically robust.

Gear 3 brings focus and momentum to your quest. The strategy you design will help channel your efforts in creating sustainable value for the end user, other significant stakeholders, and – importantly – your enterprise. That is the all-around win. During this phase, it will be necessary to analyze financial sensitivities and pinpoint risks associated with the unknown variables in your envisioned experience and alternative business models. This analysis will inform both how you configure your model and what learning experiments you will need to design to mitigate risk.

At this point in development, your team will be united in your vision. The mix of expertise in operations, finance, marketing, human resources, and other functional areas will play an important role in this phase. It will take all of these disciplines to construct an inventive and well-integrated business strategy and delivery system.

Your Goal in Gear 3

To precisely define your strategy by making important choices and designing your path forward. These steps will enable you to focus your collective energies on delivering a unique and sustainable value proposition to the market and capture value for your enterprise. That will inform your go-forward game plan.

I have broken Gear 3 into two phases: strategy formulation and activation. The balance of this chapter highlights key activities, outcomes, and development principles; provides tips on the role of data analysis and validation, as well as the mindsets, methods, and thinking modes that are most critical; and finishes with two inspired interviews that illustrate these important principles in practice. Related tools are included in part two: Tool Kit.

Fig. 15 **Gear 3 Strategy: Activities and Outcomes**

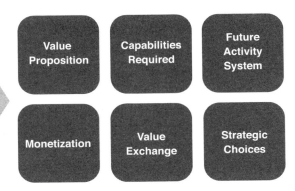

ACTIVITIES:

Synthesizing Your Proposition
Defining Critical Capabilities
Identifying Potential Partners
Prototyping/Iterating a Future
 Activity System
Assessing & Integrating Your System
Exploring Ways to Monetize Your Ideas
Assessing Value Reciprocity
Running Financial Scenarios
Making Choices

OUTCOMES:

Value Proposition
Capabilities Required
Future Activity System
Monetization
Value Exchange
Strategic Choices

Gear 3 Strategy: Activities & Outcomes

Figure 15 shows some of the activities you will undertake, along with the most valuable outcomes of Gear 3 that will strategically anchor your efforts going forward:

Value Proposition: A succinct statement of how you will create value for whom.

Capabilities Required: As a subset of your choices, a plan on how you will leverage or extend your internal capabilities or build critical partnerships.

Future Activity System: A visualization of the interconnected and synergistic activities and capabilities in which you will invest time, resources, and money.

Monetization: How the enterprise will capture value (i.e., make money) in delivering the envisioned solution to the market.

Value Exchange: How all parties exchange value to ensure a reciprocal and balanced exchange that ensures sustainable wins for all.

Strategic Choices: A clear set of choices that answers the five key questions highlighted in the first chapter of this book.

Divergent activities include the exploration of alternative models in each of these areas; now is the time to consider new ways to deliver and capture value. **Convergent** activities call for making strategic decisions.

Key Principles: Design to Win

Designing the enterprise system is the ultimate act of creativity because it translates a good idea into a well-thought out and actionable strategy. At this point, dreams often get left on the table because they have not been fully translated into a strategic path toward realization. Now is the time to capture the value for the enterprise and answer the inevitable questions, *How are we going to win in the market? How are we going to make money at this? How can we configure our system of activities so it's not easy for a competitor to replicate?* At the core of strategy is answering the critical questions presented in chapter 1:

What is our winning aspiration? The purpose of our enterprise, our motivating aspiration.

Where will we play? A playing field where we can achieve that aspiration.

How will we win? The way we will win on the chosen playing field.

What capabilities must be in place? The set and configuration of capabilities required to win in the chosen way.

What management systems are required? The systems and measures that enable the capabilities and support the choices.

Here are some important principles and considerations that will drive your strategy formulation:

Articulate your value proposition as your central promise. This is a precise statement of how your vision will deliver value to the market. By this phase, you will have undergone several activities: exploring strategic considerations, framing the market opportunity, deeply and holistically understanding people's needs, designing a compelling vision of your ultimate destination, and ascertaining the game changers. All of these inputs will inform the core value proposition that expresses who you will serve with what product or service,

Fig. 16 **Synthesizing Your Value Proposition**

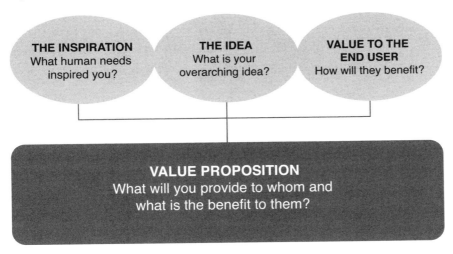

and to what end. For example, the value proposition for HSO was distilled down to *HSO builds global health services standards and innovative assessment programs so people in their local jurisdictions can save and improve lives.*

A good way to synthesize your value proposition is to pull together the high-level ingredients of your inspiration, idea, and stakeholder value as visualized in Figure 16. This value proposition will anchor everything you do in Gear 3.

Identify the essential capabilities required to deliver on your vision. With the big idea defined in Gear 2, it's time to break down your vision into what the enterprise will do to deliver that in a scalable and sustainable way. This deconstruction process will make explicit what capabilities have to be in place and the source of those capabilities to realize your new vision.

The key question you have to answer is: *What do we have to be really good at to deliver on this vision?* That might mean leveraging or amplifying current enterprise capabilities, building new capabilities internally, or strategically partnering with others. For example, HSO shifted to a greater focus on developing integrated health standards that connect points of care across the system and investing in technology to improve access and efficiencies for people in the system. Nespresso, as another example, needed to deliver on the design, manufacture, and service of its unique coffee machines. It decided to partner on those things and focus internally on what it could do exceptionally well.

The work you will have done earlier in defining the landscape of players will give you some ideas on which players you might join forces with in your quest. At the same time, your newly defined vision may call for exploration of other sources of expertise. Translating your vision into the capabilities required to deliver it makes everything strategically, operationally, and financially clear.

Visualize your strategy as a system of activities and capabilities. Based on the work of Michael Porter, Roger Martin, and others,[34] this way of *visualizing* your strategy as a distinct system will determine your long-term viability and competitive advantage. The design of a winning enterprise system is inspired by a high-value experience delivered through a collection of concrete design components and anchored in a unique and compelling value proposition. This is not a case of merely determining what it costs to make or do something and how much revenue can be generated. This is not a spreadsheet exercise.

Value is delivered, captured, and sustained through a unique system of activities and capabilities. Designing a winning set of activities entails considering and knitting together the core activities and capabilities in which you choose to invest time and money. For an enterprise strategy to be competitive, there must be something inherent in the design of the system that is unique to the enterprise and difficult for others to replicate. Otherwise, it will not justify the investment. When designing a sustainable system for a public enterprise, these factors are equally important, as your model will need to be operationally sustainable and justifiable to those paying the bills.

Activity-system modeling is a valuable way to visualize your strategy, as presented in the Tool Kit in part two of this book. As examples, I'll first expand on the high-level activity system for HSO. I will then reference how Nespresso's distinct value-creating set of activities and capabilities supported the enterprise's overarching value proposition and created a sustainable competitive advantage.

HSO's resulting strategy was anchored in a central devotion: to *Cultivate a Deep Understanding of People* – every stakeholder who matters in the quest to save and improve people's lives. (See Figure 17.) This deeply entrenched philosophy underpins all HSO's efforts to deliver value across the ecosystem. To *Create Shared Value among All Stakeholders*, ongoing co-creation ensures that every stakeholder in every jurisdiction wins. Leveraging proven evidenced-based processes and technology allows the enterprise to *Customize Processes and Solutions* and adapt what's commonly needed globally to what's needed jurisdictionally. All of these activities position the enterprise to *Build and Spread*

Fig. 17 **HSO Activity System**

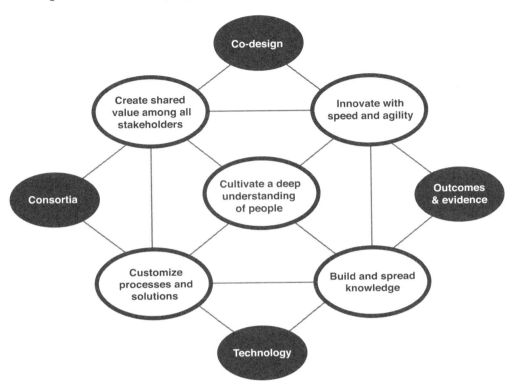

Knowledge on standards development and clinical practices, with learning transferred from one jurisdiction to another globally. By integrating the needs and inputs of people, market knowledge, and technology, the enterprise would *Innovate with Speed and Agility* to continually advance the value of HSO's products and services.

As you read in chapter 1, Nespresso (Figure 18) is another excellent example of a game-changing strategy anchored in their promise to *create moments of pleasure and indulgence for coffee lovers around the world*. Their products, boutiques, people, and marketing effort are designed to deliver a seamless *premium coffee experience* to their customer. While parent company, Nestlé, manufactures and sells consumer packaged foods largely through food retailers, Nespresso chose to create an entirely new category around a *uniquely integrated and stylish coffee system*, delivered through new channels and supported by direct-to-consumer marketing. At the heart of their strategy is a unique coffee system that leverages their ability to source and produce high-quality coffee, delivered in a convenient and proprietary capsule that is brewed through a

Fig. 18 **Nespresso Activity System**

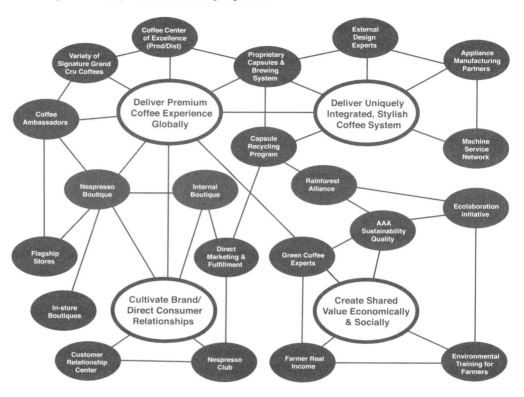

special coffee machine. The company outsourced the machine's design to high-end designers (e.g., Alessi) and manufacturers (e.g., Krups and Magimix), and built a broad-based network of qualified service providers. They actively cultivate a ***one-to-one brand relationship with their customers*** through direct marketing – an exclusive Nespresso Club membership of 10 million and growing – and direct on-request product fulfillment. They also designed their product supply chain to adhere to the parent company's commitment to ***Shared Value*** and high standards of social and environmental responsibility. They adhere to strong Rainforest Alliance standards to ensure highest quality and sustainability practices in their sourcing, farmer relations, and accredited associations as part of their Ecolaboration initiative. These choices are reflected in a strategically distinct and well-integrated system.[35]

When working with business teams, there is always an "Aha!" moment in which participants discover the power of the system: *"Now I can see that it is not just the product – it is the entire system of activities. We should always be challenged to defend how this system is different."* A distinct system is a source of competitive advantage.

Aim to deliver value at scale. With the goal of maximizing value-creation, it is often important to think about *scale* – if that is your ultimate ambition. Having the foresight to see where a big idea might lead gives you a better handle on what kinds of investments you will have to make, who your partners might be, what kinds of experiments you will do to mitigate risk, and what kinds of systems and structures you will need to design to enable the enterprise. In the case of HSO, global expansion required them to design systems, processes, and technology applications to augment their labor-intensive practices in an efficient and quality manner.

Integrate your new activity system with your existing one. As part of preparing for your quest (chapter 2), mapping your current activity system will show that you have a well-entrenched system in place that can be leveraged to give you a head start, accelerate realization, and strengthen your competitive advantage. Here are some different scenarios that you might consider:

- ▶ **Integrating an enhanced solution into an existing one.** In a scenario where your Gear 2 solution is a natural build on your current offering and model, you should strive to embed your idea (and any capability extensions) into your existing system of activities. This demonstrates *strategic fit*.
- ▶ **Resolving potential tensions with an existing system.** Sometimes the envisioned offering doesn't *quite* fit with the existing system, but complements it in a novel way. For example, the Nespresso activity system is different in many ways from the overall Nestlé activity system but it links to the core "hubs" of brand building and shared value. That can have structural implications and is why Nespresso operates as an independent business unit within the Nestlé portfolio. At the same time, they also leverage corporate synergies to deliver on the corporate aspiration. This example demonstrates *leverageable strategic links*.
- ▶ **Transforming an enterprise.** This entails moving from one strategic activity system to a new future state. In this case, you want to leverage what you are already good at and migrate in stages to a new system. For example, HSO's transition to a global standards organization began by integrating the inherent capabilities of their domestic and international organizations, and then building on that with augmentation of activities and capabilities. This example demonstrates the *strategic shift* that will take place over time.
- ▶ **Starting up a new business.** Though you might not have all of the capabilities in place to scale in the short term, every founding team has core

capabilities that are driving the vision. For example, Earl Bakken of Medtronic was an inventor at heart who worked closely with expert practitioners. That was, and still is, core to Medtronic. It might also be that you have a foundational expertise in marketing or distribution or technology. While not fully developed, these are important capabilities to leverage and build on.

Assess your envisioned system of activities for sustainable advantage. Inspired by Roger Martin's strategy work, here is a checklist of questions to keep in mind when assessing the power of your system and its ability to create a sustainable competitive advantage for you:[36]

*Does it create **value** for every stakeholder in the ecosystem?*

*Is it **breakthrough** in that it is not just more of the same but something that will truly disrupt the market?*

*Is it **distinct** in that it is different from your competitors and gives you a competitive advantage?*

*Does it **fit** together as an integrated system and support your enterprise vision and purpose?*

*Is it **sustainable** in terms of both financial viability and competitiveness? Is it a system that competitors cannot easily replicate?*

Explore ways to make, save, and invest money. Identify several options for sources of revenue and determine how to best make and save money. This will help you discover how to fund your big idea and make a case for a return on your investment. Often we believe that to generate revenue, we need to sell more widgets or services. Such is the core revenue stream for many companies, yet there are so many ways to make money that we often overlook. This is where your creativity and financial acumen will come into play. When looking at the whole end-user experience, imagine new sources of revenue. These sources include sales of your own product, selling others' products in your outlets (e.g., Apple selling peripherals such as speakers), service programs (e.g., extended warrantees offered by retailers in electronic product sales), sponsorships or advertising revenue (e.g., Google), or usage fees (as in the case of automated-teller machines).

On the flip side, you will want to be creative about how you can *save money* in delivering solutions – through efficiencies in scale (e.g., high-volume production), offshore product supply or production, automation, long-term contracts with vendors, and so many other means. You might also learn from the first two gears that you are spending money on things now that should be reallocated to a bigger, high-value idea.

When you maximize how you can make and save money, you will be able to *spend money* and invest your efforts in accordance with your strategy. Will you invest in your distribution network, like Frito-Lay does with its direct-to-store distribution system? Brand marketing, like Procter & Gamble or Nespresso? Recruiting, training, and retention, like Four Seasons?

Prototype business models and run a lot of numbers. Gear 3 offers a great opportunity to explore and prototype different ways to configure your system (e.g., internal or external capabilities), capture value (i.e., different ways to generate revenue), and mitigate risk (i.e., avoid high-risk investments or business models). For example, you may build a new capability within the enterprise or outsource it through strategic partners, as in the case of Nespresso, which chose to work with outside designers and manufacturers. You might run some numbers on your greatest opportunity for capturing value. You will also want to consider working through your solution components and determining where you might break the bank if something goes wrong. For example, a project on water-filter kiosks showed that if the machine breaks down, the company might be in a better position to broker leases rather than sell machines and bear the cost of unpredictable repair costs. Here's where looking back on your experience map and components can help you conduct a financial-sensitivity analysis on best- and worst-case scenarios. This is an important time to flex your thinking and explore options for delivering your solution to the market. It's why we use paper plates to design alternative activity systems and a lot of spreadsheets to test scenarios. Better to work this out in a design studio than in the market!

Ensure that every stakeholder in your ecosystem wins. Once you have determined your model for internal and external capabilities and explored ways to monetize your vision, it is important to make sure that every single stakeholder or partner gets value out of your venture. Reciprocity in the ecosystem is an essential principle in balanced stakeholder exchange and sustainability. It is clearly important to create value for the end user and the enterprise, but it is equally important to create value for all key stakeholders for your model to be sustainable.

When designing the value exchange among stakeholders (i.e., who gives what and what they get in return), ensure a balanced exchange. While the exchange of money is most easily measured, value can also come in the form of credibility, brand image, reputation enhancement, distribution or access to the market, or knowledge and expertise. The key is to recognize and appreciate all forms of value in the exchange. Otherwise, the system will unravel in time. For this reason, you must see the exchange through the eyes of others. Practice empathy and put yourself in the shoes of others.

To further illustrate these points, take the following simple example of a healthcare company that operates within an ecosystem in which value is exchanged among multiple partners (Figure 19). The healthcare company needs access to patients to sell new services, and it needs the endorsement of the patients' most trusted advisor, the doctor. The doctor wants information to help counsel patients in a knowledgeable (and time efficient) manner and an opportunity to earn revenue through patient visits. The patients need advice and are willing to pay for it, and ultimately they need a solution (product or service) that will improve their health.

In this scenario, one would want to ensure that the enterprise was seen to be the best source of credible, usable information. Otherwise, it could easily be substituted for another like-intentioned player and lose valuable access to the patient market.

Rethink how you manage and measure progress. Really big business ideas often call for a rethink of your processes, structures, and management systems. Success will depend on how you manage that new system relative to your existing system and how you make your big ideas "plug compatible" with the existing infrastructure of business. You may also need to rethink how you manage and measure success. For example, HSO redesigned their organizational structures and KPIs to align with their strategic goals.

Make precise strategic choices. This is not always easy, but it is essential for focus and future momentum. You may have started your quest with a long list of considerations for the five critical strategy questions. Through the development process from contextualization to Gear 2, it should become clear that

Fig. 19 **Healthcare Value Exchange**

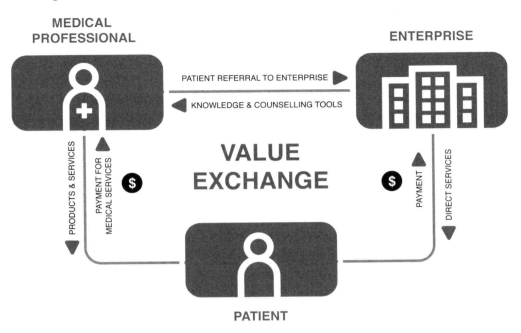

you have to make some precise choices on target, sector, geography, and products and services. In the case of HSO, they made an explicit choice to serve healthcare systems around the world and firmly establish that health-standards development was their higher-level mandate, with assessment and accreditation as important supporting services.

How you will win in the marketplace and the capabilities required to distinctly deliver on your vision will also have become clearer, based on your insights into the players, the gaps in satisfying market needs in Gear 1, and your feedback from stakeholders in Gear 2. The key is to identify the core choices you have to make to deliver with excellence and distinctiveness. What is most difficult is saying "*no.*" You obviously can't do everything for everyone. This is the time to go through the long list of considerations and not only decide what you will choose to do, but also be explicit about what choice considerations are off the table.

Once you've explored options and landed on a strategy to set you on a promising path, you will be ready to create a compelling story on how you will create new and sustainable value for both the market and the enterprise.

Building a Business Case: Data Analysis & Validation

When important strategic choices and big capital investments are on the line, facts and numbers will help you make decisions and solidify your case. There are several ways you can build a fact-based picture of the critical implications of your strategy. Here are some suggestions:

Dissect your vision into revenue opportunities and costs. Your envisioned offering can be broken down into critical products and services, for which you can estimate revenue. Similarly, your activities and capabilities will have a price on them. Your goal is to put dollars against each element – monetization opportunities and costs to deliver them.

Run financial scenarios. This when financial analysis meets creativity and prototyping. Explore options that reveal not only your greatest potential to capture value but also where your greatest costs might be. For each of those scenarios, state your assumptions.

Assess risks and probabilities. For each of those scenarios, challenge your assumptions and identify where you are at risk. This step will inform your business model in a case where the risk can be mitigated by reconfiguring your model, or it may inform critical experiments in your activation planning accordingly.

Important Mindsets, Methods, & Thinking Modes

Mindset Matters: The most important mindset for Gear 3 is *courage*. At some point in Gear 3, you will have to put a stake in the ground by making choices and leaning in on action. Research shows that courage comes from making choices to *do the right thing*. When you have done your homework through Gears 1 and 2, you should feel confident that you are making choices for the right reasons. At the same time, you will need to have some empathy for the decision-makers and project a sense of optimism.

Most Critical Methods: The most critical methods that can help you work through choice-making are tapping into your collective know-how through *collaboration*, *iterative prototyping* of alternative scenarios, and making connections through *systems mapping*. You will also draw on your *storytelling* skills in communicating how your vision taps into important new opportunities and how your strategy plays out over time. Gear 3 is design on steroids!

Regulating Your Thinking Modes: The most important cognitive mode for Gear 3 is *synthesis and decision-making*. Take all of the ideas and data you have in hand and make a compelling business case to go forward. To get there, you will need to generate and assess options, taking into account the needs of all stakeholders in your solution.

Ultimately, the design of business is not unlike the design of any other object or experience concept. This is the phase in which all dimensions of thinking come together to create a breakthrough strategy: creativity, analysis, critical thinking, systems thinking, and synthesis.

Long-run success comes from building from a base of customer devotion, embracing a clear and concrete vision of where you are headed, aligning on a clear and distinct strategy to get there, and having the perseverance to stick with it. While it is always important to remain open to new possibilities to expand your business, it is equally important to be strategic in how you do so.

Your Goal in Gear 3: Activation

To translate your vision into reality. With an exciting new vision, a focused strategy to get there, and a solid business proposition in hand, it's time to lock down your plan to get going. That takes a good business case to get the green light and an enterprise that is ready to move forward and deliver through a calculated sequence of action steps.

Gear 3 Activation: Activities & Outcomes

Figure 20 shows some of the activities you will undertake in activation and some of the most valuable outcomes that will guide your efforts going forward:

> **Business Plan:** Extending your strategic work into a case for investment of time and money.
>
> **Activation Priorities:** The top-most important development and implementation projects you will move forward.

Fig. 20 **Gear 3 Activation: Activities and Outcomes**

ACTIVITIES: OUTCOMES:

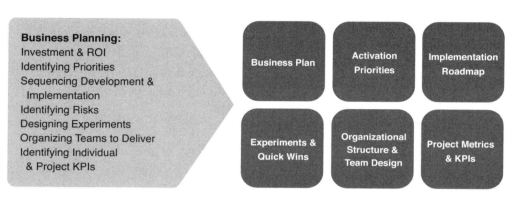

Implementation Roadmap: The measured sequence – the what and when – of projects you will move forward in concert.

Experiments: What uncertainties you will test to advance your envisioned solutions and mitigate risk along the way.

Quick Wins: What you will do right away to capitalize on your new discoveries.

Organizational Structure and Team Design: How you will organize people with clear roles and responsibilities to deliver on your critical initiatives internally and to the market.

Project Metrics and KPIs: Key management systems to measure and reward progress in delivering on priorities.

Divergent activities include iterative analysis of financial investments and payouts, prioritizing and mapping initiatives, exploring new ways of teaming, considering key risks, and rethinking ways to measure what matters. **Convergent** activities call for translating this into a clear plan that will mobilize the enterprise in the most productive and rewarding way.

Key Principles: Shift from Dreaming to Doing

Strategy is a guide to action. A comprehensive business plan with thoughtfully sequenced actions that are aligned across the enterprise is key to productivity and momentum. At this stage, it is important to be open to new ways of doing business and willing to let go of old ways of working that can hold you back. Optimism and resiliency are important as you encounter constraints and setbacks along the way. Here are some important principles from the experience of others who have carved out new paths:

Build a compelling case around your strategy. Building a business plan is a natural next step. All of the good work you've done throughout the development process will feed into a fact-based proposition: trends and market sizing, dimensionalization of needs, validation of game changers, financial sensitivity analysis, assessment of capabilities and investment priorities, monetization opportunities, and clear strategic choices will all inform your business case. This is about integrating *design magic* and *business logic*.

A solid business case can be brought to life with good storytelling that paints a compelling picture of the ultimate destination; there is still a place for magic! For example, in the Princess Margaret Hospital case in chapter 5, the team presented an inspiring movie of the envisioned patient experience to attract generous donations. In the case of HSO, an inspiring story about how the future might look set the stage for an ambitious business proposal that resulted in unanimous approval by the board.

Set priorities. There might be several streams of activity related to how to move toward your envisioned future. At the same time, you can't boil the ocean. It is helpful to define the top ten activation priorities that will leverage your learning and set your enterprise up to deliver new value. That will inform how you invest time and money to deliver payout, and how you focus the enterprise on what needs to be done and when.

Big wins come through a series of successes and failures. Years ago, it was common for businesses to perfect the grand plan and then execute it in the market at a sizable scale – Ta da! Those days are gone for most companies. Making your way to the market is now about iteratively prototyping not only in the development lab, but also in the marketplace. The agile way of working calls for testing the waters, listening to customers, and iterating based on *live learning*.

While it is important to stay the course, it is also important to remember that not everything will go as planned. That calls for enterprise agility in response to new learning and circumstances along the way. Your strategy will provide the guardrails for navigating your way forward. With a learning mindset, you will discover that there's really no such thing as failure.

Quick wins get you going and build confidence. Through all of your development work, there are some things that you can activate out of the gate to move you closer to where you want to go. Quick wins are the smaller and easier initiatives that will start you down a new path. If they fit with your general enterprise purpose and address an unmet need of your customer, there is no reason not to activate a component of your new idea as a way of getting started. For example, the healthcare company in chapter 4 expanded its fast track-system to keep at-risk patients on the healthcare radar, while pursuing longer-term systems initiatives.

As mentioned earlier in this chapter, a quick win might be reallocating investment from efforts that you now know won't create significant value to ideas that will be more in line with your future vision and strategy. Quick wins can come in the form of what you will *stop* doing, what you will *start* doing, and reinforce what you will *continue* doing.

The Business Design process will give you new insights and ideas on how to better channel your time and money right away – which builds confidence in the value of Business Design and momentum in your progress.

Design measured experiments to mitigate risk and learn. For bigger, more important moves, thoughtfully designed experiments will help you to generate valuable and actionable learning on how to advance your ideas. By testing assumptions that have inherent risk, you can validate or falsify those assumptions and find ways to adapt the execution of your ideas. Experiments can be used to vet many ideas in the early stages of development, but at this stage, your goal is to find ways to deliver on the intent of your ideas without taking avoidable risk. In this regard, experiments are about learning how to make the *ingredients* of big ideas work, not whether to pursue the overarching idea. For example, Nespresso has been experimenting with new ideas since the beginning, most recently with those related to their Ecolaboration platform.

It's important to learn and ascertain as much as possible about the elements you are less sure of. Well-designed experiments will tell you what you need to know and give you greater confidence to go to the next level of investment.

Experiments are most valuable when they are built around a clear hypothesis and measured. For example, in my work at Procter & Gamble on important experiments, we would state the hypothesis, design the experiment, and be clear about the indicated actions before we conducted the experiments. That way you aren't just trying things in an ad hoc manner; you are going into important experiments to learn and make fact-based decisions on how to execute an idea in the most effective way.

Organize people to deliver on the job to be done. New ideas often call for re-examining the way you work together to most productively deliver new solutions. That might call for designing new organizational structures and re-teaming people to align your talent and incentives to the job to be done. This is another opportunity to prototype different ways of structuring your organization or organizing teams.

For example, HSO formed teams of patients, clinicians, and health systems experts to support its standards-development and assessment process. That meant standards development would take into account the needs of all stakeholders, with the ultimate goal of improving patient health outcomes.

"A lot of experiments have contributed over time to the success of Nespresso – from the original idea, to our specific route-to-market and direct-to-consumer business model, boutiques, brand communication strategies, to trendy and designed machines. More recently, the way Nespresso has engaged and committed to sustainability through our Ecolaboration initiative, from recycling to sustainable coffees, will also contribute in a near future. As an example, AAA coffee program started in the field in 2003 as an experiment, and after eight years of learning we are starting to broadly tell our story in 2011."[37]

GUILLAUME LE CUNFF,
NESPRESSO GLOBAL MARKETING

Assess processes and systems to ensure new ideas won't get stuck. Understanding your embedded ways of working (chapter 3) will help you appreciate how work currently gets done. That can accelerate progress if it aligns with your new ideas and strategy, or it can block new ideas from getting to the market.

For example, at Procter & Gamble we had a finely tuned system for getting products into the market, based on a high-volume, manufacturing-based model. If we wanted to get a new $2.99 bottle of lotion into the market, we would just drop the idea into our enterprise system, and it ultimately made its way to the market in the most efficient way. However, that system was designed to maximize capacity utilization in our plants. You can imagine how lower-volume/high-margin products and services would not fit into that system. Management systems need to be designed to align with your enterprise strategy and envisioned solutions. It is critical to take stock of your ingrained systems and processes to determine if they help or hinder in getting your new ideas to the market.

Make talent and change management a priority. Often, big ideas and strategic evolution call for change. That can be the hardest part of gearing up for the future. While the generation of ideas and the design of strategy may be led by a relatively small group, it takes an enterprise to deliver big ideas to the market. HR is frequently one of the most important factors in driving innovation throughout the enterprise. HR plays a critical role in many aspects of the people side of business, including:

Having the talent you need and people in the right roles

Designing plans to foster engagement

Ensuring that there is ongoing communication within the enterprise

Building innovation skills and capacity

Designing reward systems for outcomes that align to your strategy

As all business leaders know, people are your most valuable asset, and designing the conditions that people in organizations need to succeed is as important as designing the business.

What gets measured gets treasured. Knowing you are on track and rewarding people across the enterprise for the outcomes that align to your strategic plan and priorities is clearly important. That entails setting up management systems to track enterprise progress, setting KPIs for teams and individuals, and tracking your innovation readiness and outputs.

Celebrate small (and big) victories. Meaningful progress takes a lot of effort from everybody, and quick wins can help motivate the enterprise on a path to future success. It's important to celebrate learning and the efforts that go into managing today's business while creating your future. As noted in chapter 2, Preparing for your Quest, continuous engagement and communication will help keep the skeptics in check and build broader confidence and momentum in your path forward.

Building a Business Case: Data Analysis & Validation

Translating ideas into reality in a measured way requires acumen in business and the design of systems to measure and reward progress. In summary of the previous points in this chapter, that includes:

▶ Analyzing and synthesizing financial data as input to the business plan and tracking ongoing results;

▶ Designing measurable experiments at a scale that will build confidence in ideas and investments;

▶ Determining the measures of success beyond the business, including metrics that track key customer indicators;

▶ Setting KPIs to align goals to people's efforts and rewards; and

▶ Establishing goals for the culture of the enterprise in terms of engagement, innovation readiness and other indicators that align with your aspirations for the enterprise.

The measurements of business performance, stakeholder assessment, people performance, and cultural assessments will complement the "softer side" of pursuing big ideas with a sense of purpose.

Important Mindsets, Methods, & Thinking Modes

Activation is the beginning of realization. The manner in which you activate and manage innovation not only enhances your odds of business success, it shapes your culture of innovation.

Mindset Matters: In this phase, all three critical mindsets of Business Design are important. It takes *courage* to put a stake in the ground and get going. As you kick into high gear and make things happen, progress is never without setbacks along the way; that's where resilience and **positivity** are important in keeping your eye on the purpose and the prize of your pursuits. At the same time, a change in ways of working can also be challenging for the people who have to make it happen. **Empathy** for the people inside the enterprise is most important in times of change.

Most Critical Methods: Every single Business Design method is in play in this phase: effective **collaboration** among teams charged with delivering on the plan, **need-finding** in designing ways to engage and motivate your people, **visualizing** the "end game" as an aspiration with purpose, iteratively **prototyping** how you might organize to get the job done, taking time for **co-creation** of ways to deliver and motivate people based on how their needs dovetail with the needs of the business, designing **experiments** to advance learning and development, applying **systems thinking** to how you design processes and management systems that integrate the efforts of the people in your organization, and inspiring people through **storytelling** as you move through your journey and celebrate learning and progress.

Regulating Your Thinking Modes: You will be in a strong **decision-making** mode at this stage. But to make those decisions, you will have to pause to **understand** the implications of your decisions in terms of the business and the people, and **generate** new ways of doing business to optimize your chances of success.

So as you can see, the mindsets, methods, and thinking skills of Business Design are at play at *every stage* of development and are applicable in everything you do every day.

The HSO stories in this book illustrate how a deep and rigorous application of Business Design can lead to a transformational outcome. Business Design can be equally effective in a venture in its formative stages as it can in an established organization with an ambition to further scale its impact. The following interview with Jeff Ruby brings to life how valuable the use of Business Design can be in a start-up mode to anchor strategy in purpose and human understanding, shape a better customer experience, identify key strategic partners, and shape enterprise culture from the very beginning. Next comes an interview with Maureen O'Neil that illustrates how Business Design can be applied to an established enterprise at a "strategic inflection point" to capture emerging capabilities in a clear proposition to further scale success. Together, these stories further demonstrate how a design-inspired approach can be used to set an enterprise on a growth path at every stage of its life cycle.

Interview with Jeff Ruby

CEO, Newtopia

" When we initially engaged in the Business Design process, we were trying to sort out two things. One was product fit: *Was the offering really satisfying the needs of our consumers?* And the second was more fundamental: *Should we even be in the direct-to-consumer business at all?* We needed to make a strategic change – what's now eloquently called "the pivot."

I call it starting over again. It's not embracing failure; it's more about redefining what success looks like. We failed in one direction and needed to restart, and so in many ways it was the point for a major pivot away from direct to consumer toward a B2B or B2B2E – "E" being employee distribution. We were trying to figure out what the offering should look like. Almost immediately after that design experience that we had together, we set out on a very different course. We learned a very big lesson around what we did and didn't want to be. That led us to our currently successful distribution model of precision health for disease prevention for at-risk employees in the United States.

My original vision for the company was to focus on disease prevention and to help individuals who were trying to stay healthy. I was inspired by my dad's experience of reaching middle age and suddenly having this disease come out of nowhere, learning that it had both genetic and lifestyle causes. But because he had been blindsided by this diagnosis, he felt like he was almost a passive spectator of his own life. So this raised the question: *How can we inspire people to live healthy as opposed to waiting until they get sick?*

But as we went direct to consumer, we realized that what individuals wanted was weight loss and a quick fix. If we were going to be successful as a weight-loss company, we needed to go after individuals who want to lose weight without sounding and feeling like the Jenny Craigs and the Weight Watchers of the world. Many consumers seeking instant gratification spend on weight loss because it's aesthetic; it's here and now, motivated by a more immediate objective, like a wedding or an event or something to get to right away. So in the direct-to-consumer world, we became an aesthetic weight-loss company, and the early customers were those who saw us as an alternative because of our genetic packaging and full lifestyle perspective.

Through a deeper understanding of the consumer, we learned the grand lesson: there's a very big difference between those who have chosen to take action to lose weight for aesthetic reasons versus those that should be concerned but who may not have that immediate driver. People don't invest in disease prevention unless there's something immediate to tie it to. If it's too far in the future, it won't capture their imagination and their wallet. The desire to stay preventatively healthy wasn't on anyone's mind.

The question that emerged from understanding and reframing was, *How do we target those individuals who are not immediately in need?*

As we started seeing the toughest cases, it led us to wonder if there was a broader market out there. We heard from consumers that if we just broadened the lens and looked at it slightly differently we could still have an impact where we thought we had failed. We realized it wasn't a concept failure but a distribution failure.

In making this pivot we also realized that our people were not necessarily going to be able to change direction. So there was a systematic rebuilding of the team to meet the new direction. In many ways, I started proactively looking for people who were much more like design thinkers or at least sensitive to user needs as part of their core DNA.

Another big learning was the separation of our customer service from our coaching. Everyone in our customer base had a coach, whether they thought they needed one or not. There was no opportunity for feedback, so anyone who didn't think they needed a coach would be turned off right away. If there was a problem with the coach, there was no one to talk to about it. So we created what we call our care specialist – a customer-experience concierge team who work with our coaches and allow them to double-check each other. That structure has been working incredibly well. So I'd say we've been shaping the team in ways of thinking and our values of experimentation and empathy and really getting into the shoes of our participants.

To keep the customer front and center of our efforts, we created a panel of personas as well. They are on the wall as you walk in. They are largely informed by the work that we did together and some of the lessons learned. We design for those individuals because the other challenge we have in this organization is that none of the members of our team fit into the risk profile of the people we are serving. Everything we do now is based on these personas.

Then there are our customer and participant councils, where we take new concepts and iterate with real individuals once we have something that's ready, which is something we never did before. Our participant council is made up of eight to ten people who help us with feedback and thoughts and ideas and make recommendations about what to include in the offering. They really spend a lot of time on this. We have someone from the original direct-to-consumer orientation – literally, from eight years ago – up to more current individuals, so they can provide a wide range of perspectives.

We also spend a lot of time thinking about the online smart-touch experience. I would say we are far from done and we are constantly looking to improve because it is a long sell cycle to get someone on-boarded and introduced to Newtopia. The Newtopia experience really combines the best of high touch with video, voice, electronic, or text-based communication to a real live person.

It's a lot of work constantly iterating on feedback and on the metadata that we collect from our users. We track how many times they are touching their coach, or logging into the app, or participating activities or social community. We've used these "arcs of success" to benchmark what we believe should be happening and then measure and track participant experience against it. When we see things that don't measure up, then we think about what we are doing wrong and iterate some more. It's constant. When your values include empathy and experimentation, you need to get into the shoes of the people you serve. You are never going to have the right answers, so you just keep iterating and use feedback to know when you are getting closer.

Aside from that, we did some thinking about the economics of distribution. We reached the point where the only way we were to achieve any success in the consumer world was to build a trusted consumer brand, and we didn't want to invest in that. So we thought if we could form relationships with partners that already had trusted relationships with our target audience, we could lower the cost of acquisition.

It was when that we came across Aetna's Metabolic Syndrome Risk Reduction Program that the opportunity became clear. This is a program which rewards employees with lower insurance premiums if they take certain steps to avoid or at least mitigate against the onset of a preventable disease. We realized that the incentive of lower premiums would motivate these individuals – which in many cases can represent up to 50 per cent of the company's employee base. Finally things were aligning to our concept.

With Aetna as a co-funding partner, we ran a randomized control trial on nearly 3,000 of Aetna's at-risk employees for a period of three years, which required us to forfeit any outside sales. We were entirely focused on this. We were basically betting the company on the trial's success. The key was to be able to prove ourselves to the market with gold-standard data, instead of simply having a silver-tongued sales pitch. If we were able to prove that it worked at Aetna, we would be able to open the door to its 20-million-plus members, and leverage the credibility gained from that to approach all of the other insurers and employers in the United States.

We are now just scratching the surface of that huge opportunity. In many ways the market is still in the innovation adoption curve, so we're seeing early choices made by the more innovative companies. But the mass employer or the mass market of employers or payers has not yet embraced this kind of disease prevention. So it's still very much on that adoption curve, and we see an explosive amount of opportunity. The way I frame it up in my mind is that a Newtopia customer is anyone – a self-insured employer or a fully insured private or public payor who owns a risk pool.

When you look at these individuals at risk, they really represent a massive unmitigated liability for companies and insurers. If they've got people who are costing \$X that, if left untreated, are about to cause an impact \$Y, you can have a multiple of as much as 10x. We have a solution that can help mitigate that risk, with proven outcomes and a performance-based model that puts our revenues at risk to guarantee our outcomes. As that begins to pick up steam, we are currently servicing organizations ranging from 1,000 up to 250,0000-plus employees/members. Imagine the cost of supporting that size of a base without mitigation.

Looking back, I would say we have learned an awful lot. When I started, I was of the mind that "if you build it they would come" and I didn't necessarily really think through the distribution economics, or how we would attract someone to it, and the differences between what individuals would pay for on their own versus if it's paid for them. I had no appreciation for that, and yet the entire success of the business rests on that understanding.

There is also what I learned about myself. I don't know what giving up looks like and I also don't like problems that can't be solved. So it's just a question of powering through it, learning, and being comfortable being uncomfortable. I just don't know how to give up. And I'm yet to see anyone in the market to do it better than us. So until we see something better in the market, we're going to keep going forward to inspire individuals to live healthier every day and ultimately change the health of the world.[38] **,,**

Interview with Maureen O'Neil

President, Canadian Foundation for
Healthcare Improvement (CFHI)

" CHSRF (later CFHI) was launched in 1996 before the creation of the Canadian Institutes of Health Research (CIHR) (2000). CIHR's new Institute for Health Services and Policy Research (IHSPR) was funding applied health-services research similar to ours. It was also becoming increasingly clear to us that the benefits of focusing directly on improving service delivery were greater than funding research that might be a duplication of CIHR's IHSPR program.

The promise of the improvement work done by the team in our EXTRA program (a leadership program for healthcare improvement) showed that with targeted assistance, change was possible in a short period. It was also a reminder that there remains a significant gap between funding for health-service research and implementation of the results of that research. No organization was funding the "beta testing" of these new ideas. Over four years, between 2008 to 2012, we shifted from research funding to working directly with health systems to help with regional transformation and more effective treatment of chronic disease.

We changed our name to the Canadian Foundation for Healthcare Improvement in 2012. In 2014 we launched our first two improvement collaboratives. One was based on an EXTRA project in Manitoba focused on the appropriate use of antipsychotic drugs in long-term care homes with dementia patients. Reduction of inappropriately prescribed drugs resulted in fewer falls, more alert patients, and no increase in aggression. It also saved money.

The other improvement collaborative from Halifax in the Atlantic was called INSPIRED. INSPIRED provided COPD patients with self-management and advanced-care planning at home rather than leaving sufferers to rely on unplanned ED visits and subsequent hospitalizations. The results were an ROI of 1 to 21.

These "spread collaboratives" provided opportunities for teams across the country who wanted to learn and adapt these innovations to their circumstances. (Later these improvements would go to scale in several jurisdictions.) By 2015, we needed to clarify our communications and more clearly project programming into the future.

Vuka Innovation introduced the principles of Business Design. In one of the most fruitful exercises, we shared stories of our successful projects, mapping in detail what we did, who was involved, what their needs were, and how they were met. It was essentially an experience design exercise. Then we looked at them all and asked what the common underlying capabilities were which led to success. That helped us spread and scale promising innovations in health service delivery and communicate effectively.

One of our core commitments to the transformation of the Canadian healthcare system has been to put patients and families at the center. This had been a major focus in two rounds of applied research support, beginning in 2010. But what, we asked ourselves, does that actually mean for improvement work? This is where Business Design helped us more precisely articulate our aspirations and goals, where to play, and what is needed to win. One of the most important things business design taught us was that if you aren't able to articulate who the true beneficiaries are, you won't be able to communicate how you're uniquely delivering value. By more deliberately applying Business Design principles, frameworks, and methodologies, we also learned that we are natural "business designers"!

Doing this work was a critical success factor in our 2015 pitch to the federal government for extended funding. Our arguments were successful, and as a result we secured the first tranche of a multiyear investment. That pitch: *Here's what we do, here's why we do it, here's how we decide who it's for, and here is the methodology.* It all ladders up to how it will be better for the patient, because if you really use this design-inspired approach, you've got to know who you're designing for. We have used this approach for every successive funding pitch.

If that is your North Star, you also need to ask about the ecosystem needed to support it. That's why you need to come back to those same strategic questions about what you are trying to do, what you need to do to make it happen, why you're doing it, and who you're doing it for. This has been our most important learning from embracing the practice of Business Design.[39]

LIST OF TOOLS & TIPS

The following tools and tips are provided in part two to help explore, assess, and focus your thinking.

7

LEADING INNOVATION & TRANSFORMATION

ENHANCING LEADERSHIP THROUGH BUSINESS DESIGN

Having now absorbed the principles and practices of Business Design and read a variety of stories about how this discipline has been put into play, you can appreciate that it takes leadership at all levels to design and activate new ideas that create new value. Here is a story about a country with vision and boundless ambition to transform both education and industry in parallel.[40] It demonstrates the value of taking a long-term view on building innovation capacity. Through my work at the Rotman School of Management, I had the honor of working with leaders in Singapore's government, education, and industry sectors, and I witnessed their remarkable adoption of design principles and practices to unleash the innovation potential of the people in Singapore and further fuel their success.

Singapore: Making a Big Bet on Design

The leaders of Singapore take a proud stance and often state, *"We are a small country with little land and resources, but we have a lot of bright people with ambition* and know-how. Our people are our greatest resource." Over the years, Singapore has consistently aspired to play an important role in the world by capitalizing on that. In 2008, I met Philip Yeo, a highly respected public figure in Singapore and chair of SRING – an organization dedicated to enabling small and medium enterprises to scale up their success. Phillip Yeo's request: *"Teach my country about Business Design."*[41]

That was the beginning of an exciting relationship with Singapore. In collaboration with Debbie Ng of SPRING, we co-created a pilot session on Business Design, sponsored by SPRING. Our shared goal was to explore how Business Design might enhance their potential for scaled success. This initial session included organizations across a variety of sectors, each of them aspiring to scale their individual enterprises and contribute to Singapore's economic growth. It was in this session that I met the Singapore Polytechnic (SP) team. After that initial pilot, the SP team grabbed the baton and took a leadership role in building their institutional acumen and bringing Business Design to Singapore.

The Challenge

The audacious goal: to transform education for a new generation of change agents and, at the same time, enable Singaporean enterprises to achieve their ambitious goals. SP took on a mandate that would set the country up for important transformation. SP made a commitment to transforming both education and industry through Business Design.

Their Journey

SP's goal was not just to add a few new courses; their ambition was to totally transform education at SP to groom future generations and to boost collective prosperity. Here are some of the things they did to ignite that transformation.

SP was fully committed to capacity building on a grand scale. To ignite this, they certified twenty-four SP faculty members across disciplines. The certification program entailed 300 hours of class time to bring them to a level of mastery of Business Design, designed and delivered by our team at Rotman DesignWorks. Through the program, they learned the theories behind Business Design and applied their learning to two rounds of project work on both industry and education challenges. In tandem with their course work, they participated in industry workshops to hone their facilitation skills. That set them up to independently deliver ongoing industry programs.

These certified trainers started to conduct workshops for their colleagues to transfer their Business Design knowledge and also mentored a new batch of multidisciplinary faculty members who worked on industry projects, using the Business Design model to scale the school's design capacity. That demonstrated not only that the principles and practices of Business Design are applicable in any discipline, but can also effectively serve as a common language in cross-disciplinary collaboration. In the words of Tan Hang Cheong,[42] principal of Singapore Polytechnic at the time, *Design is the language of change.*

They then applied this approach to institutional transformation in terms of spatial design for classroom learning. As good Business Designers, they brought stakeholders (i.e., students and staff) into the development process for the redesign of learning spaces on their campus.

SP applied their learning in re-imagining their educational model for 15,000 students. They conducted need-finding research with students created personas for their diverse student population, and co-created with the faculty's students on ideas that would help students to enhance their learning and social experiences at SP.

During SP's Escapade event in 2011, the co-creation process was elevated to a new level through a one-day campus-wide Ideafest with more than 400 high school students. Students were given a specific challenge: *What might we do to be more environmentally conscious?* Students broke out into classrooms across the campus and were facilitated through the design process by the certified trainers who had adopted this approach to problem-solving and innovation.

As an important part of their strategy to propagate this new way of thinking and showcase student talent, they formed strong industry partnerships. SP worked closely with industry on projects that would give students an opportunity to exercise their design muscle and bring fresh thinking to industry – which cultivated a shared language and appreciation for the power of design.

In parallel with their institutional transformation, SP committed to SPRING to train high-potential enterprises in Singapore to further build skill capacity. Given the level of mastery they had established through the certification program and their facilitation training in the early enterprise programs, SP took on the role of running Business Design training for organizations in both the private and public sector.

This impressive effort to groom a new generation and boost the innovation know-how of industry partners created a symbiotic relationship between the school and industry, effectively generating demand for SP talent.

The Outcome

Today, SP is the hub of high-potential talent and industry transformation. They have ignited the passion and potential of a new generation to contribute to important and well-recognized initiatives and awards, including:

▶ Creation of a Business Innovation and Design Diploma within the business stream;

▶ Redesign of the SP Engineering Academy, where design thinking is used extensively;

▶ Influence on an international engineering initiative that originated from MIT called CDIO (conceive, design, implement, operate) through design thinking;

▶ Training of Singapore's civil service and regional government bodies;

▶ The President's Award for designing a new Library@Orchard, a library with a focus on design, lifestyle, and the applied arts; and

▶ The first ASEAN Youth Award, for their efforts in Learning Express, a regional initiative to use design thinking to make a difference in developing regional economies.

Singapore demonstrates how design can enhance the skills of a new generation, impact business and public service, and transform a regional economy!

"We have made much progress over the years. It has been a long and fruitful journey!"[43]

JOH LIANG HEE,
DEPUTY PRINCIPAL, SINGAPORE POLYTECHNIC

Enterprise evolution and transformation does not happen at the wave of a wand. It requires a long-term view of the capabilities and culture one aspires to shape. It takes leadership, commitment, courage, and conviction, along with a thoughtful and well-implemented plan. If you realize the benefits of this approach through early experience and are keen to pursue it as a broader quest, there are some things that are helpful to consider up front. You may be asking, *What can we do to embed these practices into our enterprise? How can we enhance collective performance?*

That's the purpose of this chapter – to present some of the key learning from others' experience in leading new ways of working and rolling out this practice more broadly across an enterprise. The following topics are explored:

Enterprise Value: The value of embedding the principles and practices of Business Design into the enterprise.

Innovation Leadership: Ten design-inspired principles for enhancing your leadership capacity and creating conditions for innovation success.

Transformation Tips: Ten tips for success in your journey to becoming a design-minded enterprise.

Inspiring and Propagating Innovation: How to inspire and propagate design-inspired innovation through the questions you ask, the language you use, the practices you institutionalize, the spaces you create, and the knowledge you spread.

Building Your Innovation Pipeline and Enterprise Capacity: Ways to enhance and sustain innovation, including design capabilities, throughout your enterprise.

Measuring Performance and Transformation: How this fits within other human resource and operating systems and practices, how you can assess your current state of "readiness," and how you can design your own "innovation dashboard."

Getting Started: Five easy steps to activate the practice of Business Design.

The Enterprise Value of Business Design

Adopting Business Design practices can lead to delivering greater market value; it can also create value inside the organization, with the value of the core methods from chapter 1 summarized in Figure 21. For example, prototyping can allow you to explore more and bigger ideas to create market value; it can also stimulate dialogue and save money in the development process. Co-creation can lead to more relevant and robust solutions; it can also help you work out the bugs faster and more cost-effectively. Most importantly, all these practices are applicable to every stage of development, as noted in each phase of development presented throughout this book.

Embedding Business Design into your organization is much like the Business Design process itself. It involves understanding your people, defining a long-term

Fig. 21 **Value to Market and Enterprise**

Value to Market	Design Methodologies	Value to Enterprise
Create more robust and viable solutions	Multidisciplinary collaboration	Enhance viability and create greater alignment and momentum
Identify opportunities to create new value for customers	Need-finding	Create stronger customer focus and sensitivity
Design a richer, more complete customer experience	Visualization	Practice more effective and compelling communications to foster alignment
Consider more break-through ideas to deliver customer value	Iterative prototyping	Stimulate dialogue, accelerate learning, save money in early development
Design more relevant and desirable solutions	Co-creation and feedback	Work out the bugs faster at a lower cost
Ensure integrated and seamless delivery	Systems mapping	Realize greater synergies and efficiencies in your activities
Discover new, unarticulated unmet needs	Storytelling	Communicate in a more engaging and compelling manner
Determine how to best deliver solutions	Experimentation	Mitigate risk and learn how to advance new ideas

vision for the way you work, putting quick wins and experiments into place, and finding the right way to integrate this approach strategically. Business Design can inject your organization with a new way of thinking and working together that enhances market sensitivity, constantly evolving value offerings and building team alignment and momentum. It can serve as a booster for enterprise collaboration and performance that leads to agility and innovative thinking on a day-to-day basis.

Innovation Leadership: Ten Design-Inspired Principles

The question I get asked all the time – by both senior and emerging leaders – is *"What can I do to activate this practice and effectively lead innovation?"* While design thinking and Business Design are relatively new notions, innovation and leadership are not. Business Design and innovation leadership are closely linked. While many successful leaders of innovation have a natural behavior that inspires others to join their quest, I believe that the principles and practices of Business Design are inherent in their success and tied to recognized traits of innovation leadership. Business Design is more than a collection of methods for devising novel business solutions: it's a valuable part of the innovation leader's tool kit.

While it certainly takes someone with authority to recognize and support the drive for innovation, leadership can come from any level. This is my personal learning from my days at P&G and is reflected in some of the stories in this book. I am always inspired by my students: they have a fresh perspective, energy, and an ambition to make a meaningful mark on society and the economy. I believe that *someone* has to step forward and lead the way.

When it comes to cultivating a culture of innovation, Business Design has a direct impact on a leader's ability to do the following:

1. **Galvanize teams around a common purpose and ground efforts in a meaningful human-centered problem to solve.** Recognition of human needs and connecting one's work to a meaningful quest gives teams and organizations a sense of purpose and elevates their aspirations. *Being purpose-driven is the ultimate motivator.*

2. **Make innovation inclusive and harness diversity.** In the best cases, big ideas build themselves when a diversity of perspectives and know-how is considered. *Including others in the quest leads to better solutions and builds shared ownership in the path forward.*

3. **Create a safe zone for innovation.** This can be a matter of culture, space, structure, or forums – creating the conditions under which people can safely share insights, ideas, and concerns. *Build a safe space – physically and psychologically – for others to innovate.*

4. **Translate imagined futures into something to build.** When people read words on a page or a strategy document, they have their own "movie" in their heads, and that can create tensions over time on how the strategy plays out. Through Business Design, those movies are translated into tangible possibilities that approach a new reality. *Making the vision tangible establishes a concrete destination.*

5. **Manage risk and inspire a learning attitude.** Big ideas always entail an element of risk. Business Design not only helps mitigate those risks through easy, low-risk prototyping and learning experimentation; it also builds trust through empathy for others' risk tolerance and the need for measured steps forward. There's too much celebration of "failure" in my mind. It's not about

failure; it's about learning what didn't work through experiments so you can make it work better in the next iteration. *Learning through prototyping, feedback, and experiments mitigates emotional and business risk.*

6. **Effectively interpret both human factors and business factors.** Dreams and imagination can and should also be anchored in hard facts. At every stage of Business Design, the intuitive and qualitative inputs must combine with data to create confidence in the path forward. *Bridging these dual paradigms builds credibility and a stronger foundation for progress.*

7. **Move people in small steps toward a big vision.** Big ideas are exciting but can be overwhelming when it comes to implementation. Taking measured steps builds trust in the game plan and confidence in the pursuit. *Taking small steps through quick wins and learning experiments builds confidence and momentum.*

8. **Have and inspire courage.** Courage is about stepping out and putting a stake in the ground, making it safe for others to pursue higher value. Business Design focuses the team on defining needs and distinct ways to fulfill those unmet needs. It combines what's right for the end stakeholder with what's right for the business to survive and thrive. It entails making decisions that are simply the right thing to do. *Courage comes from doing the right thing.*

9. **Inspire a "can-do" stance to overcome minor setbacks in the pursuit of big ideas.** Not everything will go exactly as one would like in the pursuit of new ideas. Inevitably, there will be things that don't work or new information that enters the picture, and you have to course correct. The practice of feedback and experimentation help cultivate a learning mindset. At the same time, setbacks in the pursuit of big ideas can be tough on teams. That's when support and encouragement are most valued. *Positivity fuels creativity and resiliency.*

10. **Have a goal and a plan to get there.** While the destination might be fuzzy at the front end, the work of an effective team will make the solution and strategy clear through the process. Business Design is a logical approach that builds from insights to strategy, enabling leaders to map out how the team will get to where it needs to go. *Have a process and build trust in it.*

Transformation: Ten Tips for Success

As Claudia Kotchka says in her interview at the end of this chapter, *"If you're serious about transforming your enterprise, know what you're in for."* Here are my top ten tips to keep in mind as you go about embedding Business Design principles and practices more broadly throughout your organization:

1. **Make a long-term commitment.** Business Design is not a one-shot vaccine nor an event that you engage in periodically; it's a way of thinking, doing, and communicating every day, across every department. That's an evolutionary process that takes time.

2. **Emphasize the underlying ideology of Business Design.** Business Design is fundamentally a system of principles, mindsets, and practices. Making it part of your everyday way of thinking and doing, from top to bottom and across all areas of expertise, will help you fully leverage the insights, imagination, and ingenuity of your people.

3. **Engage all disciplines and levels of the enterprise.** Business Design is inclusive. It might take a relatively small group to design solutions or strategy, but it takes an entire enterprise to *deliver* new value. For Business Design to be an effective innovation platform, everyone must see their role in the process, as well as the relevance and value in their own discipline, on a day-to-day basis.

4. **Integrate the principles of Business Design into your existing practices.** Business Design, as presented in this book, is not meant to be a disruption, but rather an enhancement. It is not meant to displace current systems and practices, but rather to enhance development practices and be integrated into your most effective development and go-to-market systems.

5. **Build your internal capacity to innovate.** In the early days, you might need help from experts to get you going – or to get you unstuck from time to time. The aim, however, should be to enhance your skills internally. To really get the value out of Business Design and to have it adopted throughout your enterprise, you must acquire and develop the skills internally.

6. **Prepare to invest.** If you want to boost enterprise returns, you should be ready to invest energy, time, and money in all areas of your organization. If you regularly put a million dollars toward an innovation consulting project or into a sales meeting, isn't investing in the capabilities of your entire organization an equally good investment?

7. **Position this practice as an effective platform for personal and business performance.** Business Design is a way to boost performance and productivity in optimizing your path to creating greater value, as noted earlier. Enlisting well-respected and empowered leaders with vision and fortitude to lead the transformation will link this approach to performance. That's what Procter & Gamble's A.G. Lafley did when he appointed Claudia Kotchka to lead the charge for the company.

8. **Align your systems and incentives.** Chances are that attempting to operationalize and sustain your capacity for design-inspired innovation across

the enterprise will have implications for your management systems and performance incentives. Consider your internal processes, the way people are evaluated and rewarded, allowance for more experimentation and learning, and rewards for collaboration and originality.

9. **Start now with a tough challenge.** Business Design often starts off as an effective problem-solving tool, evolves into a strategic planning tool, and eventually becomes a part of your culture. Start with a pilot group to demonstrate the value. Conduct a few training and inspiration sessions. Just get started and grow from there.

10. **Inspire – don't legislate.** Business Design is not about establishing a strict process or a new set of rules. It's about a culture shift toward deeper values and shared principles. It is about giving people license to explore, create, experiment, and learn – both on big projects and day-to-day problem-solving.

Inspiring & Propagating Innovation

Business Design is a discipline that aims to elevate the level of innovation and increase your odds of success in a consistent and deliberate manner. At the same time, its underlying value lies in mindfully nurturing a spirit of innovation and collaboration; that unleashes the innate capacity to rise to any challenge across the enterprise. This has been key in shaping the culture of many highly innovative and successful enterprises.

Embedding the principles, mindsets, and methods of Business Design broadly within an enterprise requires a high-level commitment to big-picture programs and initiatives, as well as activation of everyday ways to inspire and ignite passion for design-driven innovation. These everyday signals come in the form of questions, language, space, and practices.

First, *ask new questions.* As a decision-maker, you can influence the motivations and behaviors of your entire organization. The ten questions described below have worked for others to re-energize people and foster a culture of design-driven innovation. Instead of asking, "Can you prove this will work?" and thereby likely killing any new-to-the-world idea, consider asking these questions:

1. **What unmet need does this address?** A rigorous approach to Gear 1 will answer that question. If the opportunity is based on the universal needs of your target users, it's hard to argue.

2. **What's the vision for the user experience?** This question calls for a clear articulation of the proposition and how it may eventually unfold as a

multi-dimensional experience for the user, not just a description of a new product or service alone. A good future story that aligns with the purpose and strategy of the enterprise is more likely to get the "green light."

3. **Who was involved in the development of this idea?** This question will reinforce the principle of cross-disciplinary collaboration, reveal how comprehensive the development process was, and signal how much early buy-in and future traction is associated with the idea.

4. **What other ideas did you explore?** Multiple prototyping inevitably leads to bigger, more robust solutions. Teams that explore several ideas before converging on one have demonstrated more open-mindedness and rigor than those who started with one idea and focused on making it perfect.

5. **What did you learn from customers?** The co-creation process always reveals valuable insights. Customer feedback, both good and bad, is important to capture. It is helpful to discuss what resonated, what surprised the team, and what bombed. Co-creation is a signal that they have stayed close to the customer and are truly creating for and with them.

6. **Could this create a sustainable competitive advantage?** A true breakthrough will set you apart and allow you to carve out a new space that you can own. The answer to this question lies in both a compelling idea and a distinct strategy to deliver and *own* that idea.

7. **What do you want to learn as you move forward?** It's OK to not have *all* the answers or 100-per cent guarantees. That comes with new territory. Acknowledging what is known, and what is not, is healthy. That encourages teams to pursue their path with a learner's mindset and be prepared to iterate and advance ideas along the way.

8. **How can I help?** That's a big one. Sad to say, many employees see their senior decision-makers as roadblocks to big ideas. Great leaders are happy to offer their wisdom and guidance to support their employees in their pursuit of strong visions and give them the space to experiment and learn.

9. **What did you learn that might help us right now?** Through the Business Design process, teams will most likely discover new insights that can help your business today, with immediate implications on priorities. For example, you may need to recast or enhance current, short-term initiatives, such as a promotion or a product launch. There is always something learned in the Business Design process that informs the here and now.

10. **What should we stop doing?** One of the great benefits of this process is that it leads to a clearer picture of what really matters to the customer and,

conversely, what doesn't. Such insight can lead to axing projects on your to-do list that do not create value.

Second, *use design language* in your efforts to embed Business Design into your enterprise. Aside from the way we communicate in our decision-making process, the everyday language we use is a simple cue to a design-driven approach. Discussing "needs" and "experiences" and referring to "prototypes" are small signals of a design culture. At the same time, don't overload your conversations with a lot of jargon – that can be a real turn-off for some people.

Third, *create spaces* that are conducive to creative collaboration. One of the first things converts in Business Design do is create a visible and accessible space where community collaboration and innovation can take place. You may begin by reorganizing and redecorating one meeting room to set your team up for a more creative and productive collaboration. Consider a space that is more open, has features like whiteboards and large work surfaces, and is stocked with materials like large rolls of paper, sticky notes, and possibly some proto-typing materials. Eventually, you can convert more spaces for creative collaboration, leaving the offices and cubicles to administration. Those who have taken this philosophy all the way, such as design firms and design-driven corporations, have carried it throughout their enterprise space.

And finally, you will want to *modify your practices* where there is a benefit to doing so. There are so many easy and productive ways you can work together to advance your business through Business Design. Here are some simple ways to get started that have worked for others:

Spend face time with your key stakeholders. While market research will always play a role in bringing dimension to segments, trends, and opportunities, spend-ing time with people and *listening* to their stories will give you a more holistic understanding of them and greater insight into their needs.

Have a charrette instead of a meeting. A charrette is a design session in which challenges are solved on the spot. Call together the right people and organize an agenda in which you deconstruct a problem, brainstorm solutions, and build out a prototype or two. Instead of reviewing what you said you were going to do in the last meeting, reviewing what you've done since that meet-ing, and discussing what you will do before the next meeting, why not tackle the job on the spot? There will always be a place for status meetings!

Spend as little money as possible on early prototypes. Low-resolution mock-ups can often be quite effective in helping to convey your early ideas, at virtually no cost. Try limiting your early prototyping budget to twenty dollars. People, including customers, love getting involved in the development process and are more likely to give you valuable early feedback on an idea when you haven't spent a lot of money on it.

Consider multiple options. Before you commit to one solution or idea, always consider other options. I go by the Rule of Three: generate three ways of solving a problem or addressing a need, compare and contrast with an open mind, and then create the best single solution. Most often, the solution will be none of the original three, but rather some combination of them.

Visualize more. The fastest way to communicate is often through visualization. Whether it is drawing a diagram, mapping a system of interrelated parts and forces, or creating a prototype or experience timeline, visualization brings clarity and focus to communications and collaboration efforts.

Foster collaboration across functions and business units. With the depth of talent and resources that many large enterprises have, it is ironic that sometimes the biggest barriers to innovation and, more importantly, activation are the structure of the organization itself – the invisible walls between dreams and realization. Often a big idea calls for drawing resources from and leveraging strengths across divisions. Yet when it comes time to activate an initiative, these divisions may wonder who owns the initiative and how it will play out within the organization's current structure. This struggle is common in large enterprises and must be recognized from the outset of a development project.

Building Your Innovation Pipeline & Enterprise Capacity

There are several things to consider when building your capacity to innovate through design-inspired practices like Business Design: sourcing innovation expertise, building internal capacity, and ensuring the right support systems and process are in place, including rewarding people for contributing to innovation success.

Figure 22 shows some options to consider in building your innovation capacity and pipeline:

Fig. 22 **Sources of Expertise**

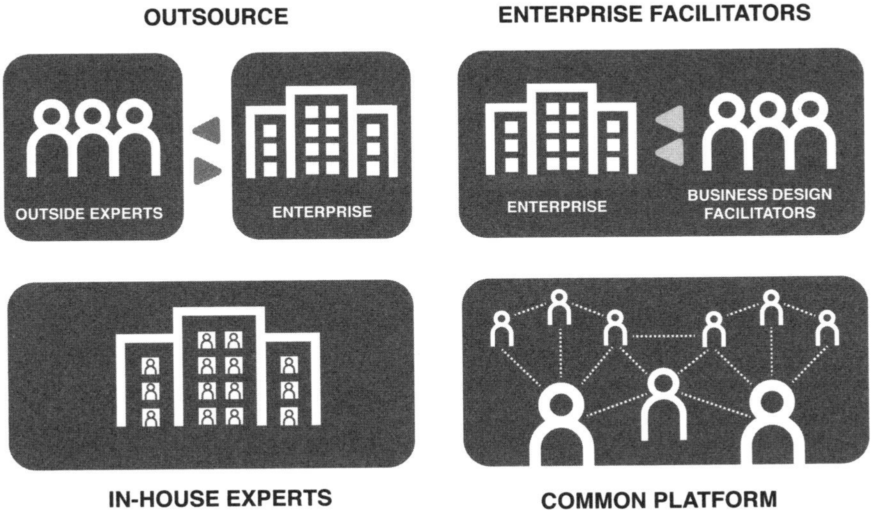

OUTSOURCE

OUTSIDE EXPERTS

ENTERPRISE

ENTERPRISE FACILITATORS

ENTERPRISE

BUSINESS DESIGN FACILITATORS

IN-HOUSE EXPERTS

COMMON PLATFORM

Hire an outside consultant to do it for you: For those that simply don't have the capacity to take on a big innovation quest, hiring outside innovation experts is an option. There was a time when organizations were paying a lot of money in retainers to outside consultants to come up with the "next big idea." However, complete outsourcing has some drawbacks: it can be expensive, may not translate into activation because ideas don't plug back into the organization, and may not cultivate a deep sense of ownership inside the enterprise. That's why more and more enterprises are looking to build internal talent.

Tap into external innovators and entrepreneurs: An extension of outsourcing innovation is to collaborate with external sources of new ideas from start-ups and "disruptive" inventors and entrepreneurs. Procter & Gamble realized the value of tapping into external innovators decades ago through its Connect & Develop program, in which it worked with inventors to commercialize new technologies. More recently, many organizations have established a more formal alliance with entrepreneurs. By tapping into fresh ideas to accelerate and scale ideas that fulfill the corporate ambition, they create a model in which everyone wins – the start-up (through access to scalability), the enterprise (through creation of new value for the market and the enterprise), and most importantly, the consumer (for whom unmet needs are addressed in a new and novel way).

Set up an innovation lab as a center of in-house expertise: Innovation labs and incubators have been set up in organizations all over the world in recent years, with great intentions. Centralized labs can be highly productive, as is the case for Fidelity Labs, but often fail for a few reasons. First, they are often disconnected from the rest of the enterprise and are ineffective in bringing about enterprise-wide innovation because of lack of visibility and enterprise engagement. I am shocked by the number of executives I meet who have no idea what is going on in their central labs. Second, they are not aligned to the overarching enterprise strategy or business-unit goals. Third, they fail to deliver a return on investment. These are the "trophy labs" that might look impressive to investors and media but can't demonstrate business impact.

Create an internal pool of skilled facilitators or "catalysts": In this approach, you train skilled facilitators to go out into the enterprise to help teams unlock fresh thinking to design *and* deliver new ideas to the marketplace. Ambitious people don't often like wasting time on theoretical exercises. For example, while Procter & Gamble established a team of facilitators with deeper skills, they also brought the entire enterprise along on the journey to demonstrate how new approaches could apply to their business. Both Procter & Gamble and Intuit have scaled the value of design-inspired methods and mindsets by training people who are both skilled at and motivated by helping others drive innovation. Experts outside the enterprise can help train facilitators to unleash the capacity to create new solutions internally.

Expand capacity by embedding skills across the enterprise: If your goal is to transform your ways of working together and enhance your culture of innovation, you might decide to enhance skills on a broader basis so everyone can participate in or lead the innovation process in some way. If you choose to engage the enterprise in skill-building more broadly, I have found that the most effective way to teach new ways to solve problems is through *applied learning* – having them learn new skills by tackling their toughest challenges, as skillful facilitators do. In this scenario, more people learn to "speak the language" and benefit from the basic principles every day. To do that, you might bring in external experts to train the trainers and build internal skills.

As you define your enterprise strategy to boost innovation capacity, it helps to have external experts and mentors as sounding boards and coaches. People who have perspective, know-how, and a few battle scars from pioneering new ways can make you more aware of what can help and hinder your progress. This assistance can take the form of a formal advisory board or an informal network of peers and mentors.

Measuring Performance & Transformation: Innovation Dashboard

The big question all performance-oriented and analytically minded companies have is, *"How do we know our efforts are going to pay off?"* In some ways, you may just intuitively believe that this all makes sense. At the same time, you might also like to have a handle on the effectiveness and impact of your programs and have some indication that your investments in business and people development are paying off. For this, I suggest you create your own "innovation dashboard." See Figure 23.

Here are some suggestions on measures to consider when creating your enterprise dashboard, based on the learning of many who have gone on this journey:

Innovation readiness assessment and tracking: Assessment tools can help measure the strategic alignment, innovation practices, and effectiveness of the processes and systems that shape your business performance and your innovation culture. As noted earlier, at Vuka Innovation, we've used one such tool to diagnose, enhance, and track innovation readiness. You may also have your own indicators of what constitutes innovation progress and success. It is important to define and assess these along the way so that innovation capacity can be tracked and strategically advanced.

Engagement and job satisfaction: Engagement is key in enterprise productivity. A sense of purpose that comes from an inspiring vision and an authentic connection to the customer has the potential to enhance intrinsic motivation. Collaboration brings teams together and gives everyone a voice. Unleashing creativity can energize teams. Progress and shared success can enhance job satisfaction. All of these intentions are inherent in the practice of Business Design.

Output and business performance: Driving progress and business results is inextricably linked to how strategies and plans cascade down throughout the enterprise and build your pipeline of promising new initiatives. At the end of the day, what you produce is most important. Monitoring your "yield" in terms

Fig. 23 **Innovation Dashboard**

READINESS   ENGAGEMENT   PERFORMANCE   ASSESSMENTS

of initiatives that go to market and create new value, as well as their projected value to the enterprise, can help you assess your return on investment and prioritize efforts. Including an "innovation pipeline tracker" in your dashboard will add an important dimension to it. While business results are one important measure of performance, big ideas often take time to realize their full potential. Performance can also be measured in terms of customer satisfaction, loyalty, and referrals to others. Performance indicators that you believe to be critical to your success can be built into your innovation dashboard.

Personal 360° assessments: This incorporates performance on a personnel level – how well an individual performs in his or her job. For example, Business Design is very much about team productivity and effectiveness. Therefore, be sure to solicit team feedback on contributions and leadership within teams. Just as in the co-creation process, feedback is the source of learning and advancement.

Getting Started: Defining the Path Forward

There are many ways to get started in your journey to boost your innovation capacity. Here are five easy steps to get you going, using Business Design principles to define your path forward:

1. **Assess where you are and where you want to be in five years.** Take stock of the market context and your current state, and decide how your desired future state will look.
2. **Take time to deeply understand your people and enterprise systems.** Create the conditions for success by starting with an appreciation for your current cultural values and ways of working.

3. **Explore ways to boost your capacity and performance.** Consider ways to spark a new way to work. You might choose to just try new ways as an experiment or embark on an enterprise-wide transformation program.

4. **Determine your strategy and roadmap to get there.** Make choices on how you will get there. Recognize that big ideas take time, perseverance, and a learning mindset.

5. **Start anywhere.** Most importantly, get going. Demonstrate the value of a design-inspired approach through a project on an unresolved challenge or a fuzzy opportunity that you don't know how to kick-start.

Every enterprise will design its own journey in Business Design. I am hoping the learning from others, as presented throughout this book, provides you with some helpful considerations. As I noted in my introduction, building a culture of innovation through the practice of Business Design is a journey in transforming the ways in which we work and, ultimately, create and sustain new value in the marketplace. May you enjoy the journey and realize great success!

The following interview with Claudia Kotchka, former vice-president of Design Innovation and Strategy at Procter & Gamble, provides insight for those who aim to fully leverage the power of design and run with it in a big way in their organizations. I asked Claudia Kotchka what advice she has for business leaders. Here's what she said.

Interview with Claudia Kotchka
Vice-President of Design Innovation and
Strategy, Procter & Gamble (2000–2009)

"My first piece of advice is, *know what you're asking for.* My experience is that some people say they want it, but when they realize it's a pretty big culture change that involves all the disciplines in the organization, they're not really so sure. So step one is about knowing what you're asking for.

My second piece of advice is *show, don't tell.* Don't spend a lot a time trying to sell it or trying to explain it. Run some pilots, get it started, and go. That was exactly how you and Roger [Martin] designed all the workshop training. There weren't a lot of PowerPoint presentations. It was just go, dive in, experience it, which scared the heck out of everyone at first. But I remember one comment: *"This is the best training I've ever attended. Because I'm being trained and don't know it. But at the same time, I'm solving a real problem; a problem that's important to my business."* It is an absolute role model for training – they're working on a real problem. It's not fake, so they're interested. They have a stake in solving the problem, so they show up. And they have no idea what they're getting into, but wow, what amazing results. I can't say enough great things about it. It's incredible! Once you experience it, you come out transformed. And that's true for every single person who experiences it.

The third bit of advice I would give is, *get help.* I always tell people "Don't try to do it yourself. You don't know how to do this. And you don't have to. You just have to make sure it happens in the end." I got help from lots of people, including you [the team at the Rotman School of Management]. When I realized I needed to teach management and staff at P&G what we were doing with design, I recognized I don't know how to teach. I'm not an educator. No one at P&G is an educator. So I decided to get help from the best – the experts at educational institutions that know how to teach.[44] "

Part Two

Tool Kit

This section presents some of the most popular tools to apply in creating new value for the market and your enterprise. These represent the core methods used in the case studies in this book. These practical tools and tips can help you get you started, or you can add them to your existing repertoire of innovation methods.

Fig. 24 **Visualization of Tools and Tips**

PREPARING FOR YOUR QUEST

Framing Your Ambition
Enterprise Readiness
Team Design
Team Profiling
Team Mapping
Team Building
Facilitation
Team Charters
Project Brief
Project Blueprint
Communication &
  Engagement Plan

CONTEXTUALIZING YOUR CHALLENGE

STEEP Analysis
Landscape of Players
Scenario Planning
Stakeholder Mapping
Activity Systems (Current State)
Activity Systems (Competitive)
Activity System Assessment
Strategic Choice Considerations

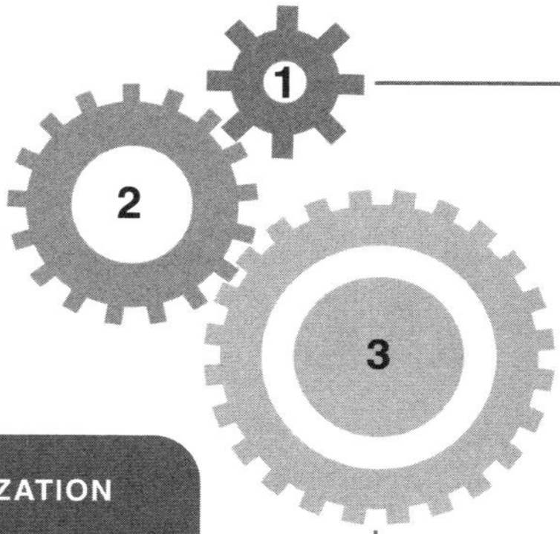

①

②

③

EMPATHY & DEEP HUMAN UNDERSTANDING

Role Play to Empathize
Need-Finding Research
Observation
User Journals
Photo Elicitation
Listening & Recording
Mind Mapping
Subject Profiles
Discovery Exchange
Motivational Mapping
Need-Mining & Analysis
Need Articulation
Need Validation
Personas
Current Journey
Design Criteria

CONCEPT VISUALIZATION

Ideation & Concept Harvesting
Role Play to Ideate
Metaphors
Iterative Prototyping
Experience Mapping
Storyboarding
Role Play to Advance Ideas
In-Person Feedback
Virtual Feedback

STRATEGIC BUSINESS DESIGN & ACTIVATION

The Proposition
Capability Requirements
Monetization
Value Exchange
Reciprocity
Market Sizing
Financial Sensitivity Analysis
Activity Systems (Future)
Activity System Assessment
Strategic Focus
Experiments & Risk Assessment
Quick Wins
Organizational Structure
Management Systems

PART TWO CONTENTS

PREPARING FOR YOUR QUEST

These tools provide ways to frame your project in the context of your enterprise, design your project road map, and identify the right people for the innovation journey. These are important considerations in establishing the conditions for success from the start. The outcome: Commitment to a shared ambition that will set you up for a productive pursuit.

FRAMING YOUR AMBITION
LINKING THE PAST TO THE FUTURE

WHY DO WE DO THIS?

To link your aspirations to the current dynamics of your business and align on what success might look like for your enterprise. This preliminary scoping exercise will help frame your ambitions and challenges and align your quest with the overall enterprise ambition and strategy. It will make your quest relevant and valuable to your enterprise, as a prelude to your project brief and your initial business case.

HOW CAN YOU DO THIS?

The following are important considerations to appreciate at the *outset* of your pursuit:

1. **State of the business.** Understand the current state of the business – in terms of financial performance and market impact. Are you struggling or on a roll? Appreciate success factors and identify barriers to future success.
2. **Leadership aspirations.** Appreciate the overarching vision and aspirations for the enterprise to help contextualize your pursuit in a meaningful way.
3. **Enterprise goals and strategy.** Understand the measurable goals of the enterprise, the current enterprise strategy, and where the organization currently focuses time and effort. Define how your quest relates to that strategy and how it will contribute to delivering on your enterprise goals.
4. **Enterprise priorities.** Identify the most important initiatives underway and how your efforts complement them and create new value. Organizations in most need of Business Design are those that spend resources on too many scattered priorities or need to recalibrate priorities for greater return.
5. **The way people work.** Identify the processes and systems (formal and informal) that guide how people spend their time and effort. These ingrained processes and systems have gotten you to where you are but can either help or hinder you in the pursuit of new ideas. Recognizing current ways of working reveals what you can leverage or what you might need to redesign up stream.

6. **Enterprise values and culture.** Identify what values drive current decision-making and how these values define your culture. Built and reinforced over time, these factors can have an important impact on how you manage potential change in behaviors and attitudes when creating a desired future.

7. **Aspirations for the project.** Synthesize your insights and articulate how your quest will fit with and contribute to all of the above. This will make your quest more relevant and valuable to the enterprise.

8. **Visualize success.** Create a picture of success in broad terms – how the organization will look and feel when you've reached your future state.

Tips

▶ Link a project to the enterprise goals to help justify putting time and resources into your quest.

▶ Solicit input from executive sponsors to gain valuable perspective and support from the start.

▶ Be candid about what you can leverage and where you will have to navigate a change in mindsets or behaviors to advance your quest.

▶ Be visual! Visualizing your "future state" can be an engaging and imaginative way to capture your aspirations. Having some big paper and markers helps!

WHAT MIGHT THIS LOOK LIKE?

In addition to capturing a snapshot of enterprise context outlined above, it is often motivating to imagine your "destination" as an organization. As an example, a development team might capture their aspirations in a visualization exercise of "What will success look like for us as an organization?" Imagining your destination allows the core team to express their aspirations in a metaphorical drawing and tell their envisioned future story.

ENTERPRISE READINESS
ASSESSING YOUR ENTERPRISE CAPACITY TO INNOVATE

WHY DO WE DO THIS?

To measure, assess, and evaluate the degree to which the enterprise is ready to generate and deliver innovation on a sustained basis. Quantifying enterprise-wide perceptions of the current state of readiness will help to stimulate dialogue, identify ways to enhance readiness, and benchmark future progress. For example, the Vuka Innovation Readiness Survey[45] cited in chapter 2 is one tool that benchmarks current perceptions of strategic alignment, ways of working, supporting systems, and culture – all factors in your ability to adapt to an ever-changing business environment. *More on that instrument is available online as fraserdesignworks.com.*

HOW CAN YOU DO THIS?

Here are some simple steps to measure and assess your readiness:

1. **Select your survey instrument and identify participants.** There are a variety of survey instruments that measure enterprise readiness as a valuable diagnostic of your current state. You can conduct this survey within a smaller group to stimulate team dialogue, or run a more extensive enterprise-wide survey to ascertain a more comprehensive picture of the perceptions of enterprise readiness.

2. **Run the survey.** Invite others to participate in this online questionnaire. For a truly complete picture, include the leadership; all employees across functions, levels, and geographies; and your board of directors.

3. **Review your enterprise profile for strengths to leverage and development opportunities.** Analysis conducted on survey results will reveal insights about your ability to respond to market opportunities in a strategic, unified, and productive way to sustain a "value creation advantage."

4. **Engage others in a dialogue about opportunities and ways to enhance your innovation readiness.** Internal workshops give people an opportunity to contribute insights on what helps and what constrains your capacity to

innovate, as well as ideas on how to build a more inclusive culture of innovation.

5. **Establish priorities and a game plan to activate.** From your discussions, you will identify easy quick wins and longer-term development opportunities. These may include clearer communications, new principles to put into practice, new ways of working, skill-building programs, new "teaming" practices, or new reward systems. The data will tell you what you can leverage and where you can improve the most.

6. **Reassess at regular intervals to track progress and make course corrections.** Set goals on desired areas of improvement. A regular checkup on readiness will enable you to continue to boost your innovation readiness and performance.

Tips

▸ This survey can be run within a select group as a means to stimulate dialogue and align on your current state and future opportunities. Expanding input to your broader organization will give you a more comprehensive picture of perceptions across the organization.

▸ Consider what many organizations face: "survey fatigue" and pressing demands on time and energy. Timing of the survey, motivation to participate, and ample time to complete the survey are important to keep in mind.

▸ Use results to engage others in a dialogue to improve readiness, including day-to-day practices and mindsets as well as more formal structures and processes.

WHAT MIGHT THIS LOOK LIKE?

In the HSO transformation presented in this book, the Vuka Innovation Readiness Survey was used to measure the readiness across all dimensions of innovation success and helped to identify opportunities to boost innovation across the enterprise. Over the course of HSO's strategic transformation, it implemented a capacity-building program to embed Business Design into its ways of working. Together with an inspiring strategy, these efforts resulted in a boost in employee perceptions on one of their KPIs – "Our enterprise is innovative" – from 50 per cent in agreement to 66 per cent in agreement.

TEAM DESIGN
IDENTIFYING KEY CONTRIBUTORS

WHY DO WE DO THIS?

To establish a multidisciplinary team that will bring a diversity of functional expertise, perspectives, and skills to the quest. Setting the foundation for fruitful collaboration at the outset of the project will ensure rich thinking and outcomes and will build momentum over the course of the project. This activity will help you to identify who can contribute to the development process as the basis for resource commitment, by helping you answer the following questions:

What functional expertise and skills will be required to create and activate a comprehensive solution?

Who are the people who will be critical to creating and delivering the solution?

Who else may inspire or support us in our quest?

HOW CAN YOU DO THIS?

1. **State your challenge and how it relates to your current business.** While the opportunity will become more clearly defined as you develop your project brief, the ingoing challenge will generally point to the expertise you will want to enroll from the beginning.

2. **Consider a diversity of skills and perspectives.** A diverse team will bring richness to the process and open your enterprise to possibilities and solutions that may be far from the obvious. This diversity will also position you to get things done in a well-orchestrated manner and create momentum as you move forward. Diversity comes in several different ways; the intent is to harness the most valuable perspectives, insights and know-how and build commitment to delivering on the outcomes. It is easy to start with the intact team, which is used to working together. To further expand your thinking, consider these general categories of diversity:

    Functional: Harnessing diverse functional expertise from the start of a project enables you to obtain to a more comprehensive breakthrough sooner.

Skills based: It is helpful to have people who are particularly good at project management, ideation, visualization, synthesis, analysis, communication, and other key skills that will enhance progress along the way.

Geographical: Across regions within a country and across countries around the world, people have valuable perspectives on their local business or culture.

Generational: Engage emerging leaders: they have fresh insights and energy. In many cases, they will have to own the future. Intentionally design the team to not only diversify expertise, but also balance the wisdom of the seasoned experts with the perspective of "emerging bright stars" in the organization.

Cultural: There are many other characteristics that offer the opportunity to diversify perspectives and bring in people who can deliver value from their experiences and unlock fresh thinking. *Who might help add a unique perspective that can help us see the world in different ways and avoid homogenous thinking?*

External: Often it makes sense to bring in someone from outside the enterprise, either as part of the development team or as a sounding board. For example, it helps to have a patient embedded in the development team in a healthcare project. The question to ask: *Who can shake up our thinking?*

3. **Define the core team.** Identify the core interdisciplinary group of individuals, beginning with *intact team members*, who have a vested interest in the project. Consider who else will add valuable, fresh insights, and know-how, both *internally* and *externally*. Also consider key partners who will be critical in creating and delivering possible outcomes (e.g., design agency or other strategic partners).

4. **Establish the team.** Once you have a diverse and committed team, align on your project brief. Your team charter will help clarify roles and guiding principles for how.

5. **Secure an executive sponsor and an advisory team.** Your sponsor will bring both wisdom to and endorsement of the project in the context of other enterprise initiatives. Consider who else's *wisdom and endorsement* will be needed to support your project as an important priority for the enterprise. An advisory board can be accessed at key points in the development process and help guide your efforts.

6. **Define roles and requirements for all team members.** Define who is dedicated as the *core team* (i.e., those doing the heavy lifting), who is *part-time*

(i.e., those who will bring expertise or inspiration at appropriate points in the process), and who will be *sponsors or advisors* (i.e., those brought in on a regular and focused basis).

Tips

▶ Diversity of perspectives will lead to more robust solutions and broader ownership.

▶ It helps to define a core development team, as well as others who can weigh in and add perspective and wisdom along the way.

WHAT MIGHT THIS LOOK LIKE?

Figure 25 depicts the team design for the HSO healthcare project presented in chapters 3 and 6. The leadership designated an executive sponsor and a development team that brought together many disciplinary and stakeholder perspectives within the organization. They also designed the process to engage board members, employees, and other key experts along the way.

Fig. 25 **Designing the Team for Strategic Transformation**

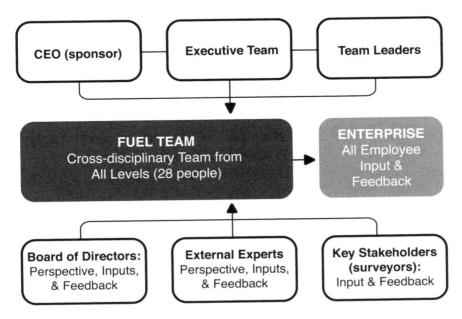

TEAM PROFILING
ALIGNING THINKING PREFERENCES

WHY DO WE DO THIS?

To gain greater self-awareness and a deeper understanding of team members and facilitate more productive collaboration. There are many profiling tools that consist of a questionnaire followed by an analysis and report of an individual's unique strengths and preferences. As noted in part one, awareness of individual thinking preferences can help enhance an individual's ability to tackle the task at hand and boost team effectiveness. The One Smart World profiling tool enhances understanding of how team members think and helps to establish a strong foundation for collaboration. *More on how this profiling can enhance Business Design effectiveness and productive collaboration is provided on fraserdesignworks.com.*

HOW CAN YOU DO THIS?

You can leverage this tool by following these three steps:

1. **Complete the survey.** This questionnaire is based on years of research in identifying individual preferences in understanding, generating, synthesizing, and deciding. It is not about ability, but rather what dimensions of thinking are most preferred and energizing for an individual.

2. **Review and share your results.** This will help you fully leverage individual team member preferences. There are no inherently right or wrong results. An effective organization will have a diverse mix of thinking preferences to maximize collective performance.

3. **Integrate your insights into your work plan.** You can integrate this notion of regulating thinking modes into your development plan and your team charter. You can also integrate these new insights into your personal development plans to strengthen your cognitive agility.

Tips

▶ Throughout development, there are times when you need to pause to understand, generate new possibilities, and synthesize and make decisions.

- Results do not infer ability, but rather one's personal preferences and operating style. Awareness of these natural preferences allows you to more deliberately regulate your thinking mode to best complete the task at hand. Every step in this Tool Kit is inherently associated with a particular mode of thinking.

- Drawing on individual preferences and rotating leadership on any given task can enhance collaboration. For example, individuals who prefer *generative thinking* can help drive ideation; individuals who prefer *decision-making* can help drive convergent activities; and the individuals who strive for *understanding* can make sure everyone understands what they are doing, why, and for whom.

- Regulating your thinking mode begins with awareness and is enhanced through practice.

WHAT MIGHT THIS LOOK LIKE?

Figure 26 is an example of one person's profile, which shows a natural preference for "envisioning" the future (over brainstorming), a preference to "tune in and empathize" as a way of understanding (over data analysis), and an inclination to make decisions based more on "belief and gut feeling" than validation.

Fig. 26 **Thinking-Preference Profile**

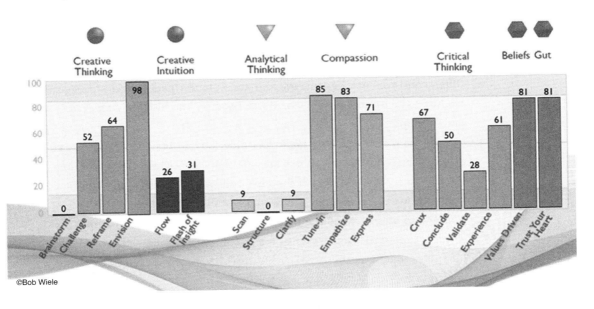

©Bob Wiele

TEAM MAPPING
IDENTIFYING TALENTS, ROLES, & PASSIONS

WHY DO WE DO THIS?

To harness diversity and build clarity around skills, expertise, and roles. Team mapping is a collaborative way to build appreciation for what each team member brings to the project and reveal personal passions related to the project. Team mapping visualizes your talent ecosystem and answers questions such as,

What expertise, skills, knowledge, and perspective does each team member bring?

What role will he or she play in the project?

What are his or her personal interests and passions related to the project?

HOW CAN YOU DO THIS?

1. **Describe competencies and interests.** Ask team members to write down four pieces of information about themselves on sticky notes: their area of expertise (*e.g., manufacturing*), their core skills (*e.g., facilitation*), knowledge and perspective (*e.g., customer insights*), and their personal passions and interests (*e.g., building strong local communities*). Write each piece of information on a separate note with the author identified by name or initials.

2. **Cluster and connect.** Keeping the four areas of information separate, begin to cluster the information on the walls. Look for and identify connections and overlaps.

3. **Identify team strengths and gaps.** Examine the clusters and identify areas of strength and areas where there are gaps that you might need to fill if they are necessary for the project. If they are, finds ways of shoring up those gaps by engaging others along the way who might fill those gaps.

4. **Appreciate and harness the diversity of the team.** Use this as input for your team charter. Discuss how personal interests and insights may play into the project, as these will bring intrinsic motivation and depth to your quest.

Tips

▶ Have these items on hand: a big whiteboard or sheet of paper, sticky notes, and markers.

▶ While posting everyone's strengths and areas of interest, take the time to have each person talk about himself or herself in more detail. This will help provide a better understanding and appreciation of everyone's capabilities and interests.

WHAT MIGHT THIS LOOK LIKE?

Through team mapping, the team members for a hospital project came to appreciate the diversity of skills and experiences they could collectively draw on during the project, as well as the individual passions that could be harnessed. Their competencies covered business expertise, architecture practices, health sciences, and information technology, all of which would be important to the hospital project they were about to embark on. Many of them had volunteered in hospitals and were passionate about helping patients. Figure 27 shows what an interactive session that stimulates discussion and appreciation for diversity might look like.

Fig. 27 **Team Mapping: Talents, Roles, and Passions**

TEAM BUILDING
ENGAGING IN FUN WAYS TO WARM UP TO WORK

WHY DO WE DO THIS?

To reinforce some design principles and practices early on and get to know each other in a fun way, work through anxieties, and foster collaboration. Here are three simple team-building exercises to create a shared experience, which you can add to your own creative icebreakers:

1. **Personal artifact and story** – To understand what makes people tick
2. **Marshmallow exercise** – To practice prototyping and collaboration
3. **Fear in a hat** – To reveal apprehensions and anxieties

1. PERSONAL ARTIFACT & STORY

This simple exercise helps team members, by referencing a personal, favorite object of theirs, tell stories and anecdotes about what motives them.

How Can You Do This?

Ask everyone to bring an object or artifact that is meaningful to him or her and to tell a story about the significance of that object. As a group, have each person explain why he or she brought that object and why it is important to him or her.

Example: In the first team session, one of the designers brought a toy car. He told a story about how he collects toys and is intrigued by things that make people more curious and playful. With that insight, we knew we could count on him to bring a fresh and imaginative perspective to any project.

2. MARSHMALLOW EXERCISE

The Marshmallow Challenge[46] is a fun and interactive prototyping exercise that encourages teams to experience simple but thoughtful lessons in collaboration and creativity.

How Can You Do This?

1. Divide the group into teams of five or six people. If you are a bigger group, it is fun to split the group up into competing teams. This also ensures that everyone is fully engaged in the exercise.
2. Gather these materials for each team:
   twenty sticks of spaghetti (the sticks can be broken)
   one yard of tape
   one yard of string
   one marshmallow (marshmallow must remain intact)
3. Give each team twenty minutes (at the same time) to build the tallest freestanding structure, using only the materials provided. The marshmallow must be on top.
4. At the end of the exercise, reflect on the following:
   What did the team struggle with?
   What did the team do very well?
   What was your process?
   What improves performance? What hinders it?

3. FEAR IN A HAT

This is a way for you to understand and appreciate the apprehensions and anxieties your fellow team members may have as you embark upon a project.

How Can You Do This?

1. On a piece of paper, everyone completes the sentence, "In this project, I am most afraid that _____." They should be as specific and honest as possible, but not in a way that could easily identify them; they should not put their name on the paper. The papers should be placed in a hat and shuffled.
2. One by one, each member of the group reads out the fear of another team member and explains, in his/her own words, what that person fears in this situation. (If you draw your own fear, put it back). No one is to comment on the fear – just listen and move on to the next person.
3. Avoid implying or showing your opinion on the fear being expressed, to prevent disrespecting or completely misunderstanding someone's fear.

4. When all the fears have been read out, discuss what the common fears were and how the team can allay and manage these concerns.
5. At the end of the exercise, reflect on the following:
   What are the common fears on the team?
   How can we use insights to develop our plan?

Example: In one team, a common fear that emerged was that all their exploration and development work would never be executed due to lack of support or conflict with the current enterprise system. Knowing that team members shared that fear emphasized the important role of the executive sponsor and raised the team's commitment to Gear 3 and clear activation planning.

FACILITATION
GETTING THE MOST OUT OF TEAM TIME

WHY DO WE DO THIS?

To harness the efforts of team members and keep everyone focused on outcomes at every stage of development. Given the collaborative, outcome-focused nature of the Business Design process, effective facilitation is critical to capturing the most value from the team and the time you spend together, and to obtaining the best outcomes in the most productive way.

SKILLS FOR EFFECTIVE FACILITATION

A facilitator's first job is to help the team get the most from their time together. Every meeting, in a sense, is a workshop. Good facilitation skills help keep the team on track and ensure that meetings are productive and focused on outcomes. An effective facilitator

- ▶ Helps build trusting and collaborative relationships within the group,
- ▶ Clarifies goals for the group and assigned roles within the group,
- ▶ Is able to stay focused on engaging everyone in the group,
- ▶ Does not impose their own ideas simply because they have the pen,
- ▶ Facilitates productive and effective communication at all times,
- ▶ Guides the group to stay on track in terms of both outcomes and timing,
- ▶ Nurtures a productive and collaborative environment, and
- ▶ Supports effective team decision-making when there are choices to make.

These are some of the core skills of good facilitation. If you are really keen to master the skills of facilitation, you can enlist an organization that specializes in facilitation and visualization training.

HOW CAN YOU DO THIS?

1. **Review the list of facilitation skills.** Each team member should review the skill requirements and determine his or her comfort with and readiness to conduct group facilitation. Be honest and open about your interest, commitment, and capabilities with regard to the role. It is an important role, but not one that everyone feels comfortable playing.

2. **Discuss and assign two to three lead facilitators to begin the project.** It is advisable to assign this role to your most willing and capable candidates at the outset of the project. You can always rotate in new facilitators as the project unfolds.

3. **Be diligent about helpful two-way feedback.** Effective facilitation is a two-way street. To be an effective facilitator requires discipline and skill; valuable and timely feedback helps the facilitator develop this skill and draw the best out of the team. At the same time, it also takes a respectful and collaborative team to realize productive and fruitful outcomes; the facilitator should give the team feedback on their behaviors and team dynamics.

Tips

▶ Facilitating group work is an incredibly valuable skill to develop in your everyday work.

▶ It is helpful to share this role and give individuals the opportunity to take the lead on an activity they are passionate about.

▶ Helping each other be more effective at facilitation is a valuable learning opportunity for everyone.

TEAM CHARTERS
CREATING A SHARED VISION FOR THE TEAM

WHY DO WE DO THIS?

To align as a team on how to work most effectively together. This is best done before project work begins, as it can serve as a simple reference to ground the team throughout the design journey. By articulating your shared vision and codes of conduct for the team, you will set a good foundation for collaboration.

HOW CAN YOU DO THIS?

As a team, create a charter that includes the following:

- Project ambitions
- Team values
- Roles and responsibilities
- Meeting and communication strategies
- Team rules and codes of conduct
- This is a great way to get values and pet peeves on the table early on.

Tips

- Refer to the outcome of your team-mapping exercise in defining individual roles.
- The key to a successful team charter is clarity, authenticity, unanimity, and candor, especially when it comes to pet peeves.
- Try to add a little candor and humor to make it less like a list of rules. One team had the rule, "No smelly food in meetings," which helped them avoid distractions during meetings.
- A team charter is an important reference when you get off track or the team becomes dysfunctional (as all teams do from time to time).
- Identifying key codes of conduct will ensure discipline and respect for team productivity. It is also a great way to get values and pet peeves on the table early on.

WHAT MIGHT THIS LOOK LIKE?

Figure 28 is an example of a simple, group-generated team charter:

Fig. 28 **Team Charter**

Team Ambition
To create a breakthrough technology-based solution that will redefine the meaning and management of money to help people take control of their financial wellbeing.

Team Values
Openness, transparency, and respect. Give everyone a voice.

Team Roles and Responsibilities
Matt (Team Lead): Design and oversee master project plan (roles, deliverables, timing)
Eugene (Creative Director): Design clear and inspiring reports and presentations
Grace (Project Manager): Manage all external activities such as research and logistics
Avi (Voice of the People Who Matter): Lead research to anchor the human quest
Srikanth (Business Strategist): Coach team and counsel on business viability
Alpesh (Methodologist): Source and design development methods
Job (Facilitator and Sense-Making): Facilitate and counsel on prototyping and synthesis

Meeting and Communication Strategies
Meeting Times: Mondays, 1–4 p.m., Meeting Room A; Wednesdays, 2–5 p.m., Meeting Room A
Scheduling: Use Google calendar, hosted by Matt
Meeting Preparation: Agenda and pre-work issued 48 hours in advance of meeting.
Communication: Use designated intranet as a portal for all document sharing, online discussions, and planning updates. No external portals.

Team Rules and Codes of Conduct
No phone calls, texting, or browsing during meetings.
On time for meetings, or you bring snacks to the next meeting.
Respond to group email in timely fashion to accommodate scheduling and work.
Individuals are accountable for their deliverables.
Decisions will be made on a consensus basis – vote is a last resort.
Constructive feedback only – "attack the problem, not the person."

PROJECT BRIEF
FRAMING YOUR QUEST

WHY DO WE DO THIS?

To crystallize the ambitions of the project, key issues, stakeholders, the business motivation, and analogous inspirations for the project. A project brief must be specific enough to make the objectives and challenges clear, while being open enough to allow for opportunities and new possibilities to emerge. A project brief brings your motivations and inspirations together into a focused framework for development and helps frame your case for investment of time and resources.

HOW CAN YOU DO THIS?

Here are some questions that can be helpful in distilling your project brief:

- ▶ *What are our goals and ambitions for this project?*
- ▶ *What are the issues or conditions that inspire this opportunity?*
- ▶ *How does this tie to our overall enterprise ambitions and strategy?*
- ▶ *Who is our primary target? Who are other important stakeholders?*
- ▶ *What is the activity around which we want to create value?*
- ▶ *What can our enterprise bring to contribute to the solution?*
- ▶ *Are there any analogies or references we can learn from?*

Tips

- ▶ The earlier tool on Framing Your Ambition will give you insights into how to make your proposition most relevant and valuable to the enterprise.
- ▶ At the beginning of a project, briefs are often too narrow or too broadly focused. The key is to "right-size" the project to what you feel is aspirational yet within scope.
- ▶ To keep your brief succinct and focused, you may capture the more detailed information as supporting documents.
- ▶ Compelling facts make for a good business case.
- ▶ New information will surface during the discovery process. While your project brief will provide an important touchstone in your development, don't ignore unexpected discoveries that can either enhance or call for a reframing of the quest.

► Your ingoing brief will be fortified by your work in subsequent phases of development; don't expect to have a comprehensive picture of the market or stakeholder needs defined up front.

WHAT MIGHT THIS LOOK LIKE?

Figure 29 is an example of a one-page project brief that illustrates how to frame the ingoing quest of a development team.[47]

Fig. 29 **Project Brief**

PROJECT BRIEF: LIVING WELL (THE ROYAL CONSERVATORY OF MUSIC)

What are our goals and ambitions for the project?
To develop a breakthrough, revenue-generating solution for the Royal Conservatory of Music (RCM) that will improve the physical and mental wellbeing of seniors.

What are the issues or conditions that inspire this opportunity?
Too often, seniors internalize ageism, disengage from activities, and deteriorate mentally and physically. They may become reclusive or dependent on support from family members, limiting their psychological independence and engagement. In an aging society, there is pressure to find solutions to support seniors in a socially and economically responsible manner.

How does this tie to our overall enterprise strategy and ambitions?
Our ambition is to make music a more integral part of everyday life and personal wellbeing.

Who is our primary target? Other important stakeholders?
The primary target is seniors, 70+ years of age, who find joy through engagement in the arts and self-expression. Other important stakeholders are the people who provide lifestyle support and care to senior family and friends.

What is the "activity" around which we want to create value?
Enhancing the physical and mental wellbeing of seniors.

What can the RCM bring to contribute to the solution?
RCM's current sponsored "Living Through the Arts" program leverages the beneficial aspects of music therapy through a variety of Outreach Programs and Creativity Workshops. The program has proven to enhance individual and community potential through artistic self-expression and creativity, with measurable, positive evidence that these programs enhance wellbeing on both cognitive and emotional levels. The RCM is the largest and oldest independent arts educator in Canada and has offered extraordinary opportunities for learning and personal development through music and the arts for more than 100 years.

Any analogies or references we can learn from?
SM(ART)S: Seniors Meet the Arts, Young @ Heart

PROJECT BLUEPRINT
MAPPING THE DEVELOPMENT PROCESS

WHY DO WE DO THIS?

To visualize how the project will unfold, including the methodologies, activities, participation, timing, and desired outcomes. A blueprint helps to guide the team and to communicate to others how the project will progress. It serves as the backbone for development by organizing Business Design tools and activities to tackle the challenge at hand. A clear blueprint will guide development and answer the following questions:

What is the flow of activities?

Who is involved?

What methods will be used?

What are the deliverables and milestones?

HOW CAN YOU DO THIS?

1. **Create a timeline.** Draw a line on a large piece of paper representing the project timeline and designate each major phase of development and the desired outcome: Contextualizing the Challenge, Gear 1, Gear 2, and Gear 3.
2. **Map the methods, activities, and who will participate.** This will show how you will sequence activities and how you move through divergence and convergence toward outcomes for each phase of activity. Identify who will participate at each step of the process.
3. **Define the deliverable and milestones for each phase.** Set target dates for important deliverables. Consider the start date and end date for each activity and phase.
4. **Supplement with project details.** For each milestone, indicate the actions and activities necessary, including research, development work sessions, and presentations. Assign roles and responsibilities to individuals on the team.

5. **Visualize your blueprint.** Synthesize and visualize your plan on one page, capturing development activities, methods, and deliverables. Consolidating your road map helps you keep all of these activities in context, providing a vision of how they all come together in one comprehensive master plan for your project.

Tips

▶ Keep the plan open and high level at the beginning. This will allow you to plot out the major milestones and deliverables before focusing on the detailed plan.

▶ Put it all on one page.

▶ Be prepared to adapt and refine along the way.

WHAT MIGHT THIS LOOK LIKE?

Figure 30 is an example of a project blueprint showing how the methodologies, activities (including who was involved in each activity), and outputs were sequenced.[48]

Fig. 30 **Project Blueprint**

August	September	October	November
Preparation & Foundation: Framing the Opportunity	Gear 1: Understanding Who Matters & What Matters to Them	Gear 2: Designing the Experience	Gear 3: Making Choices

KEY EVENTS

August	September	October	November
Foundation Sessions	Gear 1 Presentation	Co-Creation Workshops	Strategic Choices Session

ACTIVITIES

August	September	October	November
Frame the Project • Identify the Team • Frame the Challenge **Kick-off Session** • Align on the Project Plan • Envision Success & Team Building **Business Immersion Session** • Stakeholder Mapping • Landscape of Players • STEEP Analysis (Trends) **Strategic Choice Framing Session** • Strategic Choice Considerations • Alignment Activity	**Field Observation & Journey Mapping** • Observe People in Context to Understand Behaviors & Challenges (Customer Shadowing) **Need-Finding Research** • Storytelling/In-depth Interviews (Using Photos & Journals) **Analysis** • Analyze Transcripts & Synthesize Findings (Needs by Stakeholders Group) **Validation** • Conduct Quantitative Survey to Ascertain Needs & Satisfaction Gaps	**Co-creation Workshops** • Ideation • Prototyping • Experience Design & Mapping • Role Play • Co-creation & Initial Feedback **Concept Refinement & Synthesis** • Ideal Journey (Storyboards) **Feedback** • Presentation of Concepts to Key Stakeholders for Feedback (Event & Virtual Platform) • Further Refinement	**Strategy Session** • Revisit Strategic Choices • Articulate Value Proposition • Identify Capabilities Required • Design Experiments • Identify Quick Wins **Synthesis, Value Proposition Refinement, Business, Strategy, Case Development**

BUSINESS OUTCOMES

August	September	October	November
Foundation Presentation • Project Framing • Shared Understanding about Who Matters **Detailed Field Research Plan**	**User Insight Presentation** • Customer Journey Maps • Customer Needs & Personas • Design Criteria	**Solution Visualization Presentation** • Concepts • Experience Maps • Synthesis of Learning & Insights	**Strategy Presentation** • Business Case • Value Proposition • Strategic Choices & Assumptions • Quick Wins & Experiments

TEAM OUTCOMES

August	September	October	November
Alignment Skill Development: Foundational Understanding & Strategic Framing	Inspiration Skill Development: Empathic Listening, Mind Mapping, Need-Finding Methodologies	Shared Vision & Ambition Skill Development: Ideation, Positivity, Systems Thinking, Visualization	Conviction to Act Skill Development: Experimentation, Strategic Decision-Making

COMMUNICATION & ENGAGEMENT PLAN
DESIGNING FOR INTERNAL & EXTERNAL STAKEHOLDER ENGAGEMENT

WHY DO WE DO THIS?

To engage important stakeholders in the development process to solicit input and build shared ownership. Having a clear and concise communications and engagement plan will help you bring along the stakeholders (internal and external) who are essential to the success of your projects and enterprise. The plan will ensure that the right people are engaged in the right way at the right time.

HOW CAN YOU DO THIS?

1. **Create profiles of the key people you'd like to engage in your quest.** These might be important stakeholders internally (for development or feedback) or externally (e.g., key customers or partners). Gather insights and data from your experience, colleagues, or other sources (e.g., online). Create profiles for each by answering the following questions:

    Role: Who are they? Why are they important? What do they do in their work?

    Needs: What do they care most about? What weighs most heavily on their mind?

    Motivation: What would they value most from this quest? Why?

2. **Map how you will interact with them throughout your development process.** For each stakeholder profile, identify how you will interact with them and what they will experience over time. Plot the timing and nature of the interactions you will have with them onto a collective road-map template. Look for gaps and opportunities to keep them engaged throughout your development process.

3. **Design your communication and engagement strategy.** For each stakeholder (group or individuals that are of critical importance), address the following questions:

    How will you engage them in the development process?

    What will be the nature of your interactions with them?

    What do you hope to achieve from those interactions?

Tips

▶ Differentiate between internal and external stakeholders. Internal stake-holders will add insight and know-how, and cultivate shared ownership in the ultimate outcome. Engaging external stakeholders in the co-creation process will further enhance solutions and a sense of shared ownership.

▶ Assign work-session participants into groups to address different stakeholders and reconvene to share learning, fill gaps, and consolidate efforts into your master plan for engagement and communication.

▶ Identify and leverage existing communication channels (e.g., town halls, external events, meetings, etc.) to engage stakeholders.

▶ Routinely check in and iterate your plan based on feedback from stakeholders and changes to your product or service offering.

WHAT MIGHT THIS LOOK LIKE?

Early mapping for the HSO project identified how to see the efforts of the enterprise through the eyes of important stakeholders. Figure 31 is a picture of a work session in which participants grounded their planning in stakeholder personas to identify what was important to each stakeholder and then mapped out a comprehensive communication and engagement plan.

Fig. 31 **Mapping Stakeholder Engagement**

CONTEXTUALIZING YOUR CHALLENGE

By examining current market trends, industry players, stakeholder ecosystems, and enterprise capabilities and resources, you will identify market opportunities and ways to leverage your strengths going forward. This contextualization will help you identify market-based opportunities and determine key market spaces in which you wish to compete.

STEEP ANALYSIS
IDENTIFYING FUTURE MARKET-BASED OPPORTUNITIES

WHY DO WE DO THIS?

To define the most salient trends that will contextualize your quest and maximize your business opportunity. With the aim of aligning your quest to on-trend opportunities, a comprehensive STEEP Analysis will help you identify broad trends in the areas of Society, Technology, Economy, Environment, and Politics (STEEP).[49] Defining and dimensionalizing the most salient trends will help you identify the future market opportunities related to your project and enterprise, as input to building your business case.

HOW CAN YOU DO THIS?

1. **Tap into existing research and the tacit knowledge of your team.** By bringing together team members with diverse perspectives, you will be able to quickly and productively create a long list of trend considerations. Prepare to download your knowledge and insights based on market studies, articles, books, blogs, or your own observations.

2. **Explore and capture all of the trends you think are relevant to your project.** Take a broad view of the world in which you operate and create a comprehensive list of current and emerging trends across the dimensions of STEEP:

    Social: What social trends might inform your opportunity?
    Technological: What trends in technology will impact your future?
    Economic: What trends in the economy are relevant to your project?
    Environmental: What environmental trends are important to consider?
    Political: What political trends can you tap into?

    To enable easy download and assessment, capture one trend per sticky note.

3. **Assess your findings.** Create a 2 × 2 framework on a large piece of paper; label one axis "likely to occur – unlikely to occur" and the other axis "high impact – low impact." Assess each trend and organize them into the four quadrants on your map.

4. **Gather data to validate and dimensionalize top trends.** Identify which trends are most likely to occur and will have the most impact on your future opportunity. Gather statistical data to substantiate emerging trends and quantify the potential impact to your enterprise, citing credible references and sources.

5. **Synthesize and fortify your business case.** Review your findings and determine the trends that best frame the market opportunity and align to your business goals. Trends should be considered in terms of how they might impact market attractiveness, customer segment growth, competition, and customer attitudes and needs.

Tips

▶ Have these materials on hand: sticky notes and large paper for capturing and assessing trends.

▶ By capturing your team's diverse insights and perspectives in a generative manner, you can accelerate and share in the discovery process.

▶ Broadening your perspective on the world by identifying macro trends will lead you collectively to new contextual insights.

▶ Remember that "trends" are measurable shifts in the market that can be substantiated with data. They are not a "point in time" condition. Trends project into the future.

▶ Use a variety of research resources (e.g., publications, online sources, government reports, third-party research). While you might do some sleuthing on "social media" and opinion pieces for intuitive insights, you should place priority on credible sources of intelligence.

▶ Identifying these trends is not a way to predict the future but is a way to anticipate and plan for the future.

WHAT MIGHT THIS LOOK LIKE?

Figure 32 *shows the outcome of this exercise for a project on healthy eating. Results show that the rise in obesity and diabetes, government regulation of foods and labeling, health concerns, and increased consumption of prepared meals all point to opportunity gaps in the market.*

Fig. 32 **STEEP Analysis**

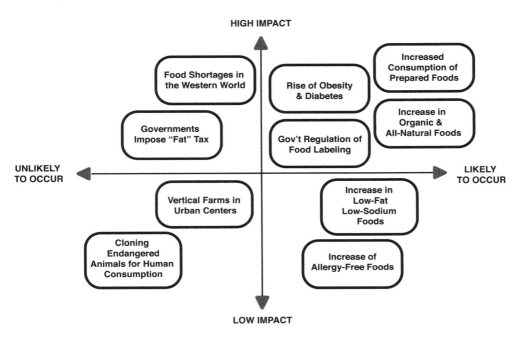

LANDSCAPE OF PLAYERS
IDENTIFYING FUTURE FRIENDS & FOES

WHY DO WE DO THIS?

To identify other players who are conducting business in your envisioned market space. This step helps you determine which players pose competitive threats and which ones could bring a complementary strength to your enterprise and be leveraged into strategic partnerships.

HOW CAN YOU DO THIS?

1. **Define the space broadly, as an activity.** Consider the target you are trying to help and how you want to help them, in general terms. As examples: helping women better manage their finances, helping healthcare providers contribute to better patient outcomes, helping children make better food choices, helping growing start-ups design a better business.

2. **Tap into the tacit knowledge of your team.** As in the STEEP exercise, you can productively create a long list of who is operating in this space, based on your market awareness and intelligence.

3. **Explore a wide range of players.** For example, if you were a packaged-foods manufacturer looking to improve healthy eating, this range might include long-standing competitors (e.g., other packaged-foods manufacturers), emerging high-growth players (e.g., nutraceuticals), adjacencies (e.g., weight-management services), and players with whom you don't compete but with whom you share a common cause (e.g., advocacy groups). There is no such thing as too many players to consider at the outset of this exercise. Identify as many possible companies, organizations, and categories that are considered to be part of the market space you have selected. An easy way to prepare to cluster players is to write each player on a sticky note.

4. **Cluster and label your findings.** Cluster your findings into four to six categories based on what each offers. For example, in healthy eating, players may cluster into product companies, retail companies, service companies, or communication companies. They may also differentiate by commercial versus public or not-for-profit.

5. **Assess their impact and prioritize.** Once you have categories on your long list, prioritize who is best positioned to make an important move in this space, both direct and indirect competitors, as well as those that may become allies. These players will be important as a point of comparison in Gear 2 or of potential collaboration in Gear 3.

Tips

▶ Have these materials on hand: sticky notes and large paper for capturing and assessing players.

▶ By capturing your team's diverse insights and perspectives in a generative manner, you can accelerate and share in the discovery process.

▶ Your STEEP Analysis will reveal some of the players in your targeted space.

▶ Consider companies from as many different industries as possible. Many companies are now crossing over into different industries; for example, from products to services or from computing to entertainment.

WHAT MIGHT THIS LOOK LIKE?

Figure 33, *a summary of a few of the players in the business of "healthy eating," demonstrates the diversity of players.*

Fig. 33 **Summary of Landscape of Players**

FOOD MANUFACTURERS	PEOPLE & SERVICES
Nestlé	Food experts (e.g., nutritionists)
Kraft	Wellness coaches
PepsiCo	Aramark Food Services
Campbell Soup	Fitness clubs (e.g., Equinox)
Del Monte	Weight management (e.g., Weight Watchers)
General Mills	Chefs (e.g., Jamie Oliver)

OTHER PRODUCT PROVIDERS	MEDIA & INFORMATION
Grocers (e.g., Whole Foods)	Online services (e.g., Diet.com)
Lifestyle products (e.g., Nike)	Health organizations (e.g., Mayo Clinic)
Supplements (e.g., GNC)	Publications (e.g., Prevention)
Pharmaceuticals (e.g., Pfizer)	Not-for-profits (e.g., Heart & Stroke)
Retailers (e.g., Walgreens)	Self-help books

SCENARIO PLANNING
EXPLORING FUTURE POSSIBILITIES

WHY DO WE DO THIS?

To envision how different the future might look from the present by identifying signals of change that could disrupt current systems. A scenario describes, in vivid detail, a potential future environment, revealing important context for designing future-forward solutions.

HOW CAN YOU DO THIS?

Scenario planning is a natural progression from your STEEP Analysis, combining and projecting signals of change to create potential scenarios you might face (or create) in the future. It is often helpful to build out three to four scenarios to compare.

1. **Reflect on emerging signals in the market and ideate on a range of future scenarios.** Review your assessment of signals and select combinations of two to three that, in your opinion, are the most probable, challenging, and relevant to your organization's future. Think at least five years out to stretch beyond the current state.

2. **Explore and build out three to four scenarios.** For each of your signal combinations, use your intuitive foresight to develop a central plot for a story that evokes an emotional response from those who will use these scenarios as a reality check in future decision-making. At the same time, use facts when you write your stories, to ensure that readers don't get anchored on current world realities.

3. **Develop indicators and assess.** Develop indicators that you can measure over time to judge whether the business ecosystem is heading toward one or more of the futures described in your scenarios. These indicators can help you evaluate whether or not your actions are helping you create your desired future, as well as whether or not certain risks are imminent. Continuously monitor these indicators so that you don't lose an opportunity to adapt.

Tips

▶ Frame the big questions that you want to address about the future of your business.

▶ Use departure questions to explore how weak signals might affect your business. For example: *"How might our supply chain be affected over the next five years by the potential imposition of punitive tariffs being contemplated by our government today?"*

▶ Don't be afraid to consider all possible outcomes – no matter how extreme or unlikely.

▶ Try to use any visual stimuli you can find to aid storytelling and spark the imagination.

WHAT MIGHT THIS LOOK LIKE?

Here is one such scenario that paints a picture of a future challenge:

You are a global food producer. As such, you are reliant on the continuous expansion and intensification of agriculture to support your volume projections. It has come to your attention that the bee population is severely threatened by the loss of wild plants and flowers due to agricultural intensification. One-third of all food production globally is dependent on bee pollination. If the agricultural expansion and intensification you depend on continues, you will literally be threatening one-third of the world's food supply – and your own future as a company. This is a wicked problem that requires a profoundly innovative solution. How can you solve for this scenario?

STAKEHOLDER MAPPING
IDENTIFYING & CONNECTING PEOPLE

WHY DO WE DO THIS?

To identify all of the people who matter to your success and how they relate to and influence each other within the "human ecosystem." This step helps to frame your challenge and reveals opportunities to increase the chances of solution success by appreciating how all the key stakeholders (users, enablers and influencers) interact and influence one another. A comprehensive map of how important stakeholders relate to the central customer or stakeholder, and to each other, is an important prelude to need-finding research.

HOW CAN YOU DO THIS?

1. **Explore the long list of the people who are important to your project's success.** These are the key stakeholders who serve, enable, or influence the actions of and desired outcomes for your central "customer." They will play a role, to varying degrees, in your future success. To facilitate iterative mapping, list each stakeholder on an individual sticky note, to be arranged on a large piece of paper or surface.

2. **Define their roles and relationships in a low-resolution map.** By defining and visualizing stakeholder roles and relationships, you will see the interconnectedness of the human ecosystem.

3. **Visualize the human system as a pathway or network.** Represent relationships in a visual manner to bring clarity to the picture. This visualization can be either organized around the user journey, as it was in the chapter on Gear 1, or depicted by a general "network map" of stakeholders pertaining to a common issue, as shown in Figure 34.

4. **Focus on the people who might play the most critical role in your success.** Identify which players might have the most impact on your ultimate customer and be important to include in your need-finding research and solution design.

Tips

▶ Have these materials on hand: sticky notes and large paper for capturing and mapping all stakeholders.

▶ By capturing your team's diverse insights and perspectives in a generative manner, you can accelerate and share in the discovery process.

▶ It is important to consider *all* possible stakeholders who influence the decision-making process and the web of interrelationships among them.

▶ Stakeholder mapping begins at the start of a project and is refined on a regular basis, as new information is uncovered that leads to a better understanding of the challenge. While you may likely do a preliminary version of this in contextualizing your quest in broad strokes, need-finding research will create a more definitive picture of the dynamics at play.

WHAT MIGHT THIS LOOK LIKE?

As shown in chapter 4, *a stakeholder map might be visualized as a **patient pathway** (Figure 34).*

Fig. 34 **Stakeholder Mapping as a Cardiac Patient Pathway**

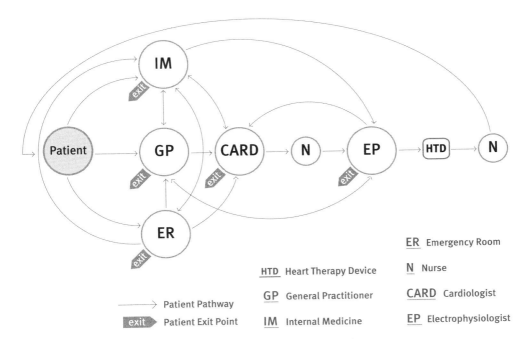

*In an analysis of Canadian healthcare accreditation, key stakeholders were mapped as an **ecosystem** with a focus on Patients, Providers, and Policy Makers (Figure 35).*

Fig. 35 **Stakeholder Mapping as a Network**

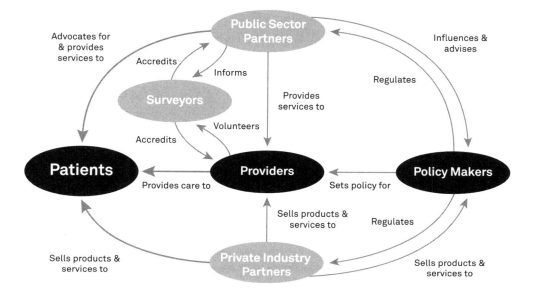

ACTIVITY SYSTEMS (CURRENT STATE)

VISUALIZING YOUR CURRENT STRATEGY

WHY DO WE DO THIS?

To align on today's enterprise strategy. Activity system modeling is a method of systems thinking and visualization that represents strategy as a combination of interrelated activities and capabilities. Doing this up front on a project will give you a clear picture of your current state, which you can reprise in Gear 3 to determine if and how your new vision and strategy fits with your current strategy.

An activity system is a strategy visualization made up of the following:

▶ **Hubs:** Core activities that together define how the enterprise uniquely creates value

▶ **Supporting activities:** Specific activities and capabilities that fortify hubs

▶ **Linkages:** How hubs and activities reinforce each other to create value

A powerful activity system is one in which a unique system of activities synergistically creates value for the market and the enterprise. This tool can also be used for assessing another company based on publicly available information (see Activity Systems [Competition]).

This exercise will help you succinctly visualize your current enterprise strategy by addressing the following key questions:

What do we currently invest time and effort into? What have we chosen to do internally and what have we chosen to outsource or partner to deliver?

What is the enterprise's current strategy to create value?

What are we uniquely good at?

How does our system compare to that of others? How strong is our current competitive advantage? (See Activity Systems [Competition].)

HOW CAN YOU DO THIS?

Here's how you can build mutual understanding and strategic clarity, using Four Seasons Hotels and Resorts as an example:[50]

Before you convene as a team:

1. **Gather input.** Ask team members to think about and list how your business creates value and all the things your enterprise does to deliver market value and be competitive. Think about the activities that create value across the entire business and every function, and answer the questions below:

   What is the overall goal or vision for your business? What is your overarching value proposition? (e.g., to offer guest experiences of exceptional quality)

   Think broadly and ask: What are the vital activities that your enterprise broadly and consistently invests time and money into to deliver value? (e.g., superior staff service attitude, consistent global branding)

   What are the specific activities or choices that bring those themes to life? (e.g., superior staff service attitude may lead to a decision to have no customer service department)

2. **Consolidate and distil inputs.** You will likely have dozens of inputs – that is normal. Aggregate all of them and cluster them into activity themes – the potential "hubs" of your strategy. Articulate these themes by phrasing them as something you actively ***do***: For example, *Focus on hotel management*. In documenting consolidated inputs, there are two lists that will be helpful: one of hubs (which may be up to ten at this point) and one of specific activities/initiatives that support these hubs (which could be a very long list).

When you get together as a team:

1. **Review and discuss your list of themes and select the most critical as hubs.** Facilitate a discussion about the overarching value proposition and possible hubs. For each hub, ask two key questions:

   How critical is that to our overall proposition and creation of value?

   How extensively does that drive our activities? What is the evidence of that?

   It is often helpful for one person who is passionate about a theme to give a two-minute "case" for this as a hub, for the group to appreciate its value. At this point, you should simply capture the essence of that theme – you can go back and refine the wording later.

Once you have discussed the potential hubs and identified which are most critical to creating value, have each team member reflect on the following questions before casting their vote for the central hubs:

Is this critical to our value creation?

Do we invest time and money broadly and consistently to support this?

Does this contribute to our competitive advantage?

To cast your votes, you may provide five sticky red dots to each team member. Have them think about the activity themes that meet the three criteria and allocate one dot per hub. Identify the top four or five hubs and probe for any dissensions or deep concerns.

2. **Fortify those hubs with specific supporting activities.** For each hub, ask, *What are the critical activities or choices that reinforce each hub?* Have participants refer to the list of specific activities.

3. **Visualize your current-state activity system.** Write each of top the four or five hubs out on large sticky notes or paper plates. Place them on a large surface or paper. Discuss as a team how each hub relates to the others and draw lines to show the relationships. Then position specific activities around the hubs and identify linkages within the system.

4. **Synthesize your current strategy and articulate your story.** Capture the strategy depicted by your activity system in a story to explain how the system works in a one-page narrative. This story should describe how you create value through the following:

> *Overarching proposition: What does our enterprise uniquely offer the market?*
>
> *Hubs: What core drivers of our business today define our strategy?*
>
> *Activities: What specific and concrete activities or choices reinforce those hubs?*
>
> *Relationships: How do hubs and activities relate to and reinforce one another?*

5. **Assess your current system for uniqueness and competitiveness.** Referring to the tool on Activity System Assessment, have participants independently rate how different they believe your system is versus the competition on a scale of one to ten (one being identical and ten being completely different) on a card and give it to the facilitator. Make a quick tally for the group and discuss your assessment based on the range of numbers.

Tips

▶ Refer to other documents on your business (e.g., strategic plans, operating plans, annual reports) for insights.

▶ Prototype! Use paper plates and sticky notes to prototype the system early on. This is an iterative process as you gather and distil your inputs and make intuitive connections within your system. Your first version will look like spaghetti and meatballs. That's okay. The key is distillation and making connections.

▶ Some initial inputs will fall by the wayside. You should have a limited number of hubs. An enterprise cannot have ten hubs and do them all well.

▶ Linkages are important. Understand how one hub connects to another, how one activity can reinforce more than one hub. That's strategic synergy.

▶ In assessing your competitiveness, it is particularly helpful to have done a similar exercise on other organizations (see Activity Systems [Competition], next tool).

▶ The process outlined in this tool requires pre-work in collecting and organizing inputs; it provides a rigorous, inclusive, and well-documented foundation. As an alternate method, you can ask members to bring their list of hubs and activities to your work session and transfer them to sticky notes to be clustered into themes and supporting activities, in a similar "organic" method to that presented in constructing an activity system for competitors (next tool).

WHAT MIGHT THIS PROCESS LOOK LIKE?

Figure 36 shows how this process might be visualized, using Four Seasons Hotels and Resorts as an example.[51]

Fig. 36 **Visualizing Your Current Strategy**

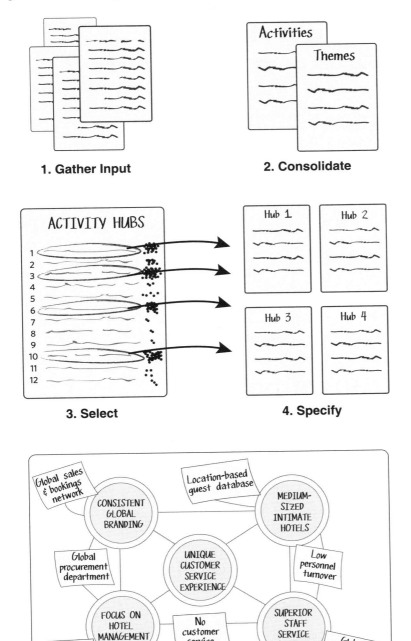

1. Gather Input

2. Consolidate

3. Select

4. Specify

5. Visualize the Activity System & Assess

ACTIVITY SYSTEMS (COMPETITIVE)
VISUALIZING COMPETITIVE STRATEGIES

WHY DO WE DO THIS?

To visualize how competing enterprises create value in a distinct way and, most importantly, relative to the way your enterprise creates value. This exercise is an excellent way to do a comprehensive deep dive into another company, using the same activity system modeling outlined in the previous tool. This exercise will help you articulate and visualize the following:

What is the enterprise's strategy to create value?

What is unique about their system (in comparison to others', particularly yours)?

How strong is their current competitive advantage?

HOW CAN YOU DO THIS?

Before constructing a competitive activity system, gather inputs. Find out as much about the company as possible by reviewing annual reports (which publicly state their vision, strategy, and financial investments) and market-facing sources of information (e.g., a website that presents a comprehensive picture of their offerings or through immersion in their customer experience). It helps also to get a sense of the customer experience by using and interacting with their products and services. Specifically, look for three things:

▶ *What do they offer? Begin by searching through their website.*
▶ *Where do they invest time and money? Begin by reading their annual reports.*
▶ *What are they really good at?*

Then you can aggregate, synthesize, and map your inputs into an activity system.

1. **Lay out what you know.** As a team, share all of the information you've gathered with each other. List all of the inputs on sticky notes (one per note) and discuss what they signify.

2. **Find patterns and cluster.** Begin to group together related inputs as potential hubs and ask, *How is this critical to their success in creating value?*

3. **Articulate, position, and connect the hubs.** Once you have four or five large clusters, begin to label each one as a hub. As noted earlier, articulate these hubs by phrasing them as something they *do*: for example, *driving cost minimization* is one of IKEA's overarching differentiating activities. Through this process you will begin to see connections between hubs. Find these connections by asking, *How does one hub relate to others? How does this combination of interrelated hubs uniquely create value?*

4. **Build out the activity system.** Position specific supporting activities around the hubs, and then identify linkages among all of the hubs and the activities. Include what they have chosen to do internally and what they have chosen to outsource. (For example, *flat packing and self-service and assembly by customers help to minimize IKEA's costs* as a supporting activity.) Identify relationships by asking, *How does activity reinforce each of the hubs?* The more connections, the stronger the system. Your final activity system should be a one-page visual representation of the organization's strategy as defined by hubs and supporting activities.

5. **Synthesize their strategy into a story.** Articulate how these activities ladder up to strategy:

   > *Overarching proposition: What does the enterprise uniquely offer the market?*
   > *Hubs: What are the core drivers of their business that define their strategy?*
   > *Activities: What specific and concrete activities reinforce those hubs?*
   > *Relationships: How do hubs and activities relate to and reinforce one another?*

6. **Assess and discuss their uniqueness and competitiveness.** Using the assessment criteria presented in the next tool (Activity System Assessment), have each participant independently rate how different they believe that enterprise's strategy is versus others on a scale of one to ten (one being identical and ten being completely different) and discuss your assessment.

Tips

▶ Use any accessible pertinent information or intelligence to create a robust picture of their strategy.

▶ Prototype! I often use paper plates and sticky notes to prototype the system. This is an iterative process as you gather and distil your inputs and make connections in the system.

▶ You should have a limited number of hubs. An enterprise cannot have ten hubs and do them all well.

▶ Linkages are important. Understand how one hub connects to another, and how one activity can reinforce more than one hub. That's strategic synergy.

WHAT MIGHT THIS PROCESS LOOK LIKE?

Figure 37 shows how that process might be visualized, using IKEA as an example.

Fig. 37 **Visualizing Competitive Strategies**

1. Lay out what you know

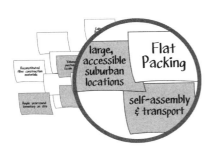

large, accessible suburban locations

Flat Packing

self-assembly & transport

2. Find patterns & cluster

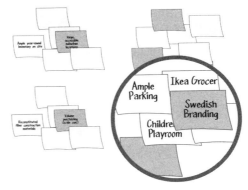

Ample Parking

Ikea Grocer

Swedish Branding

Children Playroom

3. Articulate the hubs & identify linkages

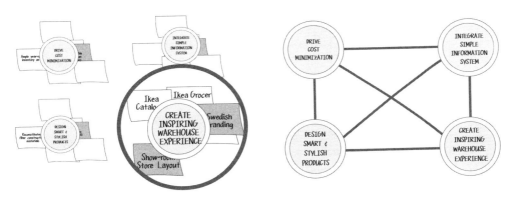

Ikea Catalog Ikea Grocer

CREATE INSPIRING WAREHOUSE EXPERIENCE

Swedish Branding

Show-room Store Layout

DRIVE COST MINIMIZATION — INTEGRATE SIMPLE INFORMATION SYSTEM — DESIGN SMART & STYLISH PRODUCTS — CREATE INSPIRING WAREHOUSE EXPERIENCE

4. Position activities around hubs, connect, & visualize

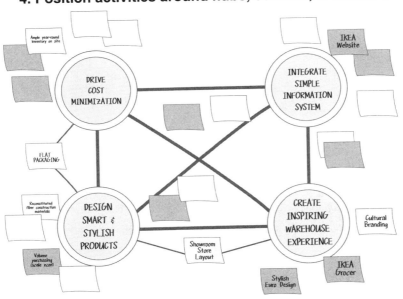

ACTIVITY SYSTEM ASSESSMENT

ASSESSING CURRENT COMPETITIVENESS

WHY DO WE DO THIS?

To evaluate your strategy – and those of others – as a distinct set of activities and source of competitive advantage. This exercise will give you a clear picture of how distinct your system of activities is relative to that of competitors.[52]

HOW CAN YOU DO THIS?

Ask yourself the following questions:

1. **Does this strategy create value?**

   How does this strategy create value for end users? How does this system of activities meet their unmet needs in a meaningful way?

   How does it create value for other key shareholders?

   How do the activities create value for the enterprise?

2. **Is your strategy a breakthrough?**

   To what extent does this activity system enable the enterprise to deliver a meaningful proposition to the market?

3. **Is it distinctive?**

   How does it compare to other enterprises within the current landscape of players?

   Is this set of enterprise activities distinctive relative to others in this game?

   Does this strategic activity system currently give the enterprise a distinct advantage?

4. **Does the system fit?**

   How do the activities complement and reinforce each other? Is it a cohesive and synergistic set of activities?

5. **Does this system create sustainable advantage?**

   How long can the enterprise sustain an advantage with this strategy?

   How likely is it to be imitated?

   What about this system is difficult for others to replicate?

Tips

▶ Now is the time to be objective and analytical about both your own strategic system of activities and those of others. If your system "fails the test," you have a clear opportunity to make it stronger and more distinctive.

▶ This exercise is best done as a group, with candor and objectivity. This will solidify your collective assessment.

▶ Get the objective input of others: it helps to call on senior mentors and trusted industry experts.

STRATEGIC CHOICE CONSIDERATIONS

FRAMING UP CURRENT CHOICES & FUTURE CONSIDERATIONS

WHY DO WE DO THIS?

To make current choices explicit and generate future considerations to explore. By identifying the choices that define your current strategy and exploring new considerations based on your contextual assessment, you will have a better understanding of what you need to learn from the activities in Gears 1, 2, and 3

HOW CAN YOU DO THIS?

Round One: Make Your Current Choices Explicit

This round will draw on the work on your current activity system and your knowledge of the enterprise and the market. It is meant to lead to a clear and focused synthesis of "what has been" or "what is, as of today," not where you might go in the future.

1. **What were your aspirations?** Look at your strategic plans and review communications that point to your overarching purpose. In a clear and concise statement, articulate your current aspirations. *This statement is often compared to a vision statement.*
2. **Where are you playing?** Identify and align on your current customer base; the products and services you currently have in play; and the segment, geographic markets, and channels in which you currently operate.
3. **How are you winning?** Align on your current value proposition, core activities, and your market advantage. What are the four to five ways in which you have won over your customer and profited to date?
4. **What are your current capabilities?** Identify the things you do exceptionally well in a repeatable and scalable manner – the capabilities within your organization that have brought you success in the market.

5. **What management systems do you currently have in place?** Identify the unique management systems (e.g., processes, go-to-market systems, and measurement systems) that have supported your success to date.

Round Two: Create Future Options

This round will draw from your work in contextualizing your challenge, considering trends, emerging players, and new market opportunities. This is an opportunity for everyone to get their thoughts on the table as the basis for development and decision-making. Unlike Round One, you will likely have a longer list, to be considered and decided on as your future direction comes into focus.

1. **What might you aspire to achieve?** This might be a matter of staying true to your current purpose or taking it up a notch for greater impact.
2. **Where might you play?** What is the longer list of potential customer segments, geographies, products, and service segments or channels you might consider?
3. **What might it take to win in the future?** Considering emerging trends, stakeholder needs, and players, in what other ways might you win in the future?
4. **What capabilities might be required?** While you will aim to leverage your current capabilities, what new capabilities do you anticipate you might need in the future?
5. **What new management systems might you need?** Knowing the nature of business and ways of working are constantly evolving, what new systems might you need?

Round Three: Compare, Cull, & Focus

Based on your current choices and future considerations, ask yourself these questions:

1. **How do these choice sets compare?**
2. **What can we leverage and further amplify in the future?**
3. **What new considerations might we explore? Which ones can we eliminate?**
4. **Where should we focus our development efforts? How will we decide what's in for consideration and what's out?**

WHAT MIGHT THIS LOOK LIKE?

Figure 38 is a visualization of how a development team ascertained their "starting point" and explored considerations for the future. There was a very long list! After they devised their envisioned future through the Business Design process, they converged on a very clear set of strategic choices for the future.

Fig. 38 **Strategic Choice Exploration**

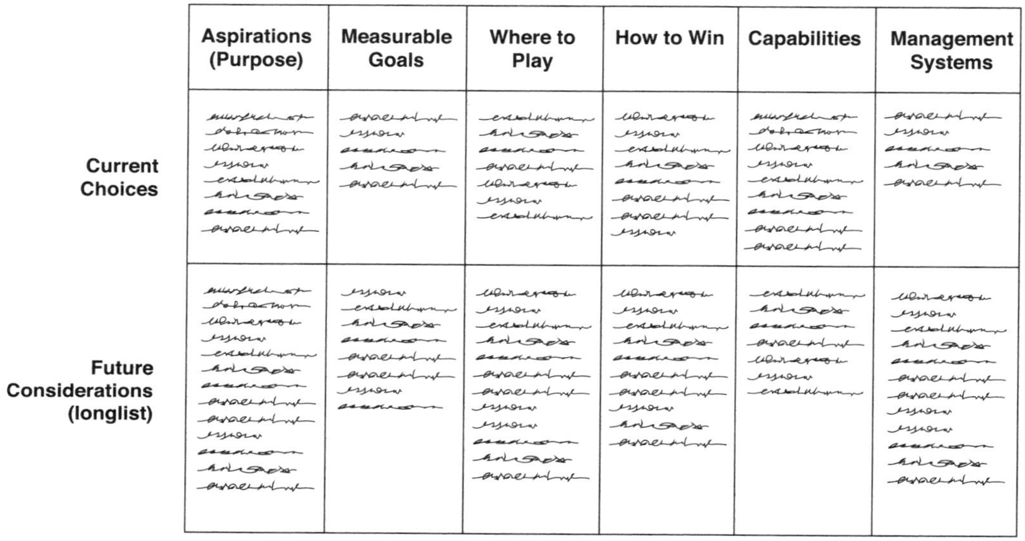
Aspirations (Purpose)
Measurable Goals
Where to Play
How to Win
Capabilities
Management Systems
Current Choices
Future Considerations (longlist)

GEAR 1: EMPATHY & DEEP HUMAN UNDERSTANDING

Human-centered value creation is rooted in understanding the world through the eyes of every important stakeholder, including both your core customers as well as others in your external ecosystem who will be important to effectively delivering your solution to the marketplace. What follows are some of the tools that will help you discover, understand, and validate stakeholder needs as a means to identify human-centered opportunities for value creation.

ROLE PLAY TO EMPATHIZE
LIVING THE EXPERIENCE

WHY DO WE DO THIS?

To build empathy by experiencing the world from someone else's perspective.
Through this exercise, you will come to genuinely understand the user's challenges and have greater empathy through a "lived experience" in a defined situation. As you put yourself in others' shoes, ask, *What does person experience and feel? What are their points of pain?*

HOW CAN YOU DO THIS?

1. **Define the target user.** Based on the challenge, identify whose perspective you would like to better understand and appreciate. *For example: Let us assume your end user is an elderly person.*

2. **Outline the challenge.** Think of a situation in which this end user struggles – it could be a situation where there is a physical or mental challenge, or a difficulty or barrier in his or her everyday life. *For example: We might understand that an elderly person has trouble with dexterity in his or her everyday life.*

3. **Describe the activity.** Create an activity that will enable you to experience the world from your target's perspective. Do this by defining the person, their situation, and an activity that presents a challenge for them. *For example: An elderly person with dexterity challenges might have trouble doing daily tasks on his or her own at home.*

4. **Recreate the experience.** Use props, aids, or artifacts that help to simulate the experience. *For example: To simulate what it is like to be an elderly person living alone, you may don thick rubber gloves to simulate challenges in lost manual dexterity.*

5. **Live the experience.** View the world through this person's point of view by living his or her life for at least an hour. Fully immerse yourself into the activity to truly experience the world from the user's perspective. *For example: To experience the normal activities of this person, try opening doors, opening a pill bottle, and making a phone call while wearing thick rubber gloves.*

6. **Reflect on experiences.** Reflect on what you experienced and how it made you feel. Define the most powerful emotions you experienced and your most compelling insight into how it must be to live that person's life.

Tips

▶ When defining the activity, a direct simulation may not be possible because of physical or circumstantial limitations. In this case, define an analogous situation that parallels the core challenges the person experiences. *For example: To appreciate living with chronic pain, put some stones in your shoes for a day – not to create pain, but to appreciate what it is like to be plagued by distraction and discomfort for hours on end.*

▶ When you do this exercise, attempt to experience the world from your users' perspective as much as possible. This means eliminating distractions and focusing on the task at hand.

WHAT MIGHT THIS LOOK LIKE?

To understand the challenges that seniors face as they age, one team member wore rubber gloves while attempting to carry out common tasks such as paperwork, making meals, and brushing her hair (see Figure 39). She found these tasks to be much more difficult and became quite frustrated and tense. Through this process, she discovered that decreased physical functions of the elderly negatively affect not only their physical abilities, but it also their emotional state.

Fig. 39 **Empathy Exercise**

NEED-FINDING RESEARCH
DESIGNING A DISCIPLINED DEEP DIVE

WHY DO WE DO THIS?

To define the people you need to more deeply understand and target who to recruit for research to ultimately define universal unmet needs. Rigorous need-finding research calls for thoughtful consideration of whose voices must be heard and which activities you want to explore. A clear plan for research will address these questions:

Who do we need to better understand?

What is the right "sample profile" to ensure we have a varied representation of each stakeholder group?

What is our methodology?

What is the central research question?

HOW CAN YOU DO THIS?

1. **Define target subjects, with an emphasis on the end user.** Reference your stakeholder map and project brief to define who matters most. Be sure to explore the needs of all of the critical stakeholders. *For example, the central stakeholder might be legal professionals.*

2. **Diversify the sample.** Diversify your research by looking at a variety of people in your sub-samples. These contrasts will help you see similarities and differences among different people in the same activity. *For instance, in understanding the legal profession, you may want to include both new lawyers, seasoned professionals, and a variety of practices – corporate council, public sector, and legal firms.*

3. **Define the research topic as an activity.** Define the broad activity that is most relevant to your project brief. *For example, you might ask lawyers about "thriving in their profession: what helps and what hinders."*

4. **Design the research methodology.** Specify the various activities you would like your research participants to take part in (e.g., user journals, photo elicitation, etc.) and how you will record and analyze the data. Be aware that the more activities you have users take part in, the more they may have to be compensated for their time.

5. **Define an action plan.** Consolidate all of this information into a recruitment and field research plan. This document should be reviewed with your team and a professional recruiter if you are not doing the field research yourself.

Tips

▶ Refer to your stakeholder map and project brief for who to include and which activity to explore.

▶ In considering how to diversify your sample, consider the ultimate question that will be asked: *Whose voices were heard?* The last thing you want is for anyone to question your sources of insight.

▶ How many people should you recruit in total? As a general rule, ten research participants per homogenous group who participate in in-depth research activities are often sufficient.[53] The key in this research is quality and depth.

▶ Prepare to over-recruit research participants to make up for participants who drop out of the study. It is normal to over-recruit two to three people for every ten.

WHAT MIGHT THIS LOOK LIKE?

In the Canadian Bar Association Re-Think project cited in part one, it was important to include a diversity of stakeholders across geographies, practices, and demographics. Figure 40 shows how interviewers were distributed across the sampling plan to ensure we defined universal needs.

Fig. 40 **Recruiting Sample Plan**

Gear 1 – Member Sampling Grid

Based on Year of Call	BC + Yukon			Prairies + Northwest Territories			Ontario			Quebec + Nunavut			Atlantic Provinces			National			Total per Practice
	Young	Mid	Senior	Young	Mid	Senior	Young	Mid	Senior	Young	Mid	Senior	Young	Mid	Senior	Young	Mid	Senior	
	< 10	10–25	> 25	< 10	10–25	> 25	< 10	10–25	> 25	< 10	10–25	> 25	< 10	10–25	> 25	< 10	10–25	> 25	
Large Firm	2	1	1 (MP)	2	1	1 (MP)	2	1	1 (MP)	2	1	1 (MP)	2	1	1 (MP)	10	5	5	20
Mid-size Firm	1	1	1 (MP)	1	1	1 (MP)	1	1	1 (MP)	1	1	1 (MP)	1	1	1 (MP)	5	5	5	15
Small Firm + Solo	2	1		2	1	1	2	1	1	2	1	1	2	1		10	5		15
Corporate Counsel		1	1		1	1		1	1		1	1		1	1		5	5	10
Public Sector	1	1		1	1		1	1		1	1		1	1		5	5		10
Total per region	6	5	3	6	5	3	6	5	3	6	5	3	6	5	3	30	25	15	Total per Life Cycle
	14			14			14			14			14						

Across all regions = Maximize diversity + 50/50 gender split + represent all provinces and territories

OBSERVATION
UNDERSTANDING CONTEXT & BEHAVIORS

WHY DO WE DO THIS?

To discover fresh insights and generate hypotheses by studying people in their natural environments. Disciplined observation entails objectivity, as opposed to relying on our preconceived notions. It calls for a structured approach to perceiving human behavior relative to objects, the environment, and other people in a specific context. This will lead to new insights, hypotheses on points of pain, and opportunities to address unmet needs.

HOW CAN YOU DO THIS?

1. **Select an observation site.** Think about the situations you would like to know more about and select a location that best suits the conditions of your project. Select a well-defined site that is relevant to your quest. *For example: Kids eating lunch at school.*

2. **First level observation: observe the facts and see things objectively.** Conduct your first phase of observation for thirty to sixty minutes. Take note only of the factual aspects of what you see and do not disregard anything. Watch for the physical items that can be objectively verified by scientific methods whenever necessary. It is important *not* to assign meaning or pass judgment on what you see at the time of observation. Collect the facts:

   What kinds of people are present?
   What objects are present?
   Where is the activity taking place? What is the environment?
   Are there any "workarounds" taking place where the user is trying to solve a problem without any existing solutions at hand?
   For example: Kids are swapping food. Some are throwing their lunches in the garbage.

3. **Develop a hypothesis.** Do this only after you have exhausted your ability to take in objective data. Based on what you have observed, develop a hypothesis for what you think is happening in the location you have selected. *For example: The kids are swapping food and throwing their lunches in the garbage because they don't like what's in their lunch boxes.*

4. **Second level observation: look for meaning.** Conduct a second level of observation for thirty to sixty minutes. Based on what you are seeing, begin to make note of what you *think* is happening – the *meaning* behind the actions, interactions, events, and objects. These aspects are highly subjective and will tap into your intuition. Ask yourself these questions:

   Why is this happening, and why are people doing these things?

   What objects are important? What role do they play?

   How are people engaging with each other, with objects, and with their surroundings?

   What is the context (social or practical) that is motivating them to do these things?

   For example: The looks on their faces suggested they thought some of the food in their lunch boxes was disgusting. The kids don't like what was packed for them at home. If they can't swap it, they throw it out.

5. **Articulate insights and observed points of pain.** Analyze your notes to see if your hypothesis was correct and if it revealed anything new about the world that you did not know before, including defining moments that reveal "points of pain" or struggles. These new insights should be captured and used as part of your user understanding research.

   For example: If kids had a choice on what went into their lunch boxes, they might be less disappointed in lunch and more likely to eat a healthy lunch.

Tips

▶ Materials that can help: You'll want to have a camera and a notepad to write and sketch.

▶ Key questions to consider in this activity include, What are the *observable facts* – the people, objects, and activities that are present? How are people interacting with each other, objects, and their surroundings? What is *really* going on here? What could that mean or suggest?

▶ Effective field observation is a structured and disciplined exercise. Unstructured observation runs the risk of focusing only on the things that interest you, rather than the objective things going on.

▶ Be mindful of ethical considerations. Remember to be considerate of local norms of conduct; mask or secure the identity of people or places you are observing, and be respectful; do not be intrusive or disruptive.

WHAT MIGHT THIS LOOK LIKE?

Figure 41 depicts the subject of an observation exercise on work styles. The notes that follow show what might emerge from the exercise.

Fig. 41 **Observation: First Level and Second Level**

Observations Notes

First level: Just the facts

It is 10:30 a.m. This man is in an open office space, at his desk, in front of his computer – it's a Mac. There is a mug on is desk. There are toys on his desk (which he keeps picking up), including a "Russian doll," a miniature Eiffel Tower, and a pink rubber brain. There are drawings and sticky notes on the wall behind him. There is a bike and helmet beside him.

Second level: What could that mean?

This man is working. All of the objects and his surroundings suggest he is in a creative role. The toys suggest he has a playful outlook. He approaches his work in a creative way and visualizes his ideas as he develops them. He has appeared to have created his own little inspiring workspace in this open office.

USER JOURNALS
UNDERSTANDING THE USER JOURNEY

WHY DO WE DO THIS?

To stimulate dialogue with participants and reveal new insights based on user-generated content. User journals are an effective way to engage users in telling their personal stories, either as a supplement to or in lieu of photo elicitation (in situations where photo taking is prohibited). This exercise will reveal new insights and serve as the basis for discovering unmet needs through a deeper understanding of these questions:

What does this experience look and feel like from the user's perspective?

What is happening, and what are the highs and lows of their experience?

HOW CAN YOU DO THIS?

1. **Select a stakeholder group.** Identify the key stakeholder group whose current journey you would like to better understand, according to your field research plan.

2. **Define the experience.** A user journal exercise asks individuals to document their experience within the context of a specific activity. They record their activities, thoughts, and feelings in a journal over the course of a few days. Your project brief will help you define the experience you would like to know more about. For example, in the project on improving the chemotherapy patient experience in chapter 5, taking photographs in a hospital was prohibited, so we asked patients, *"For each of your visits to the hospital, please document your experience using this journal."*

3. **Design the package.** A user journal package is a kit that is sent out to individual users. Each kit contains three documents: participant instructions, journal, and informed consent.

    Participant instructions – Provides an overview of the package and details contact information, exercise instructions, exercise duration, important dates and times, and a request for a follow-up interview.

Journal – Provides detailed instructions for completing the user journal exercise. It states the purpose, procedure, research activity, and thought starters.

Informed consent – Provides an ethical agreement for conducting the research exercise. It states the purpose, procedure, confidentiality, contact, and consent.

4. **Recruit and schedule participants, and deliver the research package.** When they are recruited, a follow-up interview of approximately sixty minutes should be scheduled to take place at a location that is most convenient for the participant. When they are recruited and the interview is scheduled, the research package can be placed with the participant.

5. **Conduct the interview.** Conduct a follow-up interview with the subject to discuss the journal they have created (which you should keep for reference). The purpose of this interview is to listen to their stories to gain deeper understanding into their needs.

Tips

▶ Refer to Listening and Recording for tips on conducting an interview.

▶ User journals are a handy tool to use in conjunction with a photo-elicitation exercise. Journals allow users to record their thoughts and experiences when they are not comfortable taking photographs (due to sensitivity issues) or in environments where picture taking is not appropriate or even allowed due to confidentiality or privacy restrictions (like an office or hospital).

▶ You can design the journal to elicit input on several levels, including feelings, timing, location, thoughts passing though the user's head, etc. The key is to make it user friendly and not overly complicated.

▶ Finding individuals to participate in your research is often something best left to professional recruiting firms who can source participants other than your friends and family. Work with them to identify the recruiting profile, how many participants you would like to recruit, what they will do, and how they will be compensated, as per your field research plan. A lower-cost way to recruit individuals is to access your own professional and personal network, though this may result in a less objective sample.

▶ Be sure to compensate research participants for their time. That might be cash, a gift, or a redeemable gift card.

WHAT MIGHT THIS LOOK LIKE?

In the study on the chemotherapy patient experience, we asked patients to keep a journal on their way to and during hospital visits (see Figure 42). These journals prompted them to tell stories about their experiences that revealed deeper insights and unmet needs.

Fig. 42 **Patient Journal**

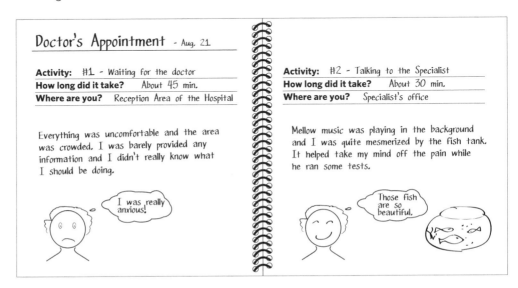

PHOTO ELICITATION
DISCOVERING UNMET NEEDS
THROUGH STORYTELLING

WHY DO WE DO THIS?

To trigger insightful stakeholder stories through subject-generated photographs. Listening to stories is one of the most powerful ways to glean new insights. Photo elicitation is an effective, open-ended way to prompt important stakeholder stories around a broadly defined activity and discover insights not normally uncovered through a more directed line of questions. It will reveal new insights and important unmet needs, as the basis for creating new human-centered value. It will help answer these questions:

What helps and hinders people in carrying out the activity of interest?

What are the POEMS (people, objects, environments, messages, and services) they encounter?

What are their unmet needs?

HOW CAN YOU DO THS?

This methodology is much like the journal exercise, but photo elicitation reveals more specific and tangible user-driven "triggers" that will reveal even more powerful stories and insights.[54]

1. **Define target participants, with an emphasis on the end user.** Reference your stakeholder map and project brief to define who matters most.
2. **Define the activity.** A photo elicitation exercise asks individuals to take pictures relating to an activity in their life, exploring ***both positive and negative*** aspects of their experience. This can easily be done with a digital camera or phone. Your project brief will help you define the activity you would like to know more about. Following are a few examples:
    "Take photographs that tell your stories about managing your health and wellness – what helps and what hinders you."

"Take photographs that tell stories about how you manage your personal finances – what helps and what hinders you."

"Take photographs that tell stories about commuting to and from work – both good and bad experiences."

3. **Design the package.** A photo elicitation package is a kit that is sent out to individual users. Each kit contains three documents:

    Participant instructions – Provides an overview of the package. It details contact information, exercise instructions, exercise duration, important dates and times, and a request for a follow-up interview.

    Photo instructions – Provides detailed instructions for completing the photo exercise. It states the purpose, procedure, research activity, and thought starters.

    Informed consent – Provides an ethical agreement for conducting the research exercise. It states the purpose, procedure, confidentiality, contact, and consent.

4. **Recruit and schedule participants, and deliver the research package.** When they are recruited, a follow-up interview of approximately sixty minutes should be scheduled to take place at a location that is most convenient and comfortable for the participant. When they are recruited and an interview is scheduled, the research package can be placed with the participant.

5. **Follow up and collect photos.** Once each individual has completed the exercise, they can either email the photos to you in advance or bring their recording device. In either case, it is valuable to retain the photos for later reference.

6. **Conduct the interview.** If you have received the photos from the individual in advance, organize (but do not reorder or edit) the photographs. Conduct a follow-up interview with the subject to discuss the photos they have taken. Your number-one job is to listen with empathy and an open mind to their stories, not to ask direct questions.

Tips

▶ Photo elicitation is a valuable exercise that requires time and focus. It is often best to use this technique on key stakeholder groups.

▶ There is no such thing as a "bad" picture. Do not filter out pictures before you begin the interview. Even bad pictures usually have a story behind them.

▶ See Listening and Recording for interviewing tips.

WHAT MIGHT THIS LOOK LIKE?

Fig. 43 **Photo Elicitation: Inspiration through Storytelling**

Here is a photo that was taken by a police officer who was undergoing chemotherapy treatment. He described the empty feeling he felt every morning when he woke up and saw his police uniform hanging in his closet. It reminded him that he was not actively serving his community and being a productive member of society. His sense of self-worth suffered during his treatment period. (That alone inspired an idea for a "chemo buddy" program.)

Fig. 44 **Photo Elicitation: There Are No Bad Photos**

This photograph shows that there are no bad photos! This dark photo was taken by a woman with an extended family overseas. While the interview team was ready to delete this photo, it turned out to provide valuable insight. The woman described the glowing computer screen in a dark room. Since her family is on the other side of the world and there is a twelve-hour time difference between her and her family, she often calls them in the middle of the night. This led to a story about the importance of keeping in touch with her family roots and the value she places on her cultural identity. That was a rich story for a bad picture!

LISTENING & RECORDING
GETTING THE MOST OUT OF INTERVIEWS

WHY DO WE DO THIS?

To glean the deepest understanding and most powerful insights out of time spent with important stakeholders. An empathic, mindful, and disciplined interviewer can draw out stories about an individual's life that reveal fresh insights and unmet user needs, and which eventually serve as criteria for creating innovative solutions. Comprehensive recording will provide a rich database to translate into unmet needs.

HOW CAN YOU DO THIS?

Interviews may use prompts (like photos or journals) or be conducted by simply asking people to tell you a story or recount an experience.

1. **Prepare and define the roles of the research team.** Interviews are best conducted in teams of two. One team member takes the lead and guides the interview. The other individual takes notes on *everything* they hear and see, making sure not to leave out any details on stories, defining quotes, or observations. It is also important that this person manage any voice or image devices you may have to record the interview. Prepare your roles, materials, and prompts (e.g., user photos or journals) before the interview begins.

2. **Explain the interview process to the participant.** The start of the interview should be used to welcome and make the interviewee feel comfortable. Below is an example of how you might begin your interview:

   "Today we want to hear your stories about [subject matter]. This is meant to help us understand your experiences on this topic. There are no right or wrong answers – this is wholly about listening to your personal stories and what matters to you."

   In a situation where photos are used as prompts, you might add, "To help you tell us your stories we want you to keep five things in mind:"[55]
   People – Who do you encounter and interact with during this activity?
   Objects – What are the things you use and interact with?

Environment – What are the places where this activity takes place?

Messages and media – What information are you looking for and how do you get it?

Services – What are the services and support systems you use?

3. **Conduct the interview, probing with open-ended questions.** Ask about their stories in an open-ended manner: *"Tell me your stories about [this picture or this subject],"* *"Tell me more,"* or *"Why is that important to you?"* It is important to ask open-ended questions to hear participant stories. Asking direct, product/service-specific questions will not reveal the same depth and breadth of insight in the search for broader unmet needs.

4. **Listen and let them tell their stories on their terms.** Conducting a proper interview with the user is key to getting the richest and most unfiltered insights. Here are some practical tips:

   Make it natural. It is crucial that the interviewee feels at ease and able to talk freely without pressure or judgment. This can be achieved through genuine empathy, with an appropriate dose of neutrality (i.e., control your reactions to their stories).

   Let them do (all) the talking. Empathy and insight will come only if you are not attempting to steer the conversation and are openly and intently listening. For at least the opening part of the interview, try asking only two questions: *"Why?"* and *"Could you tell me more?"* Product/service-specific questions will lead to largely non-inspiring responses and will rarely uncover an unarticulated need.

   Be comfortable with silence. We are often not comfortable with "dead air." It is important to overcome this discomfort, as these moments of silence will allow people to be free with their stories. Often the biggest burst of insight comes after four or five seconds (an eternity!) of silence.

   Record everything. As a note-taker, capture the stories and quotes to bring to life the pictures, journals, or other prompts. Be on the lookout for moments of excitement or frustration. Record information in the user's terms, including the obvious or seemingly unimportant. Capture any nonverbal clues there may be in emotions (*"he got teary eyed when …"*), behaviors (*"he was fidgeting during his recount of …"*), and body language (*"he looked like all his energy was zapped out of him when …"*).

Tips

▶ Materials that might be helpful: an organized note-taking template and a recording device (such as your phone).

▶ Exercise empathy and mindfulness – and pay attention to every detail.

▶ Resist the temptation to ask direct questions that are of interest to you but not to them. You are ultimately looking for unmet needs, not how to configure or price your solution.

▶ Location should be conducive to focused listening and ideally should be in the participant's natural surroundings. While you can do this virtually, it is valuable to see them and interact with them; phone interviews can be done but are far from ideal.

WHAT MIGHT THIS PROCESS LOOK THIS LIKE?

Figure 45 depicts the interviewing and note-taking process graphically.

Fig. 45 **Interview Roles and Note-Taking**

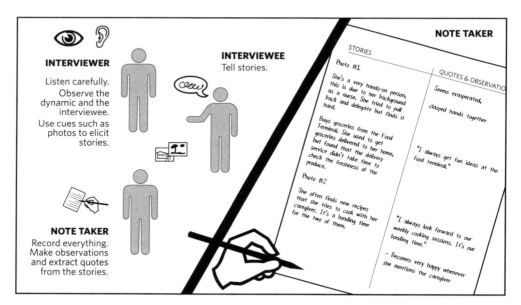

MIND MAPPING
MAKING CONNECTIONS TO
UNDERSTAND THE WHOLE PERSON

WHY DO WE DO THIS?

To appreciate the "whole person" and help make connections between seemingly unrelated data points and observations from an individual interview. This method of visualization is a thinking tool that helps make the thoughts and ideas (the "stuff" in your head) explicit for you and other people. It is used for a variety of purposes, including interview debriefing, organizing your thoughts, or making sense out of the research findings. It helps you think through questions such as, *What's really motivating this person? What are the main themes emerging from this interview and how do they connect?*

HOW CAN YOU DO THIS?

1. **Begin with the user.** Start in the center of a piece of paper with the interviewee's name. Draw a line to the first theme or topic it makes you think of in the context of the interview. Refer to your interview notes to help you recount what you heard. Ask yourself these questions:

    What was the most surprising insight from that interview? What does that mean?
    What was the overall theme behind what they said?
    How does that connect with other things they said?

2. **Expand the map.** Work outwards in all directions, putting similar ideas closer to each other. This process encourages you to recount the stories you heard in a fluid and natural way.

3. **Look for patterns and connections.** When you believe you have most of your insights out on paper, consider how it all links together. Use circles or lines to highlight these connections. Ask yourself, *What's really motivating this person? What are the main themes emerging from this interview and how do they connect?*

Tips

▶ Things to have on hand: user journals, interview photographs and notes.

▶ Make sure your paper is large enough, so you have room to expand upon your thoughts or ideas.

▶ This is an excellent way to debrief an interview with your interview partner(s).

▶ Try not to filter what you put down; write down every thought or idea that comes to you. Along the way, ask yourself, *Why is that important to this person?* (See the Motivational Mapping tool for tips on how to do this.)

WHAT MIGHT THAT LOOK LIKE?

Figure 46 is an example of a mind map based on an interview with a patient.

Fig. 46 **Mind Mapping: A Patient Interview**

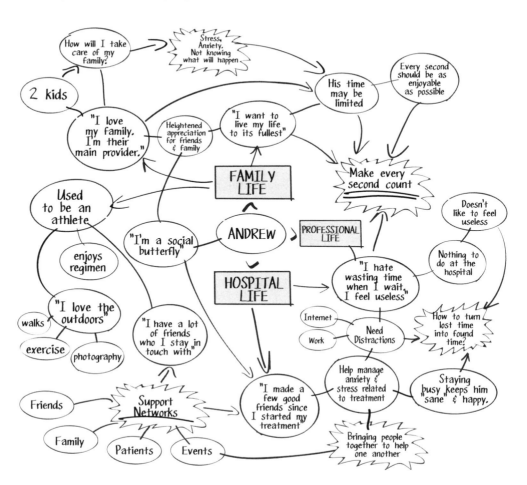

SUBJECT PROFILES
SYNTHESIZING AN INTERVIEW

WHY DO WE DO THIS?

To synthesize and record the important aspects of an interview and provide a quick reference of the individuals you have interviewed. It can serve as a helpful reference for individual interviews, including key motivators, defining quotes, and insightful aspects of this person's story. You will have many interviews, and proper recording of each one will ensure thoughtfulness and robustness in your research.

Tips

▶ Draw from your interview notes, mind map, and motivational mapping.

▶ Include defining quotes – these are valuable in keeping your discoveries in understandable language and are helpful in articulating need statements.

▶ Keep the subject profile brief and succinct – one page is best and will force you to synthesize; you may have dozens of interviews to consider.

▶ Use the subject profile throughout the research process as a quick and easy way to recall different interview subjects at a glance.

WHAT MIGHT THIS LOOK LIKE?

Figure 47 is an example of a summary of an in-depth interview.

Fig. 47 **Subject Profiling**

Participant Name	Ben Shipley
Participant Age	62
Date & Time	05/07/10 @ 12:30 a.m.
Interview Location	Coffee Shop
Interview Team	Alex, Alana
Interview Duration	1 hour

Provide a brief overview of the user

Ben has been the owner and operator of the Over the Top Sox Co. for over twenty years. He has a background in management and has helped sustain and grow the eighty-year-old company his grandfather started. He is an extremely hard-working owner, who works twelve hours a day and never seems to tire of the constant challenges his manufacturing business has to offer. Ben is proud of his staff, his business, and especially of all the socks they make and sell … "Everyone always thinks of socks last, but we always think of socks first!"

Describe your user's habits and practices relevant to the project

Ben is a huge believer in the power that technology brings to his business. He feels that without technology, he wouldn't be efficient enough to compete with goods produced in China. Though the company does manufacture socks, a big part of their competitive advantage is R&D for large clients. Ben is a makes a habit of constantly using the latest knowledge to further their understanding of product development and how technology can help him. In the plant, much of the production is automated, which cuts down much of their labor costs.

Ben makes sure to visit all of their large clients face-to-face to establish a good rapport. He also realizes the potential of great staff; he has many potential hires coming his way due to the recent downturn in manufacturing jobs. He tries to choose those who have great skill and something to offer, even if there is currently not a position for them at the plant.

What is this person all about – what drives him/her?

Ben is an entrepreneur and business enthusiast. He loves that fact that every day there is a new challenge to tackle and he can use his management skills to solve it. He values his employees. He sees the silver lining in everything, so he always sees problems as opportunities.

What is this person's biggest point of pain?

His biggest point of pain is competing against large brand names who can easily undercut his prices. This can lead to a loss of profit and can easily affect the established relationships he has with his clients. Control of his inventory is another point of pain: Ben needs to be aware of what is going on in his warehouse at all times to make sure things are running smoothly. He has to keep the cash register ringing to keep the people he values on the payroll.

DISCOVERY EXCHANGE
MAKING CONNECTIONS & BUILDING A FRAMEWORK FOR DATA ANALYSIS

WHY DO WE DO THIS?

To visually capture collective research insights, as a means of both sharing discoveries across the team and providing a framework for subsequent analysis. As team members share their stakeholder stories and insights, you will build collective understanding and intuitively formulate a hypothesis on common user issues and needs. During this exchange, patterns, themes, and common needs will begin to emerge, and you will be able to make intuitive links across many interviews and volumes of data and formulate a framework hypothesis for analysis.

HOW CAN YOU DO THIS?

1. **Assign a facilitator and visualizer.** They will record the exchange and lead the group discussion. All team members should be prepared to share their interviewee stories and should have their research notes handy.
2. **Begin with one compelling story.** One team member should begin by recounting an interview story that first comes to mind. It is most powerful (and empathic) to *recount the story in the first person* (i.e., as if you are the interviewee) and not interpret or filter the story through your own lens. While story is being recounted, the visualizer should mark down defining quotes, key themes, or words that emerge from the story. The visualizer will start to create a consolidated map of the research findings.
3. **Build on insights.** Other team members who have similar stories or related insights should share them. This will help to build on the number of insights and help to flesh out the visual map.
4. **Share stories.** Once the first story and insights have been exhausted, the next team member should share another (quite different) research story that they feel is important. The team should do this until a good cross-section of stories has been shared and clear patterns emerge.
5. **Pause for reflection and look for connections.** Use circles or lines to highlight patterns and connections, looking for important themes and common needs.
6. **Articulate a short list of hypothesized needs.** Based on your exchange and the patterns that emerge, articulate a short list of needs that you believe are

common to a particular stakeholder, keeping SPICE in mind to define needs holistically. Ideally, you will get this down to no more than five to seven initial needs. This list will serve as an initial framework for need analysis.

Tips

▶ Some useful things to have on hand for reference: user journals, interview photographs, mind maps, and subject profiles.

▶ It is preferable that the facilitator be someone other than the primary interviewers – someone who can bring an open mind to the process of listening and capturing the insights of everyone in the group.

▶ Capture defining quotes. *(For example., "I was terrified on my first day of school. Everything was new.")*

▶ Use a large whiteboard or poster paper to ensure that you have enough space to develop connections and links.

▶ This is an intuitive process. Look for deeper meaning and common needs across all of the interviews. Motivational mapping can help take the conversation to a deeper and more meaningful level.

WHAT MIGHT THIS LOOK LIKE?

Figure 48 is an early stage visualization of a discovery exchange about how people find value and meaning in life. Discussions generated a shared understanding through insight-rich stories and revealed common patterns around community, cultural identity, and balanced living.

Fig. 48 **Capturing Stories and Making Connections**

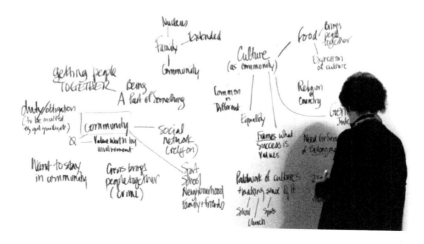

MOTIVATIONAL MAPPING
SEARCHING FOR DEEPER MEANING

WHY DO WE DO THIS?

To think more deeply about what you saw and heard across your interviews, and articulate the underlying motivation and unmet need. Motivational mapping will help give deeper meaning to observations, elements of stories and quotes, and reveal more than the obvious statements and insights. It will help you translate your collection of insights into deeper universal needs, as input to your need-finding analysis. Motivational mapping can be used in conjunction with the interview mind mapping, your discovery exchange, or analysis of needs.

HOW CAN YOU DO THIS?

1. **Select an interesting comment from a story.** In the center of a piece of paper, write down a comment or activity for which you believe there is deeper meaning. *For example: "I sat for hours staring at the wall with nothing to do while I just waited endlessly."*

2. **Define insights.** Branching off of your initial observation or quote, consider what that might mean to them on a more subjective level. *For example: "I have no time to waste. My time is valuable."* Consider other insights the central statement might suggest and draw another branch on your map.

3. **Articulate the need.** Go one level deeper to consider what unmet need that may point to. *For example: "I need to find time and make the best use of it" or "I need to be productive."*

Tips

▶ If doing this as a group, it is helpful to either use a whiteboard or a big piece of paper.

▶ Like the observation exercise, motivational mapping will enhance your empathy and understanding on a deeper level.

▶ Look for needs that are deep enough to do something about, but not so abstract that they seem vague and uninspiring.

- Intuition plays an important role here. Through all of your research, you will have an intuitive sense of what really matters to and is motivating to your user.

WHAT MIGHT THIS LOOK LIKE?

Figure 49 is a visualization for the Princess Margaret Hospital project:

Fig. 49 **Motivational Mapping**

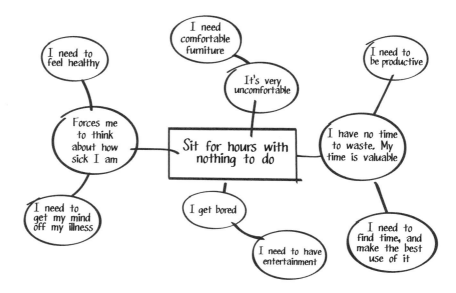

NEED-MINING & ANALYSIS
TURNING SOFT DATA INTO HARD DATA

WHY DO WE DO THIS?

To bring rigor to need-finding and provide a strong foundation of meaningful needs as the springboard for solution development. Need-mining will ensure that your discoveries are broad-based and meaningful, as opposed to just momentary inspirations. Keeping the SPICE framework in mind will ensure you consider the many dimensions of your users and other stakeholders and will lead to a well-rounded and clearly defined set of universal needs. There are many approaches to analyzing needs; here are two distinct approaches:

- ▶ An organic method in which you cluster insights on sticky notes will give you a sense of the patterns of insights and needs to inspire fresh thinking.
- ▶ A more rigorous analysis (as presented below) is recommended if you are undertaking a significant project for which you would like a stronger ongoing foundation to reference on a continuing basis.

This process should leave you with four to six deep, unsatisfied needs that will serve as the criteria for innovation and value creation.

HOW CAN YOU DO THIS?

This process is guided by the framework you will have intuitively built in your initial group debriefing and discovery exchange. It is best done if you have transcribed all of your interviews into a typewritten format from your interview notes or from an audio recording. (A transcription service can quickly and cost-effectively do this for you.) You will continue to discover "hidden" insights and needs within these stories and quotes as you deconstruct them into a comprehensive collection of data points.

The spreadsheet described below will show you how you can turn your wealth of data into a powerful foundation for innovation.

1. **Deconstruct your interviews into insightful quotes and snippets of stories.** Reference the full text from each interview. The quotes and snippets you pull from each will become your insight "data points." Insights can come

from the stories you've heard, a great quote, or something relevant that you've observed in the environment or the interviewee's behavior. Record each of these insight in individual cells of an excel spreadsheet. Using excerpts from the stories and quotes from your interview transcription, begin to identify insights that are:

Revealing – a glimpse into deeper motivations and needs

Authentic – supported by the story/observations

Practical – triggering ideas on ways to help the subject

2. **Analyze the insight and connect it to your initial need framework.** Referring to the list of hypothesized needs identified in your initial framework (see Discovery Exchange), consider which of these needs may be underlying each insight. One insightful story or quote may point to more than one need. During this process, be cognizant of emerging new needs and be prepared to adjust your need analysis framework and revisit insights in light of newly identified needs.

3. **Tabulate the universality and intensity of these needs.** This will give you an indication of the intensity and universality of needs by cross-referencing the interview insights with the intuitively hypothesized needs. You can do this by creating a spreadsheet with columns as follows:

Spreadsheet Column A – Identify the subject (the interviewee).

Spreadsheet Column B – Profile the interviewee briefly.

Spreadsheet Column C – Capture each interview "snippet" with either a single insightful quote or a segment of their story that you feel revealed a profound insight.

Spreadsheet Column D+ – Each column will represent one of your hypothesized needs (maximum of seven needs).

For each entry in Column C, connect it to the appropriate needs in columns D+ by putting a "1" in each column with which you believe the data point is associated. Tabulate the intensity and universality of needs by calculating each column on the spreadsheet. This will help you to verify the needs in your initial need framework and provide you with a flexible database of all of your interviews that you can use to analyze and substantiate your need-finding conclusions.

Tips

▶ All you need to translate soft data into hard data is Excel software!

▶ Use the outcome of your collective discovery exchange as an initial framework going into analysis, but be prepared to alter it – it is only an ingoing hypothesis.

Don't force-fit needs to your ingoing hypothesis. If a new need emerges, add it to the list of core needs and revisit the assignment of data points to needs.

▸ This is a highly iterative and intuitive process, though it culminates in an analytical output.

▸ Needs often cannot be articulated by individuals themselves and surface only when the need-finding process is complete. Motivational mapping can help define a deeper need.

▸ Any given data point may be associated with multiple needs. Ask yourself, "Could this comment relate to other needs?" For example, a comment on "waiting for hours" could be related to a need to be more engaged and productive or a need to have more information.

▸ New technologies and tools are emerging all the time. Keep an eye out for language-processing software that can help you make the most out of your database of insights.

WHAT MIGHT THIS LOOK LIKE?

Figure 50 is a section of a spreadsheet that illustrates how the individual insights and quotes from the hospital project were broken out, analyzed, and linked to needs.

Fig. 50 **Spreadsheet Analysis of Soft Data**

COLUMN A	COLUMN B	COLUMN C	SUPPORT & CONNECTIVITY	ENGAGEMENT	EFFORTLESS SIMPLICITY	EMPOWERMENT	HEALTHY HEALING
SUBJECT	**PROFILE**	**STORIES & QUOTES**					
(1) Police Officer	48 years old Married 3 months of chemotherapy	I get anxious just sitting there (waiting room)		1			
		I never talk about cancer	1				
		I have no time to waste		1			
		Going to work is the greatest part of my life				1	
		Waiting is the most painful time		1			1
(2) Retired nurse	63 yrs old Active in her community Just starting chemotherapy	I cover my face a lot – my face looks good, but in my heart I cry	1		1		1
		There is nothing to help pass the time		1			
		Spending time with my grandson is "happy time"		1			
		There are a lot of people with different backgrounds (hard to start a conversation)	1		1		
		The walls are gray and the air is stale		1			

NEED ARTICULATION
DEFINING A PLATFORM FOR INNOVATION

WHY DO WE DO THIS?

To articulate unmet needs in a way that inspires the development team and creates a vital platform for innovation. Creating new human-centric value stems from a deep understanding of people's needs. This step is the culmination of all of your need-finding research. In combination with your Personas and a depiction of the user's Current Journey (both tools come later in this section), these needs will serve as the basis for creating and evaluating human-centered new solutions going forward.

Now is the time to turn your "hard data" back into "soft data" by capturing needs in a human and compelling manner as an inspiring springboard for innovating.

HOW CAN YOU DO THIS?

1. **Headline the need.** Summarize the motivating need in a short phrase, using user language and avoiding abstract or generic terms. You will need a short handle to refer to in development. *For example, on the Princess Margaret Hospital project, one of the key needs was "Engagement."*

2. **Define the need clearly.** Provide a clear definition of what you mean by that need, and ensure that everyone understands and buys into that definition. There is nothing that can derail you in Gear 2 more quickly than looking at a need and asking, "That's clever, but what does that mean?" *For example, on PMH, "Engagement" meant "Turning lost time into found time by giving patients the means to make more productive use of their time (both waiting for and during treatment) and engaging them emotionally, physically, intellectually or spiritually."*

3. **Provide a defining quote.** Looking back through your transcripts, select a quote that captures the spirit of the need, as voiced by a real person. *For example, a defining quote for "engagement" was "Waiting is the most painful time. I'm here for five hours. There is an opportunity to learn and make me productive."*

Tips

▶ Things to have on hand: user journals, interview photographs and notes.

▶ Needs should be articulated in a human way that is easily understood (i.e., something a *real person* would say) and reinforced with insightful and compelling quotes.

▶ Needs must be relevant to the project and must inspire a broad set of solutions. They must be broad enough to create opportunity but not so broad that they are vague and do not inspire solutions.

WHAT MIGHT THIS LOOK LIKE?

The following are some examples from the hospital project of how you might articulate and define needs:

Engagement: I want to stay active and engaged.

> Patients want to feel less like passive observers and feel more in control of their treatment process. They want to be stimulated and maximize every opportunity they have to grow and heal.

> "I am here for five hours. There is an opportunity to learn and make me more productive."

Healthy Healing: I want to recover in a healthful manner.

> Chemotherapy treatment can be a very difficult process that can take a mental, emotional, and spiritual toll. Patients need to be free of any unnecessary stressors that will negatively impact their recovery process.

> "I enjoy the walk to the hospital through the parks. It's the only time I will be outside all day."

NEED VALIDATION
DIMENSIONALIZING THE OPPORTUNITY

WHY DO WE DO THIS?

To validate needs and quantify human-centered opportunities. Need-finding is an exercise in building empathy and understanding, but it is also an exercise in building a business case. Ascertaining universal needs and dimensionalizing the opportunity through quantitative research is an important part of making a sound business case.

HOW CAN YOU DO THIS?

1. **Design your research sample.** Define who you would like to include in your research sample. Aim for a diverse, representative sample of important stakeholders.

2. **Decide on a scalable survey tool.** This could be a paper questionnaire that is given to a large group of people, or a simple online tool that makes completing the questionnaire easy for participants and analyzing data easy for you. There are many tools available, including SurveyGizmo.

3. **Articulate the need.** Consolidate your insights into simple "need statements" that your informants can understand: e.g., *"Develop the skills that put me at the top of my game."*

4. **Implement the survey.** Invite participants to take this short survey and ask them to rate the following two statements on a scale of one to five for each need statement:

   How important is this need to you? (1 = Not at all important, 5 = Very important)

   How satisfied are you that this need is being met? (1 = Not at all satisfied, 5 = Completely satisfied)

5. **Gather and analyze your data.** Review the results and determine how you will use these in your business case.

WHAT MIGHT THIS LOOK LIKE?

Figure 51 shows the results of such a survey for the Canadian Bar Association project, based on research conducted to better understand member needs and levels of satisfaction with services members currently had access to. These discoveries were validated through quantitative surveys to gauge the gap between the importance of these needs and member satisfaction in these needs being met. What they found were significant need/satisfaction gaps across the board. For example, while 81 per cent of members identified "skills for practice success" (distinct from knowledge of the law) to be highly important, only 28 per cent of them were satisfied with that their needs were being met. This signaled a sizable opportunity for the CBA to fill that gap.

Fig. 51 **Validating Universal Needs and Dimensionalizing the Opportunity Gap**

NEEDS		AVERAGE SCORE ACROSS ALL QUESTIONNAIRES OUT OF 10	PERCENTAGE OF HIGH RATINGS (8, 9, OR 10)
Access to Knowledge	Importance	8.5	84%
	Satisfaction	5.9	28%
Skills for Success	Importance	8.3	**81%**
	Satisfaction	6.1	**28%**
Advocacy	Importance	8.1	76%
	Satisfaction	6.6	46%
Reciprocal Support	Importance	8	74%
	Satisfaction	5.2	38%
Personal Efficiency	Importance	8	73%
	Satisfaction	5.2	24%
Valued Contribution	Importance	7.4	62%
	Satisfaction	5.5	26%
Personal Wellbeing	Importance	7.4	59%
	Satisfaction	5.5	46%

Note: Based on a Needs Questionnaire Completed by 167 Lawyers across Canada

PERSONAS
CREATING HUMAN ARCHETYPES

WHY DO WE DO THIS?

To capture the archetypes of important stakeholders in holistic terms and put their needs into context. Personas are fictional composite characters based on data from real people. They are used to keep your development centered on *real people* throughout the development process.

HOW CAN YOU DO THIS?

1. **Define important stakeholder groups.** Select the most critical stakeholders, with priority always on the ultimate end user of the solution. *For example, the Canadian Barr Association project focused on practicing lawyers.*
2. **Determine if there are important differences within these groups.** Based on the data generated from research, look for differences within groups in terms of motivations, attitudes, and behaviors. If one stakeholder group clearly contains more than one type of character, create more than one persona if you believe there is a danger of overgeneralizing about one group and eventually creating solutions that could alienate others. *For example, on the Canadian Bar Association project, all lawyers shared the same set of underlying needs, but these needs were expressed in different ways among distinct subgroups of lawyers, as shown in Figures 52 and 53. Profiling them separately ensured all lawyers were served.*
3. **Personify.** Characterize each of the distinct stakeholders you've identified to put their needs into context. Your personas should depict key differences you have observed. Craft your persona to feel like a real person by bringing them to life in the *first person*, citing defining quotes and including visuals that reflect their personal interests and lifestyles. Remember to create fictional characters based on real research data – make them *real*, not bland or idyllic.

Tips

▶ For inspiration, reference the needs you have identified, as well as your interviewee profiles, observations, and interview notes.

▶ Personas serve as criteria for innovation. Done well, they can aid others in empathizing with your users and inspire you throughout the development process, as well as help keep the *human factor* at the center of value creation.

- While needs may be universal, each persona should have a clear and distinct point of view. This will stretch your solution development in a way that maximizes universal appeal.
- Respect confidentiality: do not use real names, personal data, or photos from your users.

WHAT MIGHT THIS LOOK LIKE?

In the case of the Canadian Bar Association, six personas were created to bring universal member needs to life across diverse profiles of lawyers, from young lawyers to seasoned professionals. These personas have been used since the project to keep the members front and center of decisions, as noted by Cathy Cummings in her interview in part one. Figures 52 and 53 are two of those personas, demonstrating how two seemingly different "people" can share the same needs.

Fig. 52 **Persona**

Quinlee

Life – 35 years old, engaged, thinking about having kids

Career – Mid-sized firm, Senior Associate, British Columbia

Cares most about – Her future

I feel like I'm at a crossroad in my life. There is so much going on in my work and personal life. Six years ago, after graduating from law school in Singapore, I moved with my fiancé to Canada, as we felt it offered the best job opportunities. It took us a little while to qualify as Canadian lawyers, and often we weren't sure who we could turn to, to help us figure things out.

Now I'm turning 25, and my fiancé's family has been bugging me constantly about children. I want to have kids, but I feel like it has taken me so long just to become a senior associate at my current firm, and secretly I was hoping to make partner track soon. But I've seen how parental leave can be a "career killer" for lawyers. I've heard so many stories about women coming back and struggling with their practice and client base, while also raising their kids. It just seems almost impossible to balance both.

Although, even with my aspirations, I'm really questioning the firm that I'm at. Sometimes I just feel so underappreciated. I've reached out to someone I met 4 years ago, a partner at another firm, and asked for her thoughts. I just don't think that anyone at my firm would really understand the situation I'm in. All they seem to care about is whether or not I've billed enough hours over the weekends. I just want to be able to make the right choices, but I'm not sure how to do so at the moment.

"I'm worried about how my choices affect my future."

Fig. 53 **Persona**

Stanley

Life – 64 years old, re-married, 2 grown-up kids

Career – Large firm, Managing Partner, Ontario

Cares most about – Success

I've worked at this law firm my whole life. It hasn't been easy, but I've been a managing partner for the last 15 years. I'm proud of what I've been able to accomplish and keep to a small circle of friends that I've come to know and work with here. This kind of success is not for everyone, and I've seen many lawyers leave due to the demands of this profession. Personally, I've sacrificed my first marriage and missed watching my kids grow up.

I remember when I first started out at my firm, we all knew that we had to work really, really hard. If a partner wanted us to walk through a wall, we would do it, no questions. There was no other way for me to climb the ranks than by applying myself 210 per cent, making sure that the partners saw me as a rising star. My partners and I still look for that kind of dedication in our associates, especially if they want to be on the partner track. Bottom line is that every waking hour counts. We are in the business of selling time. If you want to be successful, you have to keep up your client base and bill more than your neighbor.

At the end of the day the clients are at the heart of it all. It's the one-on-one relationships that build this business from the ground up. It's that side of the business that you really can't teach, so it's a good thing I'll be around at least another 10 years.

"Time and money is what drives our business."

CURRENT JOURNEY
CONTEXTUALIZING THE OPPORTUNITY THROUGH STORYTELLING

WHY DO WE DO THIS?

To bring to life the current experience by describing actions, struggles, and feelings in a way that creates empathy for others. This is a powerful way to evoke empathy for the central user. It will humanize and contextualize the opportunity for those on the development team as well as others with whom you will share your project. Throughout Gear1, you will gather new insights into the user's journey and the feelings, people, and places that are part of it.

HOW CAN YOU DO THIS?

1. **Create a timeline.** Begin to sketch out their story by drawing a line on a large piece of paper that represents the appropriate time frame for a current user experience. This timeline may represent a few hours, a few days, or even a few months.

2. **Plot the experience stages.** Using your insights gathered from Gear 1, plot the beginning, middle, and end of the experience along the timeline. Consider the people, objects, environments, messages, and services the user encounters.

3. **Detail the journey.** Thinking about the logical progression of events uncovered by your research, create a narrative story that encompasses the typical journey for your user as they currently experience it. Consider the user's struggles, emotional state, functional requirements, and interactions with other stakeholders along the way. To avoid being vague about stages in the experience, shape your depiction by injecting it with tangible elements from the POEMS framework. If you get stuck, reference your interview notes, needs, and personas

4. **Visualize your story.** Bring your story to life by illustrating the current journey through pictures, sketches, graphics, and even a short inspiring slide show or movie set to music. The story will be most powerful – and most likely to create empathy for the user – if it captures their struggles on both a practical and emotional level.

Tips

▶ Highlight the needs and behaviors of the users without going into unnecessary detail, capturing the journey in a holistic and human manner.

▶ An effective way to communicate the experience to others is to use presentation or basic movie-creation software to make a simple animated movie from still images, text, and music.

WHAT MIGHT THIS LOOK LIKE?

Figure 54 is a script from the Princess Margaret Hospital project – a simple yet compelling three-minute depiction of the opportunity to improve patient experience by capturing the despair of the current journey and the needs that inspired a new vision for a journey of hopeful healing. The use of select copy, the transition from slow and sad music, and transition from the black-and-white photography of the current scene to colorful visuals and inspiring music set the tone for the creation of a new vision.

Fig. 54 **Current Patient Journey**

MUSIC	STORYLINE – WORDS	VISUALS
Sad and slow	PMH Systemic Therapy Treatment Centre 2007	Long, dreary hall with chairs lined up against one wall
	This is where patients enter …	Gray wall with an old framed print
	This is what the see …	Lineup of institutional chairs with no space between
	This is what they look at …	A dull wall with a thermostat and a glaring light
	This is what they can do …	Tattered old magazines
	This is where they sit for hours …	Crowded treatment room, with a chair facing the hallway
	This is where they rest …	An institutional gurney extending into the hallway
	This is what they see …	A bright fluorescent panel of light and an air vent
	This is their experience. How can we make it better?	Dull, dreary shot of an endless corridor of waiting
Transition	Through generous support and the vision of PMH … This space is a canvas to create	Big empty white space (a racquetball room)
Inspiring and upbeat	An experience that gives patients hope	Skyline with sunshine breaking through the clouds
(Build)	Where they know support is always there	Team of friendly and caring healthcare professionals
(Build)	Where confidence is acquired through knowing	Scheduling board (airline arrivals)
(Build)	There is a constant sense of calm … comfort … and peace	Zen roof garden Comfortable living room Woman in a robe meditating
(Build)	A place where relationships are created	Smiling nurse with patient
(Build)	… and waiting is just a frame of mind	Woman painting a canvas in a sunlit studio
(Build)	Where your mind is at work … and play	Close-up of a workstation Close-up of a chessboard
(Build)	Where new discoveries … help you forget that you are in a hospital	Gallery wall of art Close-up of woman watching a goldfish in a bowl
Optimistic	There can be such a place … Princess Margaret Hospital	Princess Margaret Hospital Brand imposed on the big empty white space (a racquetball room)

DESIGN CRITERIA
SYNTHESIZING THE PRINCIPLES FOR SOLUTION DEVELOPMENT

WHY DO WE DO THIS?

To define the criteria for development of new solutions. Taking your knowledge of market-based opportunities and your deep understanding of what people need and consolidating both into design criteria will guide your development process in a disciplined way to ensure your ideas create new and distinct value.

HOW CAN YOU DO THIS?

1. **Start with user research.** Review the needs that you've identified through your research. Think about how you might meet those needs and write down your thoughts as action statements. *For example, in the case of HSO, people needed useful information that improved understanding and sharpened their focus.*

2. **Define what would make your solution most relevant in the market context.** Drawing from your work in Contextualizing Your Challenge, identify what will make your future solution most salient and valuable to the market and set you apart from your competitors. *For example, in the case of HSO, there was a huge market opportunity to connect people, actions, and information across the healthcare ecosystem.*

3. **Consolidate the criteria that will allow you to create the most new value.** Establish a set of design criteria that will meet the needs of important stakeholders and create game-changing value in the market.

Tips

▶ Align these criteria to you overarching enterprise mission and brand.

▶ Consider how you might deliver on these design criteria in terms of your current relationships with your stakeholders.

WHAT MIGHT THIS LOOK LIKE?

In the stories about Health Standards Organization's journey in strategic transformation in chapters 3 and 6, a set of criteria was synthesized from its work on market context and universal stakeholder needs. These criteria anchored all of its subsequent development work, keeping its future vision focused on addressing market opportunities, human needs, and where the enterprise might uniquely add value.

Put the person (and their health) at the center.

Actively consider and engage the right stakeholders in the right way.

Cultivate trust and accountability.

Connect people, actions and information across the healthcare ecosystem.

Provide useful information that improves understanding and sharpens focus.

Enable the right actions by the right people at the right time.

Transparently communicate the link to better outcomes.

Adapt to specific needs and situations that continually optimize outcomes.

GEAR 2: CONCEPT VISUALIZATION

—

242 *This section presents a variety of methods for exploring and prototyping ideas and concepts through collaboration, experimentation, and continuous refinement. You will learn how to formulate a concrete vision for success, identify potential solutions for evaluation, and validate important game-changing ideas.*

IDEATION & CONCEPT HARVESTING
EXPLORING NEW POSSIBILITIES

WHY DO WE DO THIS?

To expand the field of possibilities for creating new and meaningful value. By tapping into the experience and imagination of a diverse team, collaborative idea-generation can yield new and exciting ideas. Inspired by unmet human needs and engaging personas, new possibilities will emerge. Ideation and concept harvesting together address the important question: *How might we best meet this person's needs?* By generating a LOT of ideas for satisfying unmet needs, you will be able to identify three to four new and exciting multidimensional concepts.

HOW CAN YOU DO THIS?

Part 1: *Ideation* will generate hundreds of ideas!

1. **Begin by picking one persona and one need.** You can start with any one of the personas or needs. It is important to focus on one at a time to maximize your sense of empathy in serving a personal and specific need.
2. **Frame the need as a question.** Identify your persona and one unmet need. Use these two inputs to create a question based on the unmet need. For each need, begin with a question like this: *"How might we (the enterprise) help (the persona) to (unmet need)?"*
3. **Generate ideas.** Thinking freely and without judgment, generate ideas that address this need. The goal is to generate as many ideas as possible in a short amount of time. Aim for quantity over quality in your ideas: the more ideas, the better.
4. **Repeat for every need and persona.** This will give you a wealth of ideas from many different perspectives, all of which touch on a different dimension of human need and collectively feed the creation of a rich and multidimensional solution. Every round of ideation will generate fresh ideas, taking all needs and personas into account.

Part 2: *Concept harvesting* translates seemingly disparate ideas into **big ideas**.

5. **Cluster and identify larger concept themes.** Across your vast pool of ideas, common solutions will emerge. Look for patterns, cluster similar ideas together, and identify the bigger concept in these clusters. *For example, several ideas may add up to a personalized coaching service that may be relevant to all personas and serve more than one need.*

6. **Expand on the most breakthrough concepts.** Choose your top three concepts using the following criteria:

    Does this concept address a need and create value for the user?

    Is this a breakthrough concept that could dramatically enhance the user experience?

   One concept at a time, ask yourself, *"What might that look like? How could that work? What kind of POEMS (people, objects, environments, media/messages, and services) could that entail?"*

Tips

▶ Allow yourselves to think outside your current business offering. Often, the *intent* of concepts that are totally outside your business can be reconfigured in other ways. Don't edit at this point.

▶ Defer judging ideas until the end; build on the ideas of others. Every idea is valid; sometimes breakout ideas are right next to the absurd ones.

▶ Keep ideas flowing by capturing the essence of the idea and quickly moving on. Don't stall by going into detail.

▶ Doodle or sketch to make your ideas visual. Visuals are easier to understand and will in turn stimulate new ideas.

▶ Use metaphors or analogies to come up with ideas. Imagine a successful company, then ask yourself what kind of ideas they would come up with to address the needs frame. (This is covered more in the tool Metaphors).

WHAT MIGHT THIS PROCESS LOOK LIKE?

Figure 55 illustrates how this process might look schematically:

Fig. 55 **Ideation and Concept Enrichment**

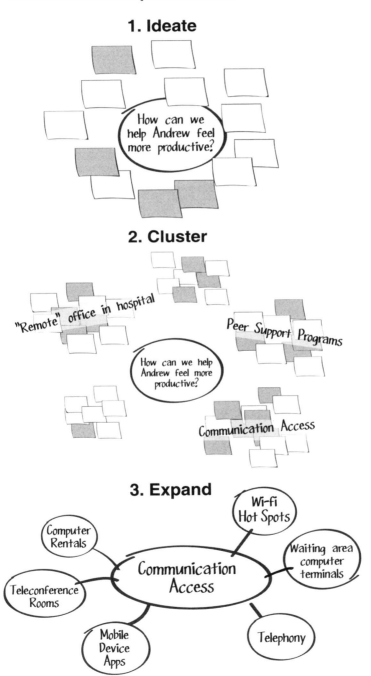

1. Ideate

How can we help Andrew feel more productive?

2. Cluster

"Remote" office in hospital

Peer Support Programs

How can we help Andrew feel more productive?

Communication Access

3. Expand

Computer Rentals

Wi-fi Hot Spots

Waiting area computer terminals

Communication Access

Teleconference Rooms

Telephony

Mobile Device Apps

ROLE PLAY TO IDEATE
EMPATHIZING TO GENERATE SOLUTIONS

WHY DO WE DO THIS?

To develop ideas by experiencing the world from a user's perspective.
Through this exercise, you will come up with ideas to address the user's challenges and develop a repository of options to be advanced as you design your
solutions. This tool is similar to the earlier tool Role Play to Empathize, where
you were trying to understand what that person might be experiencing. By
role playing to ideate, you will be generating solutions along the way. Generating situation-based ideas to feed your ideation and concept development is
sometimes referred to as "*body storming*."

HOW CAN YOU DO THIS?

1. **Define target user and outline the situational challenge.** Based on the
    challenge, identify whose pain points you would like to address. Think of
    a situation in which this end user struggles – it could be a situation where
    there is a physical or mental challenge, or a difficulty or barrier in their
    everyday life.
2. **Describe the activity.** Create an activity that will enable you to experience
    the world from your target's perspective. Do this by defining the person,
    their situation, and an activity that presents a challenge for them.
3. **Recreate the experience.** Use props, aids, or artifacts that help to simu-
    late the experience. View the world through this person's point of view
    by living their life for at least an hour. Fully immerse yourself in the
    activity, but keep your creative mind open to ideas that will resolve the
    various challenges throughout this person's journey.
4. **Capture your ideas.** If possible, have a member of your team record your ideas
    along the various stages of your experience in the user's circumstances.

Tips

▶ Reference the work you did in Current Journey to pinpoint the critical times in a user's journey and their "points of pain."

▶ Keep your needs and personas in mind to help keep your ideation focused and relevant to the user.

WHAT MIGHT THIS LOOK LIKE?

In a project on making a home more "kid-friendly," one might get down and crawl on the floor like a toddler. What you'll see might be frightening! You might see exposed plugs, small objects buried in the rug, food that someone dropped that has spoiled, or sharp edges on furniture. You can imagine the ideas (and empathy) that would come from such an ideation exercise.

METAPHORS
STIMULATING IMAGINATION

WHY DO WE DO THIS?

To stimulate imagination by creating an analogy between two unlike things.
Metaphors can be used to fuel brainstorming by transferring qualities or traits from one context onto another. Identifying and brainstorming off an analogous reference or inspiring metaphor can help to expand the pool of breakthrough ideas.

HOW CAN YOU DO THIS?

1. **Describe the "feeling" or outcome you would like to create.** Based on your unmet needs, describe the ideal outcome you would like to achieve through a new experience. *For example, in the activity of early childhood education, you found that kids wanted it to be more fun and engaging.*

2. **Think of analogies.** Based on that desired response or outcome, think of other things that elicit or deliver that reaction. Look to different industries to help open up a broader range of possibilities. *For example, if you were trying come up with ideas to help kids learn in a fun and engaging way, you would think of other ways that kids have fun – such as sports and video games. If you chose sports as the metaphor, you would pose this metaphorical question: If learning were a sport, what might that entail? What might that look like?*

3. **Transfer those attributes to your own challenge.** This step will help you to find alternate solutions and build on the ideas you already have. *In the case of childhood education, sports are active, competitive, interactive, and rewarding. A possible idea may be a math competition in schools where teams of students compete in physical and mental challenges to win prizes.*

Tips

▶ The greater the difference between the two things you are comparing, the more powerful the metaphor you will create (*e.g., education as a sport or a game*).

▶ Finding metaphors may take some practice to do correctly; it may take time to find one that is truly inspiring.

WHAT MIGHT THIS LOOK LIKE?

In the Princess Margaret Hospital project, a first-class airline seat was used as a metaphor to create a new chemotherapy experience. The need: to turn lost time into found time. Since patients sat in a chemo chair for hours on end, the team thought about other situations where people had to sit down for hours with limited mobility. They felt that a first-class airline chair was an appropriate metaphor. First-class chairs on airlines are designed to be luxurious, comfortable, and provide many amenities to passengers. While this metaphor may some day lead to the design of a new chair, it also inspired new services and access to activities to pass the time during treatment.

ITERATIVE PROTOTYPING
MAKING THE ABSTRACT CONCRETE

WHY TO WE DO THIS?

To stimulate thinking and dialogue by making abstract ideas tangible. Proto-typing helps you think through your ideas by building them out in a low-resolution, physical form. This exercise will help advance concept development through experimentation and is useful in getting instant feedback from users, particularly in combination with role plays or the presentation of experience maps or storyboards. Creating physical repre-sentations of key elements of your envisioned experience will help you think through and express:

How might this idea work?

What elements are critical in our envisioned experience? What is the role of each key element? What might it look like?

What aspects of this idea need to be further developed?

HOW CAN YOU DO THIS?

1. **Pick an idea that's only "conceptual" at this point and identify the most critical component.** Based on your early concepts, select one of the import-ant components that you would like to develop further. It may be one of those ideas that everyone gets excited about, but everyone may have a different picture in their heads about what that might look like or how it could play out. For example, it might be an object or an environment.

2. **Prototype that element of your idea.** Make it tangible by using inexpensive and easy-to-acquire materials (e.g., cardboard, markers, popsicle sticks, etc.). When building your prototype, think about what it might look like, how it may play out, what contest it is in, how it could be "built" to satisfy the user need. Your prototype should not resemble a finished, polished product, but should rather communicate the desired intent. A rapid prototype (i.e., one you devise during development) is:

   Quick and timely – The less time spent, the better.

   Inexpensive and disposable – Use inexpensive means and materials.

   Plentiful – Produce as many possible "expressions" of the concept and its component as you can.

3. **Explore how it works.** Place the prototype in the context of use to see how it functions or operates. Use role playing or storyboarding to present and communicate the prototype to gain feedback (*see Role Play to Advance Ideas, Storyboards, and In-Person Feedback*).

4. **Iterate and enhance.** Use your own intuition and feedback from others to improve the prototype for further testing. Critical feedback and continual testing will help to create a solution that satisfies all stakeholders.

Tips

▶ Low-resolution prototyping refers to physical representations of ideas that can be made with a small investment of time and money. Creating low-resolution prototypes helps you to visualize ideas, learn quickly, and reduce risk.

▶ You don't need expensive or sophisticated materials to create initial prototypes, just your imagination. Remember when you were a kid and made a house out of a big cardboard box? Be resourceful and improvise.

▶ Prototypes should not be of a higher resolution than what is needed to communicate the desired intent.

▶ It helps to use this method in conjunction with role playing and storyboarding. Doing this will aid you in both playing out your solution as a team to close the gaps and in presenting your low-resolution concepts to stakeholders in In-person Feedback.

WHAT MIGHT THIS LOOK LIKE?

A student team wanted to test an idea of an in-home organic waste disposal system. To explore how that idea might work in the home, they mocked up their concept in low-resolution, physical form with easily accessible materials (tape, cardboard, markers, pipe cleaners) and role-played their idea (Figure 56). They found that placement of the organic waste disposal within the kitchen and how it fit into their natural kitchen habits was important. This discovery inspired them to find ways to easily dispose of their waste and keep it out of sight and under the sink.

Fig. 56 **Prototyping a System for Organic Waste Disposal**

EXPERIENCE MAPPING
DESIGNING A NEW & IDEAL EXPERIENCE

WHY DO WE DO THIS?

To imagine how a big idea might play out as a seamlessly integrated user experience. Experience mapping tells the story of how a new solution will play out over time. Visualizing your ideas and concepts as a seamless, multidimensional experience will help close the gaps and enhance user value, moving from knitting together the "mechanics" to creating a compelling story. Designing an experience will help you think through these issues:

How does this new solution come to life in a seamless manner?

Are there gaps in this experience?

How does this experience address unmet needs?

Are there aspects of this experience that need to be further developed?

HOW CAN YOU DO THIS?

1. **Create a timeline.** Begin by drawing a line on a large piece of paper that represents the span of time your user will experience your envisioned solution. Depending on the amount of time it takes to complete the full product or service experience, this timeline can represent a few hours or be done over a few days.

2. **Plot the experience stages.** Along the timeline, create stages that begin with the user dilemma and move through the user's discovery of your solution, their experience with it, and the outcome or memory. Consider specifically how the user first finds out about the solution, how the user interacts with various components of the solution, and how the user reflects on how well the solution met his or her needs.

3. **Build out the experience.** Thinking about the logical and seamless progression of events in this experience, create a story that encompasses the ideal experience for your user, keeping in mind the POEMS framework. Consider the user's points of pain, emotional state, functional requirements, and

interactions with other stakeholders; be as detailed as possible. If you get stuck, role play from the user's point of view.

4. **Visualize the experience and tell the story.** Illustrate this experience by using pictures, sketches, and graphics. Create a compelling narrative to capture the full experience and the role of key design elements.

Tips

▶ Things to have on hand: Selected ideas from work you did in Ideation and Concept Harvesting, as well as the Need Articulation and Personas tools (always keep the user at the center of your designs).

▶ Having difficulty deciding where to begin your experience map? Begin with the moment of discovery and usage – where the "big idea" peaks. This may be in the middle of the journey. From there you can work out the "after stage" (where it leads) and the "before" stage (how the user got there).

▶ The ideas that you did not move forward with from the ideation phase can filter back into your experience map, to help fill in gaps and enhance the solution.

▶ Avoid being vague about stages in the experience; be as detailed as possible by using the POEMS framework to guide your exploration. Weave the POEMS components into your narrative in a relevant and natural way.

WHAT MIGHT THIS LOOK LIKE?

Figure 57 is a simple schematic that shows a segment of a patient experience, depicting how ideas were built into that experience along a timeline to continually enrich it and close the gaps.

Fig. 57 **Experience Mapping**

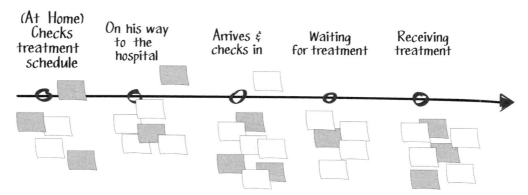

(At Home) Checks treatment schedule On his way to the hospital Arrives & checks in Waiting for treatment Receiving treatment

STORYBOARDING
CAPTURING THE STORY IN KEY FRAMES

WHY DO WE DO THIS?

To visualize your ideal solution as a stage-by-stage story of the ideal experience. Storyboarding is a cost-effective way to capture an experience to elicit feedback about the concept from the user. It is a more distilled and consolidated alternative to playing out the solution for users in In-Person Feedback, and can also be used as a synopsis of your idea in internal presentations by capturing the storyline of your experience and key design elements. It's like preparing to make a little movie or TV commercial.

HOW CAN YOU DO THIS?

1. **Create a narrative.** Reference the exercises you did in Experience Mapping to create a frame-by-frame story, including

    the *beginning*, which introduces the point of view, where the story takes place, and the conflict or situation;

    the *middle*, which describes the experience offered to the user in key stages – how they become aware of the solution, their experience with the solution, and the completion of that experience; and

    the *ending*, which concludes the story and summarizes the outcome.

2. **Select critical events.** Select the important parts of the story that reveal the design moments, considering the POEMS framework. (Design moments are parts of the solution that help influence the outcome of the story.) These can be captured in five to ten frames, depending on how multidimensional and extensive your concept is.

3. **Detail these moments.** List the actions and key components that need to be visualized though photography or drawings. Be as descriptive as possible and make note of the imagery that needs to be created to visualize the critical events. Create rough sketches to work through the visualization. This step helps to provide a coherent plan and focus communication.

4. **Complete the storyboard.** Refine your visuals and combine them with the written story to create a clear story of how your experience plays out.

Tips

▶ A storyboard is much like a comic book or the frame-by-frame reference for commercials or films. The story is communicated using text and key images to deliver important messages.

▶ Make the design elements as tangible as possible and avoid using generalities.

WHAT MIGHT THIS LOOK LIKE?

Figure 58 shows a few frames from the PMH storyboard to convey the ideal experience for a patient, beginning at home and traveling to the hospital.

Fig. 58 **Storyboarding Key Experience Points**

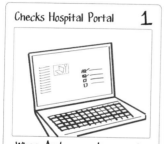

Checks Hospital Portal   1

When Andrew wakes up, he checks his treatment time online. The portal allows him to book his treatment pod and select his personalized services.

Uses Hospital Shuttle Bus   2

The shuttle bus that comes every 10 minutes picks up Andrew at the designated station and takes him straight to the hospital.

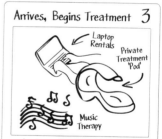

Arrives, Begins Treatment   3

Andrew begins to receive the treatment in his personal pod. He has access to a laptop, which is connected to the Internet, his e-mail, media channels, and a variety of music.

ROLE PLAY TO ADVANCE IDEAS
PLAYING OUT THE EXPERIENCE TO CLOSE THE GAPS

WHY DO WE DO THIS?

To play out solutions to identify gaps, solicit feedback, and create a natural and seamless experience for the user. Role playing uses improvisational acting to describe a multidimensional experience. Structurally, it's like storyboarding, but in real time. Role playing uses actors, props, a set, and a good storyline to communicate and demonstrate a new idea in real time to enhance your ideas. It can also be done with users, to get feedback on your ideas in co-creation. Creating a "play" on how your idea works will stimulate thinking, discussion, and helpful feedback.

HOW CAN YOU DO THIS?

1. **Develop a plot.** Based on your newly envisioned experience, define, and develop a plotline to demonstrate how the experience would work for the user.
2. **Set the stage.** Define and design the set, props, and roles that people on your team will play. The set and props should not be highly detailed and polished; rather, they should simply imply the setting and give a sense of the environment and objects.
3. **Role play.** Walk through the experience as a role play. The key is to improvise without a detailed script. Do this first with your team (to discover gaps or unnatural actions) and then (when you are ready) in front of others to gain feedback on what's working and what is not.
4. **Refine.** Evaluate what worked and what didn't work. Reference the In-Person Feedback exercise for tips on eliciting feedback.

Tips

▶ Use your experience map, storyboard, and prototype props in designing and playing out your solution.

▶ It is important not to make the role play too comical or absurd. Humorous interpretations of sensitive subject matter, such as personal or healthcare situations, must be handled with respect and care. Also, a role play is supposed to reflect real life; a comical interpretation may take away from the message being communicated.

This exercise should be coupled with the In-Person Feedback exercise to gain user feedback to help improve the experience.

WHAT MIGHT THIS LOOK LIKE?

To gain feedback from their target users, the Nestlé Confectionary team created multiple role plays that were targeted to different types of consumers, using low-resolution prototypes as props (Figure 59). The team gained instant and valuable feedback, which they used to enrich their concepts.

Fig. 59 **Role Playing an Experience Using Props**

IN-PERSON FEEDBACK
SOLICITING FEEDBACK & CO-CREATING

WHY DO WE DO THIS?

To engage others early in the development process as a way to enhance ideas. Co-creation enables others to provide honest, open feedback about new concepts. Bringing in perspectives from a variety of "users" of the solution will give you valuable insights into what will work and what will not. You can use an experience map, storyboards, or role playing to communicate how your idea works. *Most importantly, this is not a method of "evaluation," but rather one aimed at making your solution as relevant and rich as it can be.*

HOW CAN YOU DO THIS?

1. **Setup.** Before users are brought in to see your experience concept, be sure to assign individual team members to present, tell the story, take notes, and observe.

2. **Introduce the exercise.** The presenter should introduce the team and explain the purpose of the exercise and the feedback session. Be clear that the ideas are not final and that you would like their open, honest feedback.

3. **Present the experience prototype.** Present the experience to the user for no more than ten minutes. Be professional when presenting. Empathy is important in engaging the participant in a genuine effort to help serve them better.

4. **Solicit user feedback.** The presenter should lead the feedback session by asking the following questions:

   Is there anything you'd like us to clarify about how this might work?
   What's working for you?
   What's not working for you?
   How could it be better?
   What do you find most valuable?
   What parts of the solution do you consider game changing?

   As the user provides feedback, someone else should take detailed notes. The other team members should sit to the side and not to distract from or influence the discussion. They can ask questions once the presenter is done.

5. **Debrief as a team and iterate on your idea.** Discuss and capture the opportunities to enrich your ideas. If you presented a storyboard or experience map, work through the entire idea and note what worked, what did not, and how it could be improved. Discuss what you learned about where and how the idea added value for the user.

Tips

▶ There are a variety of prototyping methods that can be used for co-creation – role plays, experience maps, and storyboards. In early development, it is often preferable to use low-resolution methods to give the audience the sense that you are "inviting them into the development lab." The most important thing is being clear about your idea. Have a cohesive and compelling story to tell.

▶ Give the users a lot of credit. They are imaginative, intelligent, and generous in their effort to give you valuable feedback.

▶ Avoid defending your ideas in front of the user. Be open to their criticism and graciously accept their comments.

▶ Remember that this is a learning experience for the team. Ask open-ended questions and let the user freely express their opinions.

▶ This exercise also reveals new insights into your user, which may inspire more ideas that enrich the concept.

WHAT MIGHT THIS LOOK LIKE?

The Nestlé Confectionary team wanted to test out a new idea that targeted teens. Acting out the experience provided the team with insights into how teenagers would experience a new idea. The team played out a typical day in the life of a teenager, moving from a scene by the lockers in the hallway of a school to a mocked-up convenience store, to a computer in their room at home (Figure 60). The teenagers the team invited in for feedback totally grasped the low-resolution ideas and were eager to help make them better!

Fig. 60 **Co-creation and Recreating the High School Experience**

VIRTUAL FEEDBACK
SCALING FEEDBACK THROUGH TECHNOLOGY

WHY DO WE DO THIS?

To broaden engagement and scale feedback. This is a good way to capture insights from people who can't be reached in person. When timing and costs prevent you from conducting in-person feedback sessions, a virtual platform can be substituted. This approach can expand your engagement reach and help to scale more diversified feedback. It can also help you identify the "game changers."

HOW CAN YOU DO THIS?

1. **Select the concepts you would like to put out for feedback.** Pick a range of ideas to stimulate discussion on what works, what doesn't, and why. That will give you good insights.

2. **Select your virtual feedback platform.** It may be an existing platform that is available to use or license, or you may want to design your own customized version for ongoing use.

3. **Design your feedback plan.** Identify those you would like to engage (and how you will recruit them), what you would like to probe, and how participants might interact with each other or build on each other's comments.

4. **Put your concepts online.** Take photos of your prototypes, make a video of your role play, or present storyboards. Load them onto your virtual feedback platform.

5. **Solicit feedback and reflect.** Invite participants to weigh in. Then gather inputs and debrief with your team.

Tips

▶ Since you will not be there in person to explain your concepts, be sure that concept presentations are clear and represent your idea on their own.

▶ Make it easy to comment specifically on the key components of your idea(s) as well as its overarching concepts.

WHAT MIGHT THIS LOOK LIKE?

In the project for Canadian Bar Association, we uploaded nine concepts in storyboard form to a virtual platform. We rolled out a series of in-person meetings from east to west and then opened up the virtual community platform to the broader member community in each area. We asked them to weigh in on the concepts by providing comments and "liking" (or not) each other's comments. More than 2,000 members weighed in! At the end of this process, the winning (and losing) elements of the concepts became clear, and the ideas evolved to be more relevant and valuable.

GEAR 3: STRATEGIC BUSINESS DESIGN & ACTIVATION

—

264

This section presents a variety of methods to help you solidify your value proposition, identify key capabilities and potential partners, monetize your idea, and formulate a strategy in which all stakeholders win. From there, you will design a game plan, establish priorities for developing and testing initiatives, and organize people in your enterprise for innovation success. This process will help you establish strategic and tactical clarity in your path forward.

THE PROPOSITION
SYNTHESIZING THE VALUE OF YOUR IDEA

WHY DO WE DO THIS?

To capture the outputs of Gears 1 and 2 and translate them into a clear and succinct value proposition. This exercise will help clarify and summarize how your idea uniquely creates value and will anchor your business strategy.

HOW CAN YOU DO THIS?

Summarize your progress as a team by articulating and synthesizing the following:

1. **The Inspiration (Gear 1): Who is our target and what need will we satisfy?**
   Reprise your defined needs and personas.
   What need inspired your big idea?

2. **The Idea (Gear 2): What is your big idea?**
   Step back and discuss the big idea and the intent behind it.
   What is the overarching idea that captures the gestalt of how your game-changing components will satisfy needs?
   How would you explain your idea in one sentence?

3. **Value to the End User (Connecting Gear 1 to Gear 2)**
   How does your idea add value to their life in a meaningful way?
   How will they benefit most?

4. **What's the Overarching Proposition? (Synthesis of the above)**
   What will you uniquely offer the market?
   This proposition is a synthesis of target, offering, and need fulfillment (i.e., benefit).

Tips

▶ A strong central proposition will serve as the anchor in your strategy and a "lighthouse" in your ongoing quest to deliver the ultimate vision.

▶ Prompt discussion by asking, *What inspired you in the first place? How does this idea benefit end users in the most meaningful way? What appealed to them most?*

WHAT MIGHT THIS LOOK LIKE?

A good way to synthesize your value proposition is to capture the most inspiring need, your offering, and the value you bring to your primary target. In one of our Singapore projects, the team devised a new idea to "provide travelers with an authentic and unique gift collection of carefully selected, locally produced Singaporean bakery items to share with friends and family back home." Figure 61 illustrates how that translated into a clear and concrete proposition.[56]

Fig. 61 **Synthesizing the Opportunity**

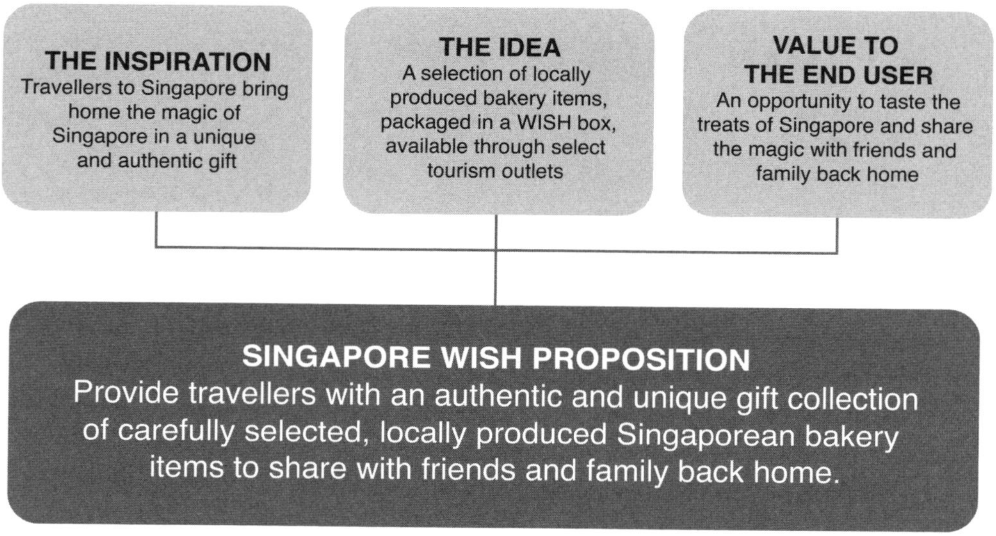

THE INSPIRATION	THE IDEA	VALUE TO THE END USER
Travellers to Singapore bring home the magic of Singapore in a unique and authentic gift	A selection of locally produced bakery items, packaged in a WISH box, available through select tourism outlets	An opportunity to taste the treats of Singapore and share the magic with friends and family back home

SINGAPORE WISH PROPOSITION
Provide travellers with an authentic and unique gift collection of carefully selected, locally produced Singaporean bakery items to share with friends and family back home.

CAPABILITY REQUIREMENTS
DELIVERING THE BREAKTHROUGH

WHY DO WE DO THIS?

To identify the capabilities that will be required to effectively and efficiently deliver your solution. This exercise translates design tactics into enterprise capabilities and then aligns those to internal or external resources. It is a useful way to identify new or enhanced capabilities and options for strategic partnerships.

HOW CAN YOU DO THIS?

This exercise is best done in tandem with designing your activity system and will shape your strategy for developing capabilities, defining what you do internally and externally. Your task is to determine the jobs to be done and who best to do them.

1. **List the components of your envisioned solution.** Identify the key components in the experience that need to be designed and delivered, including the people, objects, environments (spaces), media and messages, and services (POEMS).

2. **Identify the capabilities required to execute each component.** Capabilities are the expertise and capacity required to offer a product or service. *For example, if you are designing a new coffee system (as Nespresso did), you will need machine design, manufacturing and service access, and expertise.* At this point, don't concern yourself with whether you will do this yourself or partner with someone else.

3. **Identify internal capabilities.** Determine which current enterprise assets and capabilities can be leveraged to fulfill those requirements. If capabilities do not exist now, you will come to decide whether you will develop them internally or externally.

4. **Define your capability-building strategy.** If capabilities do not exist within your enterprise today, identify options to develop or access those capabilities through strategic partnerships.

5. **Estimate costs to develop new capabilities internally.** If you do not know specific numbers, use your intuition and define the relative measures of

high/medium/low as working measures. The amount of effort is also a good measure of the cost.

6. **Determine external expertise.** If capabilities are not available internally, begin to identify external sources of expertise through potential partnerships and suppliers.

7. **Assess your options and make choices.** Weigh the pros and cons of each scenario.

Tips

▶ It is helpful to refer to your final experience map or storyboard (if you have created these) and consider all components and design elements that make up your new idea.

▶ Consider both the "visible" and "invisible" elements of your success. For example, a direct-to-customer program will require some serious data management behind the scenes.

▶ Have your current-state activity system in hand to identify which current enterprise activities and capabilities could be leveraged.

▶ Keep your stakeholder personas and needs on hand.

▶ Brainstorm possible options for how you could build these capabilities.

▶ Strategic partnerships are an ideal way to leverage the capabilities of other organizations, if those capabilities do not exist with your own.

WHAT MIGHT THIS LOOK LIKE?

Figure 62 is a simple illustrative example of assessing the capabilities required to deliver Nespresso's vision:

Fig. 62 **Capability Requirements**

TACTICAL COMPONENT	CAPABILITIES REQUIRED	CURRENT ENTERPRISE	COST TO DEVELOP INTERNALLY	EXTERNAL SOURCES OF EXPERTISE	DEVELOPMENT STRATEGY
Coffee Capsule	Quality coffee and delivery technology	Sourcing, patented technology and production expertise	Medium (to advance, perfect, & expand)	Not needed	Develop internally
High-Style, Quality Coffee Maker	World-class industrial design	Limited	Medium (but not currently core expertise)	Alessi	Work with top external designers
	Appliance expertise and manufacturing capacity	None	High	Krups, Magimix	Develop strategic partnerships
Brand Marketing	Branding & communications	Access to world-class marketing expertise & agency partners	Low-medium	Marketing partners	Develop internally, working with brand marketing partners
Direct Marketing	Database management, call center, & fulfillment excellence	Some corporate experience, though not core practice	Medium	Direct marketing partners	Work with marketing partners
Fair Value Program	Grower relations & practice expertise	Nestlé expertise and established practices	Medium, if leverage parent company	Not needed	Develop in tandem with Nestlé

Gear 3: Strategic Business Design & Activation

MONETIZATION
EXPLORING HOW TO CAPTURE VALUE

WHY DO WE DO THIS?

To identify opportunities to monetize your envisioned solution. There are often opportunities to monetize a solution beyond how you would normally charge the customer for your product or service. Now is the time to explore ways to capture value and define your business model. In combination with market sizing (see the Market Sizing tool), identifying monetization opportunities will help you make a business case for how your idea will boost existing sales or create new streams of revenue.

HOW CAN YOU DO THIS?

1. **Explore ways to monetize your envisioned experience.** Begin by examining your envisioned experience and consider what your broad spectrum of stakeholders might be willing to pay for. Ideate on how you might capture value:

   Will you sell more of your existing products? (e.g., cross-sell more of your portfolio of products by integrating them as a synergistic system)

   Will you sell new products? (e.g., a new product that expands your portfolio)

   Will you sell others' products and make a profit? (e.g., Apple selling peripheral products, such as speakers)

   Will you leverage your reach and sell advertising on your site? (e.g., Google)

   Will you generate revenue through event sponsorships? (e.g., Red Bull)

   Will you generate data that others will pay for? (e.g., Facebook)

   Will you sell services? (e.g., IBM selling consulting services)

   Are there other ways in which you can charge for the value of your products, services, expertise, or knowledge?

2. **Size up the market of "payers."** For each of your monetization ideas, identify who will pay and how many of them are there. As presented in the Market Sizing tool, you might begin by estimating the total available market (a function of the "payers" you choose to serve). You can then scale that back to the serviceable available market – the subsegment you are able to reach geographically or through technology access (a function of where you decide to operate). Then you can estimate what share of that market you might capture, based on your offering and competition.

3. **Estimate what market payers might be willing to pay.** Based on the perceived value of your offer, competitive offerings, and any price research you may have conducted, estimate the value of what you are selling. You might want to look at a range of pricing schemes to test your options.

4. **Assess your options.** Considering the number of payers that might find value in your proposition and the price you might charge, then run some numbers to test the potential of revenue streams. Prioritize your sources of potential revenue gains and determine which options enable you to capture the most value. Identify the top three sources of potential revenue gains.

5. **Focus your business model.** Run the numbers on the scenarios that offer the greatest opportunity for you to capture value. The result of this exploration and assessment will form the basis of your business case to invest in your new idea and realize a return on that investment.

Tips

▶ Look at a broad set of considerations, drawing inspiration from other business models, as noted above. This is an iterative prototyping process!

▶ Done in combination with your work on the landscape of players, concept visualization, and market sizing, you will be able to develop a viable revenue model and business case.

▶ Run lots of numbers to ascertain where the greatest yield might be.

▶ Be careful not to be overly optimistic. For each scenario, consider competitive benchmarks, pricing alternatives, and potential number of customers. Look at the best, worst, and most likely projections.

▶ Be careful not to rely on selling "data" if you do not yet have the traction and scale you need to make a reasonable business case, though that is a valid upstream monetization opportunity. However, if you have good data on your users, there is value in offering a targeted channel for others to promote their products and services.

WHAT MIGHT THIS LOOK LIKE?

As an example of possible streams of revenue, imagine a company that gives away free open-source software to enterprises and upsells customers to their professional services to help customize and optimize adoption of that software: this company's model is sourcing revenue from "services" rather than a "product." You can also imagine how broad adoption of that "free software" might translate to a huge customer base that generates numerous insights useful to other interested parties.

VALUE EXCHANGE
DESIGNING A SUSTAINABLE BUSINESS ECOSYSTEM

WHY DO WE DO THIS?

To map and assess the value exchange among key stakeholders in your solution.
This exercise helps to ensure balanced exchange and, therefore, sustainability.
To create a balanced exchange of value in the delivery of your new solution, it
is important to address these questions:

> *Who are the stakeholders involved in buying, contributing to, or delivering our
> solution?*

> *What kind of "value" is being exchanged? Where is the money?*

> *How is value exchanged among stakeholders, including our enterprise?*

> *Do all stakeholders win?*

HOW CAN YOU DO THIS?

This exercise is best done in tandem with defining your stakeholder map,
capability requirements, monetization, and designing your strategic activity
system (which might include capabilities that you will fulfill through outside
partners).

1. **Define stakeholders and their roles.** Identify all of the relevant stakeholders
   involved in your solution, including those who will buy it, influence purchase,
   or help deliver it. *For example, in delivering a unique gift collection of locally produced Singaporean bakery items (called WISH), the role of the producers could be
   to produce, manufacture, and co-pack multiple products from various producers.*

2. **Define the key design elements (POEMS) and how they are delivered.**
   Detail how the design elements will be created, produced, and delivered
   to the end customer. *For example in WISH, referrals by tourism partners (e.g.,
   airlines), the flagship shop, and the WISH box itself were critical components
   in delivering the overall idea.*

3. **Look for ways to efficiently scale through the ecosystems.** Think of both
   the cost of developing capabilities, as well as the effectiveness of the value

chain. *In the example of WISH, existing capacity was utilized as the most cost-efficient approach in production and co-packing, as opposed to outsourcing co-packing to a third party, which would add extra cost to the value chain. Also, collaboration with others in the tourism business would mean quick and broad access; so too for distribution through existing high-traffic retailers.*

4. **Define how all parties may benefit and make money.** Define, in the broadest sense, what each stakeholder contributes to value creation and what they get in return, including if and where stakeholders make money. *In the WISH example, the most obvious source of revenue is the sale of the WISH box (for which retailers and the producers benefit), but there are other partners that need to be paid to create and deliver all the necessary design components.*

5. **Visualize the exchange of value among them.** Prototype the ecosystem by linking stakeholders to the delivery of the solution. Use sticky notes and large surfaces to prototype your value-exchange system.

6. **Look for additional sources of financing and revenue.** While you may already have identified the obvious ways to make money (such as selling a core product or service) look for additional revenue streams. *In the case of WISH, others interested in the promotion of Singapore were invited to join the network and contribute their expertise or sponsorship.*

7. **Prototype, iterate, and refine.** Start with an initial prototype and ask yourself, Is this the most effective and efficient way to deliver our envisioned solution? Are there other ways to go about this, ways to do this more cost-effectively or establish other potential streams of revenue? *In the case of WISH, there are future possibilities to capture revenue from tourism sponsors and public supporters promoting Singapore.*

8. **Evaluate the unique role of your enterprise.** Determine how you are uniquely positioned to create this solution and succeed. Reflect on the existing capabilities and interdependent relationships, and determine if these can be distinctly leveraged to attain success and competitive advantage. *In the case of Singapore WISH, the tight network of producers that deliver authentic Singaporean treats is not something anyone else could pre-empt or replicate, as it is the source of products that are unique to Singaporean tradition.*

Tips

▶ Your envisioned experience map will be an important reference, as you will want to preserve the intent of your envisioned solution.

▶ Your stakeholder map, personas, and needs are helpful references to ensure that you deliver value to key stakeholders – the end user in particular.

▶ This is an iterative process; stakeholders and elements can be rearranged to reveal different models of value exchange. Using tools such as sticky notes and an erasable white board will allow you to quickly plot and reorganize your visualization.

▶ Consider ways to refine the exchange system and improve both viability and efficiency by looking to external partners and technology. The landscape of players you may have developed earlier will come in handy. Imagine all possible partners who could help you deliver your new idea and how they could both bring and receive value.

WHAT MIGHT THAT LOOK LIKE?

For the WISH project, the team devised a new idea to "provide travelers with an authentic and unique gift collection of carefully selected, locally produced Singaporean bakery items to share with friends and family back home."[57] *To bring this WISH Box to life, they tapped into the motivations and capabilities of a variety of local stakeholders, and defined the role of each of the stakeholders in developing and delivering key components of the envisioned experience. Figure 63 illustrates how everyone wins! Dollar signs indicate where financial benefit lies for stakeholders.*

Fig. 63 **Singapore WISH Value Exchange**

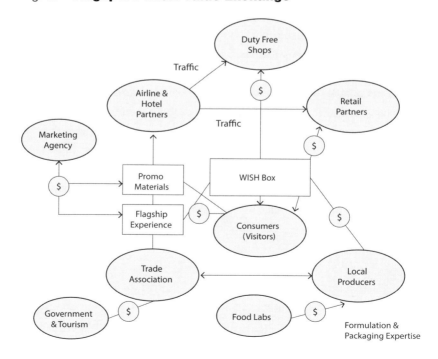

RECIPROCITY
BALANCING VALUE EXCHANGE
WITH KEY PARTNERS

WHY DO WE DO THIS?

To ensure a balanced give and take between your enterprise and critical strategic partners within your value-creation ecosystem. Reciprocity is a key consideration in designing a sustainable business system. Compared to the broader value exchange the previous tool focused on, this tool zeros in on key strategic partners. Reciprocity will ensure that you are in a *balanced exchange* of value with each of your key partners, in both financial and non-financial terms. It will address the critical question, *Are we set up for a sustainable partnership?*

HOW CAN YOU DO THIS?

1. **Identify the partners that are critical to your success.** They are key to activating your strategy, creating value, and fortifying your competitive advantage.

2. **Articulate what value each of them give to and receive from your enterprise.** The value could be financial (they receive money), reputational (their status or brand image is enhanced), or practical (e.g., they obtain access to new markets or information that benefits them).

3. **For each designated partner, assess the balance of give and take.** However value is defined to that partner, it is important to design for a fair and balanced exchange.

4. **Assess how your enterprise adds unique value to your partners' pursuits.** Most important is to ensure that your enterprise is uniquely positioned to both deliver on your proposition and bring distinct value to them, and that you cannot be swapped out for another enterprise. This factor is critical to strategic sustainability.

A picture of reciprocity is easily captured by creating a simple "balance sheet" chart, as shown in Figure 64.

Tips

▶ Value is neither just about money nor strictly two-way transactions. In this exercise, you address the broader motivation of and benefits for your partners in your value-creation system.

▶ Committing to a strategic-partnership exchange requires ongoing effort in understanding the needs of your important partners, as well as a continuing search for ways to fortify your position over time. Maintaining this balance is key to sustaining the ecosystem.

▶ It is helpful to refer the exercises on Capability Requirements and Activity System (Future), along with the work you'll generate from them.

WHAT MIGHT THAT LOOK LIKE?

An excellent example of an enterprise that has a well-balanced ecosystem is Nespresso. It has multiple stakeholders – consumers, retailers, farmers, environmental alliances, machine designers, manufacturers, and servicers. It is fully committed to everyone winning and it continually brings value to every stakeholder in the system. It also brings unique capabilities to the system in marketing, proprietary capsule technology, quality assurance, and global access. The chart in Figure 64 gives you a simple snapshot of what some of the stakeholders give and receive, and how Nespresso adds value for them.

Fig. 64 Assessment of Balanced Exchange

STRATEGIC PARTNER	WHAT THEY GIVE	WHAT THEY RECEIVE	HOW NESPRESSO ADDS VALUE FOR THEM
Machine manufacturers	Manufacturing capability and capacity	Capacity utilization, revenue, quality brand-name visibility and association	Access to global distribution, proprietary capsule technology, commitment to quality, marketing expertise, and a strong brand
Retailers (outside the flagship boutiques)	Consumer access through mini-boutiques	Revenue from sales, merchandising support	Marketing expertise and strong brand image / demand
Coffee bean growers	Quality beans	Revenue, help in business and growing practices	Shared value thorough a commitment to fair trade and expertise in business and growing practices

MARKET SIZING
QUANTIFYING THE MARKET OPPORTUNITY

WHY DO WE DO THIS?

To size the market opportunity for your envisioned solution. By understanding how many users and/or buyers your target market represents and how many you can potentially reach, serve, and (ultimately) sell to, you will be able to build a business case for potential revenue. This exercise is best done in tandem with Monetization to estimate the revenue potential of your idea.

HOW CAN YOU DO THIS?

A simple way to view and quantify your market is the framework of Total Available Market (TAM), Serviceable Available Market (SAM), and Serviceable Obtainable Market (SOM).

1. **Define your TAM.** Start by estimating the number of customers for your solution, assuming there are no market-access constraints or competitors. TAM can also be thought of as the total market demand for your product or service, initially without any constraints by choice, competition, or conditions. *For example, you might have an idea for a technology product that serves entrepreneurs. How many of them are there in the world?*

2. **Define your SAM.** Next, adjust that number downward based on the geographies and languages you might serve, your capacity to reach and serve them, and the conditions under which they might access your solution. Consider geographic constraints, your current internal capabilities to serve them, and other conditions, such as technology-access regulatory restrictions. *For example, you might preliminarily choose to offer a product for English-speaking entrepreneurs in developed markets with good Internet access.*

3. **Define your SOM.** Finally, consider the current and potential competitors in your defined space and estimate what share of the market you might capture. *For example, your market assessment might lead you to conclude that you could potentially capture 10 per cent of the SAM based on the competitive landscape and the (range of) pricing you envision.*

4. **Review and reflect.** Consider your SOM in terms of your aspirations and the expectations of your stakeholders, and re-evaluate the feasibility and viability of your solution.

Tips

▶ This exercise draws on the work you did in some of the other tools – Landscape of Players (*Who else is operating in this space?*), Concept Visualization (*How unique is your idea?*), Monetization (*Who will pay and how much?*) – and, ultimately, on the markets in which you choose to operate.

▶ Be realistic, not hopeful. Work with realistic constraints and don't overestimate your potential market share. Those who invest in ideas are often looking for a conservative estimate to ensure they are placing their bets on idea with a reasonable return.

▶ While TAM and SAM are very fact based, SOM requires some judgment; where there is judgment, there is risk. Run lots of scenarios. Investment decisions will be based on the potential upside, downside, and most likely scenarios.

WHAT MIGHT THAT LOOK LIKE?

Figure 65 visualizes how your business goal is a subset of the larger universe of customers.

Fig. 65 **Market Sizing**

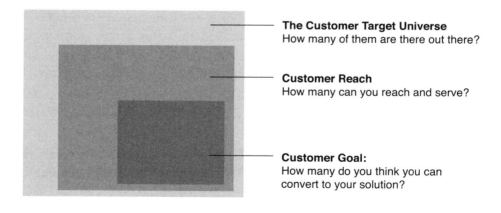

The Customer Target Universe
How many of them are there out there?

Customer Reach
How many can you reach and serve?

Customer Goal:
How many do you think you can convert to your solution?

FINANCIAL SENSITIVITY ANALYSIS

ASSESSING UNCERTAINTY & RISK

WHY DO WE DO THIS?

To assess and mitigate investment risk by identifying what could have significant impact on your financial outcomes. A financial sensitivity analysis will inform how you design your development plan and enterprise strategy to maximize success. It will define which experiments you will conduct (see the Experiments and Risk Assessment tool) and will also inform the work you do on the Capabilities, Activity System, and Value Exchange tools.

Most companies have strong financial acumen and can run lots of numbers to calculate revenue scenarios and variations in known costs. The following tips are geared to helping you isolate and examine the unknown variables (often operationally based) that can have unexpectedly negative financial consequences if not considered and tested properly. Having defined tangible solutions and the play-by-play of the experience, you will be equipped to determine which variables present risk. At this point, you need to take a critical and analytical look at what could go wrong, what the financial impact might be, and most importantly, design your experiments to test assumptions and your strategic system to reduce risk and maximize the chances of success.

HOW CAN YOU DO THIS?

1. **Deconstruct your experience and assess the certainty of executing design elements.** Identify the key components that compose the solution and identify which are more certain and which are unknown. *For example: If you are strong at manufacturing familiar products, you can likely predict quality and the cost of delivered goods. If your solution calls for a new mode of delivery, such as distribution through new sites or technologies, you may be unfamiliar with how that works and with the associated costs.*

2. **Identify the variable costs and revenue drivers associated with that experience.** For each stage of your solution, identify the following:

   Variable costs – expenses that change in proportion to business activity (e.g., call-center activity, service calls) and operational uncertainties, particularly things that might go wrong; and

Revenue drivers – activities that determine the amount of money a company receives over time (e.g., sales by channel of distribution).

3. **Isolate the unknown factors, state your assumptions, and test financial sensitivities.** Based on your collective experience and intuition, determine which of the unknown variables can have the biggest impact on financial performance. These are the ones you will want to explore first in spreadsheet form, then test in the real world. If you have negative outcomes, redesign your delivery model to mitigate risk. *For example, you may explore the relative daily sales through two different points of distribution (e.g., an office site and a convenience store).*

4. **Design learning experiments.** Experiments are not necessarily aimed at go/no go decisions (though they can be) but, more importantly, at testing your underlying assumptions and gaining knowledge of what you need to consider and do to maximize success.

Tips

▶ It is helpful to refer to your experience map with an eye to the costs and uncertainties in delivering that experience and each component.

▶ This exercise does not include fixed costs, such as capital and building a website, though they will definitely factor into your overall payout plan. This exercise focuses on identifying high-risk variables.

▶ Conversely, those elements that represent low risk may proceed in development or be rolled out as quick wins. (See Quick Wins.)

WHAT MIGHT THAT LOOK LIKE?

Imagine this scenario: A manufacturer of packaged goods has envisioned a new experience that involves giving consumers on-location access to their products through a novel new vending-machine technology. Consumers love the idea of the machine, but the company has no experience in producing, selling, or maintaining this new technology. When they examine their envisioned experience, they see a rise in vending-machine durability and potential maintenance costs. Their financial analyses for a scenario with high traffic (good for revenue) and a range of "breakdowns" due to low durability (bad for costs) leads them to rethink their business model and their role in selling and manufacturing vending machines versus subcontracting this role to deliver their envisioned experience. This rethinking, in turn, leads to some important strategic decisions.

ACTIVITY SYSTEMS (FUTURE)
DESIGNING A STRATEGY TO WIN

WHY DO WE DO THIS?

To translate your new vision into an enterprise strategy to win and provide a framework for activation. Visualizing your strategy as a distinct system of interrelated activities will define how you will create value in a distinct and competitive way. It will focus your efforts on the areas of activity and capability-building that matter most to your success.

HOW CAN YOU DO THIS?

Like much of the Business Design process, Gear 3 is an iterative process and incorporates the work you do in other areas, such as capability requirements, value exchange, and reciprocity. Your envisioned activity system takes these elements into account and sets the stage for activation. Here is a general guideline on how to go about designing your new activity system, once again using Nespresso as an example.

1. **Reprise your proposition.** This is your synthesis of the opportunity and value proposition that serves as the anchor in your quest. *For Nespresso: Creating moments of delight for coffee lovers worldwide.*

2. **Decide which combination of activities will be most critical to your success.** These are the key four or five "hubs" that will enable you to deliver on your proposition and create the most value for your customer – and, ultimately, the greatest return on investment for the enterprise. They will include both what you will do internally and what important alliances you will cultivate external to your enterprise. Because they are activity based, it is helpful to articulate these themes by phrasing them as something you actively ***do***: *For example, Deliver a Uniquely Integrated Coffee System, Deliver a Premium Coffee Experience, Cultivate Direct Brand/Consumer Relationships and Create Shared Value* (environmental and social responsibility). These are the core, interrelated hubs in the system.

3. **Define how these hubs relate to one another.** All good systems are synergistic, and activities are mutually reinforcing. In the case of Nespresso, many of the hubs are mutually reinforcing. *For example, delivering a premium coffee experience is related to delivering a uniquely integrated and stylish coffee system.*

4. **Identify specific activities and capabilities to activate these hubs.** These are specific activities that focus efforts on delivering tangible outcomes. *In the case of Nespresso, partnerships with appliance manufacturers specifically reinforce delivery of an integrated and stylish coffee system. The proprietary capsule reinforces both this coffee system and the delivery of a premium coffee experience. Nespresso boutiques reinforce both the premium experience and personalized relationships.*

5. **Assess, iterate, and define your strategy as a distinct and synergistic system.** As with the exercise of capturing your current state, this process of synthesis and visualization is iterative. You work through the design of your system until you believe you have a tightly connected, synergistic, and unique system of activities.

Tips

▶ Designing an activity system is an iterative thinking process that leads you to a tightly integrated set of choices. Don't try to be too perfect at the beginning; as noted in earlier tools, you might use paper plates and sticky notes to work through your thinking as a "prototyping" exercise.

▶ The earlier tools on Value Exchange and Reciprocity will inform how you configure your activity systems, and that will clarify strategic partner relationships. *For example, you might choose not to do something that one of your partners could do for you (as with Nespresso choosing to outsource design and manufacturing).*

▶ It is valuable to capture the strategy depicted by your activity system in a story to explain how the system works and uniquely creates value. This story should describe how you create value through the following:
   Overarching proposition: What will we uniquely offer the market?
   Hubs: What are the core drivers of success that define our strategy?
   Activities: What specific and concrete activities reinforce those hubs?
   Relationships: How do hubs and activities relate to and reinforce one another?

▶ In fully assessing your new activity system, refer to Activity System Assessment, the tool that directly follows this one.

WHAT MIGHT THAT LOOK LIKE?

Figure 66 shows how your paper-plate and sticky-note exercise might look as you work through your visual depiction of your future strategy. Figure 67 shows a more refined version of Four Seasons' system.[58]

Fig. 66 **Prototype of Nespresso Activity System**

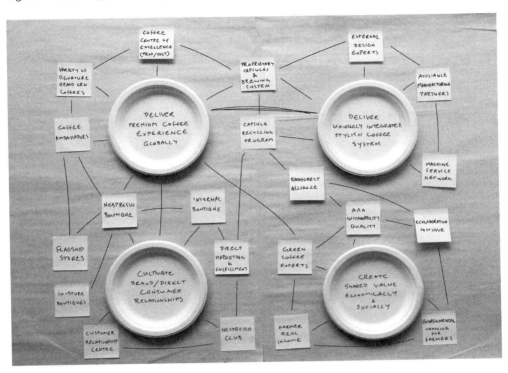

Fig. 67 **Four Seasons' Activity System**

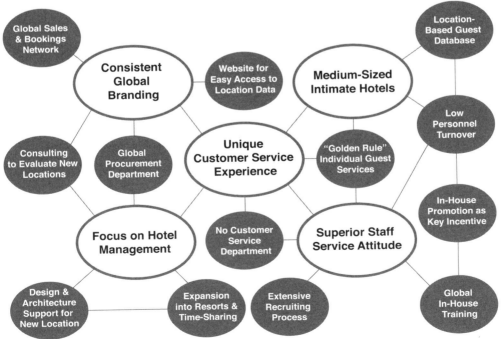

ACTIVITY SYSTEM ASSESSMENT

EVALUATING YOUR ENTERPRISE STRATEGY

WHY DO WE DO THIS?

To evaluate your future strategy as a means of creating and sustaining new value. This is the ultimate test of your strategy, as it will define your sustainable competitive advantage. Your goal is to advance your future distinctiveness and potential to create and sustain value beyond your current position, as defined earlier in this Tool Kit (see Activity System [Current State]).

HOW CAN YOU DO THIS?

Ask yourself the following questions:

1. **Does your envisioned strategy create value?**

    How will the envisioned strategy create value for end users? How will this system of activities meet their unmet needs in a new and meaningful way?

    How do the activities create value for the enterprise?

    How does the strategy create value for other key shareholders? How will they win? (Refer to the Value Exchange tool.)

2. **Is your strategy breakthrough?**

    To what extent does your new activity system enable you to deliver a meaningful and new proposition to the market?

    How does it change the rules of the game vis-à-vis the competition and within the current landscape of players?

    Does it represent a meaningful evolution of your current strategy?

3. **Is it distinctive?**

    Is your market-inspired idea and set of enterprise activities distinctive in the market relative to known competitors in this game? (See Activity Systems [Competition].)

    Could it preempt other (anticipated) players in the landscape?

    Does this strategic activity system give you a distinct advantage?

4. **Does the system fit?**

   How do the activities complement and reinforce each other? Is it a cohesive and synergistic set of activities?

   How does it leverage what you are already good at doing? Does it fit with your current strategy or does it represent a significant departure from your current strategy?

5. **Does this system create sustainable advantage?**

   How long can you sustain an advantage with this strategy?

   How likely is it to be imitated?

   What about your envisioned system is difficult for others to replicate?

Tips

▶ Now is the time to be objective and analytical, not enthusiastic because you are in love with your ideas and vision. If your system "fails the test," revisit it and design ways to make it stronger and more distinctive.

▶ This exercise is best done as a group, with candor and objectivity. You'll find it solidifies your collective commitment.

▶ Get the objective input of others; call on senior mentors and trusted industry experts.

STRATEGIC FOCUS
CLARIFYING YOUR DEFINING CHOICES

WHY DO WE DO THIS?

To focus the strategic choices that will enable you to deliver on your new value proposition. Making clear choices is the final step in solidifying your strategy. An unambiguous and precise encapsulation of your strategy and activation priorities will guide your enterprise forward.

HOW CAN YOU DO THIS?

1. **What are your aspirations and goals?** Articulate your renewed aspiration to reflect the breakthrough thinking you've had as you went through the 3 Gears of Business Design. Set measurable goals.

2. **Where will you play?** Review the results of your market scoping and sizing activity, as well as your new business model, and list the specific customer segments you will target, geographies you will serve, channels you will use, and product or service segment in which you will compete.

3. **How will you win?** Review your value proposition and activity system to focus how you will compete in your chosen market(s). Define the four to five ways in which you will uniquely win.

4. **What capabilities will you need?** Identify the capabilities that are essential for the development and delivery of your value proposition. Decide whether you will source those capabilities in-house, or outsource to vendors or partners.

5. **What management systems will you need?** Identify the unique management systems (e.g. processes, tools, and metrics) that will support your efforts and enable you to win.

Tips

▶ Key inputs include the work you did with the following tools: The Proposition, Capability Requirements, and Activity Systems (Future).

▶ Aim to be razor sharp in your choices.

▶ Assess your set of choices for distinctiveness. Ask yourself, *Will this position our enterprise to distinctly deliver on our promise?*

▶ Be clear on how you will measure progress and ultimate success.

WHAT MIGHT THIS LOOK LIKE?

Figure 68 illustrates how the Canadian Foundation for Healthcare Improvement synthesized their choices on one page after going through the Business Design process, as recounted in the interview in chapter 6. Based on the clarity of their strategy, they secured a significant increase in federal funding because their proposition was so clear, compelling, and distinct.[59]

Fig. 68 **One-Page Strategic Synthesis**

Canadian Foundation for **Healthcare Improvement** Fondation canadienne pour **l'amélioration des services de santé**

CFHI Strategy

Aspirations:

- To deliver demonstrable results for Canadians by improving patient/family experience and care, population health and value-for-money
- To be recognized as the leader in supporting the implementation, spread and scale of healthcare improvement across Canada
- To remain adaptable in a changing environment and achieve longer-term sustainable funding

Goals:

- Evalutate, analyze and communicate widely the results of CFHI's collaboratives
- Initiate new collaboratives, one of which will include palliative care
- Work with multiple jurisdictions to support culturally appropriate and safe care for Indigenous Peoples in Canada
- Continue the EXTRA program
- Seek renewed funding from the federal government
- Identify and receive revenue from sources beyond the federal government

Strategy:

Where to Play

- Pan-Canadian (e.g. multi-jurisdictional)
- Jurisdiction or system specific scale
- Appropriate care for patients who need it most (e.g. the 5% and complex chronic conditions)
- Palliative care
- Healthcare delivery organizations committed to improvement
- Cross sector & inter-professional teams
- Where improvement capabilities make a difference and achieve better patient care, better health and better value

How to Win

- **Build leadership and skill capacity:** We enhance organizational capacity to champion and lead improvement
- **Enable patient, family and community engagement:** We catalyze healthcare innovation by involving those who experience, and need care as experts in improvement and co-design
- **Apply improvement methodology:** We use improvement tools and methods to drive measureable results towards better patient care, better health and better value
- **Create collaboratives to spread evidence-informed improvement:** We bring together "coalitions of the willing" and support these networks of change agents to implement improvement across Canada

Mission:

The Canadian Foundation for Healthcare Improvement identifies proven innovations and accelerates their spread across Canada by supporting healthcare organizations to adapt, implement and measure improvements in patient care, population health and value-for-money.

Key Measurements:

A suite of measures, including:

- Changes in patient experience of care over targeted time (e.g. care transition measures, Hospital Consumer Assessment of Healthcare Providers and Systems)
- Changes in patient health outcomes over targeted time (e.g. exacerbations, adverse effects, evidence of lives improved, patient-reported outcome measures)
- Changes in per capita costs of care over targeted time (e.g. utilization rates)
- Number of patients, providers and leaders reached by CFHI programming

- Changes in leaders' capacity to assess, design, implement and measure improvement over targeted time
- Changes in improvement team effectiveness score over targeted time
- Changes in collaborative maturity scale over targeted time
- Changes in improvement team ability to sustain and spread over targeted time
- Spread of knowledge and growth of improvement leadership network over targeted time
- Longer-term sustainable funding from multiple sources

EXPERIMENTS & RISK ASSESSMENT

TESTING THE UNKNOWNS

WHY DO WE DO THIS?

To gain valuable learning that will shed light on uncertainties and potential risks, giving you the confidence to move to the next level of development and rollout. Experiments are a form of prototyping that provide observable and measurable learning outcomes about whatever part of your new idea has never been done (by you, and even others). Experimentation is a good way to "test the waters" on market uptake and to explore risk variables from your financial sensitivity analysis. The goal of experiments is to gain learning on how to design the best means of delivering your vision and fortify your **reason to believe**.

HOW CAN YOU DO THIS?

1. **Isolate the elements of your idea that present the most uncertainty and potential risk.** These are the elements that, if they go wrong, put the whole experience or business model at risk, and they are often revealed through financial sensitivity analysis of variables. You are dependent on these elements for success. Clearly state your underlying assumptions.

2. **Create a hypothesis.** For each experiment, use your intuition to predict how it will help you learn how to increase the odds of success. To generate a hypothesis, use the critical assumptions that present the most risk. *Examples of working hypotheses: Doctors appreciate and use patient counseling tools; Customers will be drawn to a product that is made available at a new site; Customers will use and appreciate a technical hotline; An institutional dispensing machine be usable and durable in a designated high traffic site.*

3. **Design an experiment.** Create a small-scale experiment to test your hypothesis by brainstorming several options to gain more insights or information. Make sure you are clear on what needs to be measured and how you will measure it. *For instance, if you are wondering about the relative sales of a product through two different channels or the impact of having a salesperson on site or not, set up a paired comparison experiment.*

4. **Define your expected use of results.** It is important to anticipate the range of results you might get, including worst-case scenarios. Define what kinds of results are you hoping for (in measurable terms) and what you will do if you don't achieve those results. This is not necessarily a go/no-go experiment, but rather a way to gain learning so you can design alternatives to mitigate risk and be more assured of the path you subsequently decide to take. Even if you fail, you will gain valuable insights on how to resolve or improve your solution.

5. **Execute, evaluate, and refine.** Determine what you will do with the learning to move the idea forward. Use this information to refine each element, or use it to revisit your activity system, or as evidence that your idea will work and your strategy is sound.

Tips

▶ Reference your envisioned experience map, prototypes, activity system, and financial sensitivity assessment when identifying key experiments.

▶ Time and money spent testing and validating executional variables at an early stage can help you to both "test the waters" on market interest and avoid costly mistakes – which will improve your payout in the long term. With a small investment of time and money, you can create experiments to help you enrich your idea and ultimately grow your business. Try imposing financial constraints to think of new ways to test your assumptions. *For example, re-skin an existing piece of equipment in a new location instead of redesigning something new that will take more money and time.*

▶ Experiments should produce measurable outcomes and actionable learning.

WHAT MIGHT THAT LOOK LIKE?

In the early days of Nespresso, former CEO Jean-Paul Gaillard's team went out to home-appliance outlets in Geneva, Lausanne, and Nyon and started selling machines to individual customers. His goal was to try this for a week to see if they could sell 100 machines. In the end, they sold 58 (in addition to 25 sold to offices), which helped Gaillard and his team learn that there was a market for these products. Previous market research had concluded that there was no market. From there, Gaillard moved ahead and launched Nespresso nationally in Switzerland.[60]

QUICK WINS
CAPITALIZING ON LEARNING OUT OF THE GATE

WHY DO WE DO THIS?

To activate your new learning and ideas in a way that will benefit your business in the short term and set you on the path toward your new vision. The Business Design process will yield value at every stage of discovery and development. Unlike an experiment, there is little or no risk associated with a quick win. On the contrary, quick wins enable you to leverage new insights and ideas to make an immediate positive impact on your business.

Sometimes quick wins are about improving on something you were already doing. Sometimes they are about replacing a tactic that doesn't create much user value with one that does. Often, a quick win can be knocking something off your to-do list that wasn't really going to create value at all. These are all quick wins, and this is where Business Design can save you time and money. Take stock of all of your learning and ideas and ask, *How could we create value* **now**?

HOW CAN YOU DO THIS?

1. **Reflect on the learning from your development process that is relevant to your current business.** This may be a new insight that inspires a tactical move to help you address a short-term challenge, or an idea from your grander vision that fits well with your current strategy and activities.

2. **Identify the smaller, tactical elements of your idea that can benefit your business today.** These are the elements for which you are confident that there is virtually no downside but good potential upside. Such elements could include ways to better serve the end user or to enhance the motivation and engagement of an important enabler. These are the ideas that you should not hold back: they are valuable to the stakeholders and/or the enterprise today. Ideas may come in any form – process improvement, revenue-generating opportunities, new distribution channels, better communications, or an improvement to a product or service that can make it better almost right away.

3. **Leverage your learning and make a plan to activate quick wins.** You have gained new understanding of your stakeholders and can show value for your efforts right away.

4. **Execute, gather learning, and celebrate your early wins.** This is a great way to build confidence in the value of the Business Design. It will also signal the start to pursuit of your longer-term vision and will motivate the team.

Tips

▶ Ideas do not have to be expensive. Sometimes a small, simple tactic at the right place and time can generate surprising outcomes.

▶ Don't forget to cut things off your current project list that you now know aren't going to create value.

WHAT MIGHT THIS LOOK LIKE?

Here are two examples of low-risk/high-value quick wins:

New insights might lead to you recast a short-term promotional effort to be more relevant and in keeping with your new vision.

In the healthcare case presented in chapter 4 (on Gear 1), implementing an expanded "fast track" initiative for patients who presented specific symptoms was immediately doable and valuable.

ORGANIZATIONAL STRUCTURE
TEAMING UP TO GET THE JOB DONE

WHY DO WE DO THIS?

To organize people to most effectively deliver your solution to the market-place. New ideas often call for re-examining the way you work together to most productively deliver new ideas. Bigger, transformational ideas might call for a radical restructuring. Smaller projects might call for a flexible way of "teaming" people around a specific initiative. In either case, the key is to align your talent and incentives to the job to be done. This is an opportunity to prototype different ways of structuring your organization or your teams.

HOW CAN YOU DO THIS?

1. **Center team design on the solution to be delivered.** Reflect on your strategy and your envisioned experience, with the customer at the center. *For example, in the case of HSO (chapter 6 story), its core strategy to win is to integrate the voices of all stakeholders into its standards-development process.*

2. **Identify the critical expertise needed to most effectively deliver your solution to the market.** Consider whose perspective and know-how will lead to the best outcome and customer experience. *In the case of HSO, an integrated team of patients, clinicians, and health-systems experts all bring valuable insights to standards development aimed at improving patient outcomes.*

3. **Design the team and how its members might work together and with the rest of your enterprise.** Determine if these teams are part of a business unit, a central team that serves the broader organization, or a specialized delivery team embedded into your operations. Ask, *What is this team responsible for and how do they fit into the broader operations and structure of the organization?*

4. **Establish goals, roles, and responsibilities.** Define the team's collective goals and how team success will be measured: *Business results? Customer satisfaction? Internal performance?* Designate one person to bring together and lead the team, and designate the roles of each individual on the team. Decide what role they will each play and what they will be accountable for.

5. **Prototype, experiment, and refine.** Explore a variety of ways to work as a team and chose one that best fits operationally with your business and experience goals. You might not get it perfect from the beginning, so be prepared to iterate and build quickly.

6. **Formalize accountability, performance measures, and incentives.** As you optimize your team structure, formalize and set the new team in motion. Be clear on who's accountable for what and align that with both collective goals and personal incentives.

Tips

▶ Prototype! As in every aspect of Business Design, explore and assess several options before jumping into a solution that will set people in motion.

▶ Seek input – from senior executives, the proposed working team, and others in the organization. They will bring valuable perspectives on how this might work – or not – and on how to optimize your team in the context of the broader organization.

▶ Start on a small scale to avoid massive disruption. Be prepared to refine and then formalize on a broader scale.

WHAT MIGHT THIS LOOK LIKE?

Here are two examples of how others have formed new structure and teams to deliver on their strategy and customer experience:

With an aim to deliver solutions that integrate the voices of many stakeholders, HSO established a formal team of patients, clinicians, and health-systems experts to support its standards and assessment development process. This structure ensures that the needs of all stakeholders are considered and that patient outcomes are kept at the center of its development process.

Newtopia, a healthcare tech start-up, separated customer service from coaching and created a two-person "care-specialist team" to enable customers to choose the level of coaching they wanted. Based on the assessment of this team, Newtopia could channel the customer early on into the care and coaching track that best suited the customer's needs.

MANAGEMENT SYSTEMS
DESIGNING SUPPORT SYSTEMS & MEASURING WHAT MATTERS

WHY DO WE DO THIS?

To design support systems for the job to be done, and to define what needs to be measured to assess performance against goals. New value-creating solutions and a new enterprise strategy often call for an evolution or even revolution in management and measurement systems. Inserting a new solution and strategy into existing systems can sometimes be counterproductive. By identifying the support systems required and the measurements needed to gauge success, the enterprise will be able to make business decisions that support responsible progress. It is critical to be explicit in these areas and ensure alignment at the outset. The key questions you will need to address are, *What systems need to be put in place to execute effectively? What do you need to measure, and how will you measure the things that matter most?*

HOW CAN YOU DO THIS?
Management Systems

Consider the management systems needed to support your quest, using the following guidelines:

1. **What systems need to be in place to execute effectively?** These could include new go-to-market systems, inventory-management systems, quality-control systems, communication systems, or recruiting practices. Systems are important because they bring order and alignment, accelerate progress, and enable you to scale effectively.
2. **What systems are currently in place?** In an existing enterprise, these are often a key factor in your go-to-market and operational success.
3. **Leverage and reconcile.** You may have some systems that will give you a good start. You may also have systems that could impede progress because they support the current way of doing business but not the new strategy. Identify the systems you can leverage, those that you will need to establish, and – importantly – where there may be conflict.

4. **Design how your system will integrate and be explicit about conflicts.** This is important in assessing how you will manage your new initiative or strategy and getting alignment from others on how you will move forward.

Measurement

Define the metrics and methods of measurements that will be most relevant and actionable. You can take an approach similar to designing management systems: *How will you measure progress? How does this fit with your current decision-making measures?* Often a new idea calls for measuring new dimensions of progress. Here are some things to consider:

1. **Business results.** Define your goals and the key factors by which you will assess business performance, and include sales (dollars or units), costs, profit, points of distribution, turnover, etc. These may be the same measures you currently use, or you may adjust them. *For example, moving from a low-cost mass-market product to a premium high-end product may require an adjustment to dollar sales (if you are historically a volume-driven manufacturer that aims to maximize capacity utilization).*

2. **Quantitative tracking research.** There are key indicators that you might want to track. Keep your eye on these quantitative measures and course correct as necessary. *For example, net promoter scores are regularly used as an indicator of customer satisfaction.*

3. **Qualitative research.** This will provide new insights that may emerge unexpectedly and which can give you new ideas on how to enhance customer value or correct a deficiency. If certain measurements aren't being met, explore that openly with customers. *Who knows better about what is working or not than your customers?* Instead of assuming that something is broken, conduct interviews with your customers as a source of ongoing discovery, inspiration, and valuable feedback.

Other Tips on Measurement

▶ Prioritize measures, putting what matters most at the top of the list. Focus your measurements on those that are of high value, both in the short term and the long term. This way, you can begin to gather valuable learning and take short-term measures to maximize success.

▶ As with the design of management systems and processes, it is critical to get alignment with key decision-makers on measurements up front. Be clear on what will be measured and why, and how you will measure it. Also include decision-making criteria, much as you defined "expected use of results" in experiments.

ACKNOWLEDGMENTS

A second edition requires some rethinking and retooling to be sure it retains the timeless learning of the first edition, while advancing knowledge and best practices. New learning draws from the insights and skills of a new collection of people. I'll start with those who made this second edition possible, and then recognize the people that help set the foundation in the first edition.

Revised & Expanded Edition

Important new content was generated in collaboration with five key groups: the clients who leveraged Business Design though Vuka Innovation, the people who worked on these projects at Vuka, professional partners who contributed to the deeper thinking and application of Business Design, the Business Design graduates of Rotman who have gone out to test this approach in the real world, and important collaborators in bringing this book to market.

I have had the opportunity to work with some visionary clients. Included in this book are new stories from leaders at Health Standards Organization (Leslee Thompson, CEO), Canadian Bar Association (Cathy Cummings, Re-Think Project Director), Newtopia (Jeff Ruby, CEO), and Canadian Foundation for Healthcare Improvement, (Maureen O'Neil, President). Within the educational realm, Singapore Polytechnic (Joh Liang Hee, Deputy Principal) continues to thrive on design, as its story illustrates in chapter 7. I also drew insights from the work we did with other organizations, including PepsiCo (Kelly Sepcic), Canadian Patient Safety Institute (Chris Power and Kim Stelmacovich), Reliance Home Comfort (Chris Chapman), Higher Education Quality Council of Ontario (Harvey Weingarten and Fiona Deller), Canadian Broadcasting Corporation (Heaton Dyer and Elizabeth Lancaster), and MaRS Solution Lab (Joeri van den Steenhoven).

The team at Vuka Innovation did some incredible project work over the past five years, particularly Stewart Shum, Job Rutgers, David Brown, Tyrenny

Anderson, Dayna Griffiths, Azadeh Houshmand, Patrick Suen, and Matt Zilli. Matt not only contributed to our projects, he led our R&D efforts at Vuka Labs, including development of the Innovation Readiness profiling tool and a pipeline of new digitized tools. Through our evolution of the discipline, all of these people brought devotion and the right skills at the right time to help take the practice of Business Design to a new level.

I deeply value the wisdom and know-how that my long-standing professional partners have contributed to both project work and development projects: Louise Pauze of Happico (collaborator on CBA Re-Think), Job Rutgers (collaborator in education and in our work at Vuka), Mengze Shi (co-creator of Vuka's Innovation Readiness instrument), Helen Giffin (who brought an important HR perspective to Vuka's Innovation Readiness initiative), and Bob Wiele (founder of One Smart World).

I am always inspired by my Business Design students at Rotman and have kept in touch with many of them over the years. It makes my heart sing to see them making such an important impact through their work since graduation. Ashwini Srikantiah is a wonderful example, as exemplified by her Fidelity story in chapter 3.

Bringing a book to life is a major production. University of Toronto Press's Jennifer DiDomenico provided valuable ongoing support through reviews, design, and management of the project, as she did in the first edition. Will Novosedlik helped transform interviews into insightful stories, brought his talent for editorial clarity and "reduction" to the book, and put his design skills to work on the figures. Many of Eugene Grichko's figure designs from the first book are carried over to this edition. Designer Ingrid Paulson gave the new edition a fresh new look. Editor Catherine Plear brought further clarity and precision to the content. Janice Evans translated the final manuscript into a well-presented book. Ashley Miller played the critical role of managing all of the moving parts in writing, clearances, edits, and figure design.

As noted in the first book, my family is always supportive of my pursuits. My husband, Neil, is an innovator at heart, and his executive perspective on the strategic and pragmatic aspects of Business Design is always helpful. He gave me the space to write and was a helpful sounding board along the way. My daughter Ceilidh, a talented and ambitious designer, is always an inspiration to me in everything I do and reminds me of the importance of finding meaning in our everyday work. My late parents continue to be a memory of inspiration for combining their talents for analysis (my dad) and creativity (my mom), and doing what you love with remarkable people in your journey.

First Edition

This revised and expanded edition would certainly not be possible without the foundation of the first book, and the people who made that possible. At the top of that list is Roger Martin, former dean of the Rotman School of Management at University of Toronto – a visionary leader with the foresight to stake out important new territory in explicitly integrating design into business education and practice. He was an invaluable coach to me as we built Rotman's Strategy Innovation Lab, DesignWorks.

DesignWorks would not be a force today if not for the support of our benefactors who were committed to advancing business education. Marcel Desautels's generous contribution to the Rotman School funded the start-up of DesignWorks. The late Joseph Rotman, whose name is on this world-renowned school, also spent time with students on many occasions, instilling in them the need for entrepreneurial thinking and a design-inspired approach to building a business.

Within the educational space, there are some particularly important people who contributed to the early integration of design and business. David Kelley, a life-long innovator who co-founded IDEO and established Stanford's d.school, was one of our original collaborators, as was Patrick Whitney, Dean of the Institute of Design at Illinois Institute of Technology, and Vijay Kumar in the early days of our Procter & Gamble training. Jules Goss of the Ontario College of Art & Design University (OCADU) brought his design perspective and industrial design students to our first summer fellowship program and our first joint course in 2006. Job Rutgers, also of OCADU, contributed to our quest in Singapore and has been an ongoing design partner in advancing our educational collaboration. During our early years, I collaborated with Jeanne Liedtka of the University of Virginia's Darden School of Business, Sara Beckman of the University of California's Haas School of Business, and Nathan Shedroff of the California College of the Arts to bring value to our respective students, culminating in our shared 2010 award from the Academy of Management in teaching design principles and practices to MBA students.

Our early days DesignWorks pursuit would not have been as relevant or pragmatic if not for enterprise leaders who embraced the principles of Business Design as a means to unleash greater potential in their organizations through both training and project work. At the top of that list is Procter & Gamble, with Claudia Kotchka leading the charge of expanding design thinking across the organization globally, and sharing her wisdom in the last chapter of this edition. Cindy Tripp was instrumental in codifying and expanding design thinking training to every corner of the P&G world.

Other industry pioneers who gave us a canvas to hone training methodologies and demonstrate the potential of Business Design through projects showcased in the stories in both editions of this book include the world-class Princess Margaret Hospital (led by Sarah Downey at the time), the team at Medtronic, and the Nestlé Confectionery team (led by Sandra Martinez and Elizabeth Frank). There were a host of other companies who engaged in learning programs and supported research projects that contributed to important learning.

At a higher economic level, Singapore is a country that has fully embraced the potential of Business Design. Philip Yeo saw huge value in bringing Business Design to Singapore in his role as chairman of SPRING and special advisor for economic development in the prime minister's office in 2008. Debbie Ng helped make that happen. The Singapore Polytechnic team, led by Principal Tan Hang Cheong and Deputy Principal Joh Liang Hee at the time, took on the mission of bringing this new discipline to their country as a means of both educating a new generation and bringing out the best in established entrepreneurs. Back in Canada, Glen Murray, Minister of Research and Innovation for Ontario in 2010/2011, saw the tremendous potential of Business Design to boost the Canadian economy and brought the Singapore program back to Canada.

There were others with whom I did not work directly, but who generously offered their insights and stories in the first edition, which are brought forward into this edition: Guillaume Le Cunff and Hans-Joachim Richter of Nespresso shared insights on their path to success; Isadore Sharp of Four Seasons Hotels and Resorts graciously shared his insights on both the human and the strategic side of building a successful enterprise; Sir Richard Branson, the visionary behind the Virgin Group, shared his insights on how to build a customer-centric business and an enterprise culture of breaking the mold in a strategic way (with the support of Andrew Bridge and Christine Choi); Earl Bakken, co-founder of Medtronic shared his wisdom on the value of dreams and intuition.

Our early body of knowledge and evidence that Business Design *works* would not be where it is today without the commitment of the early team at DesignWorks. Haris Blentic was the first to enlist in the P&G challenge. Mark Leung and Eugene Grichko signed up in 2006 and contributed to important research projects, including the Princess Margaret Hospital project presented in this book. Grace Park brought energy and fresh insight to our executive workshop programs and enterprise coaching. Stefanie Schram contributed to projects while developing and delivering our executive training programs. David Brown brought his entrepreneurial spirit to our quest in Singapore, along with Stewart Shum who managed this huge undertaking. Carolyn Meacher brought her experience and expertise in innovation coaching to our work. Danielle Waxer helped orchestrate the many interviews and clearances required for the publication of the first edition. A special thanks to Alpesh Mistry, a long-standing member of the early DesignWorks team and my primary collaborator on the first edition. This core team made an important contribution to MBA student learning, executive training, research, and the publication of the first edition.

There were other important Rotman collaborators who brought expertise and insights to our early work: Mengze Shi (my partner in the first MBA Business Design Practicum), Brian Golden (who opened the doors to the Princess Margaret Hospital project), Melanie Carr (leadership and personal development expert), and Maria Rotundo (organizational behavior and culture expert).

I have tremendous gratitude and respect for all those who generously offer their wisdom, support, and energy in contributing to the shared goal of helping people create new value in this ever-changing world.

NOTES

1   Singapore, *Report of the Economic Strategies Committee* (Singapore: Ministry of Finance, 2010).

2   Quotations from enterprise leaders in executive workshops held between 2005 and 2016.

3   Eric Goldschein, "11 Incredible Facts about the Global Coffee Industry," November 2011. https://www.businessinsider.com/facts-about-the-coffee-industry-2011-11.

4   Hans-Joachim Richter and Anna Lundstrom, Nestlé Nespresso S.A. Corporate Communications, correspondence with Heather Fraser, August–October 2011. Supplemented by https://www.nestle-nespresso.com/about-us/facts-and-figures and https://www.pressreader.com/bahrain/bloomberg-businessweek-europe/20160704/281599534810855.

5   Developed in 2005 by Heather Fraser and Roger Martin in collaboration with David Kelley and Patrick Whitney.

6   Participant from a Singapore Polytechnic management workshop held at Singapore Polytechnic in Singapore, February 2011.

7   A.G. Lafley and Roger L. Martin, *Playing to Win: How Strategy Really Works* (Boston: Harvard Business School Press, 2013). Reprinted by permission of Harvard Business Review Press. From *Playing to Win* by A.G. Lafley and Roger L. Martin. Boston, MA, 2013, pages 14–15 . Copyright © 2013 by Harvard Business Publishing; all rights reserved.

8   Heather Fraser, "Business Design: Becoming a Bilateral Thinker," *Rotman Magazine*, Winter (2011): 70–6.

9   Business Design Process, Vuka Innovation, 2016.

10   One Small World, Bob Wiele.

11   Isadore Sharp, *Four Seasons: The Story of a Business Philosophy* (New York: Portfolio, 2009).

12   Isadore Sharp, interview by Heather Fraser, 4 May 2011.

13   Based on a strategic planning initiative led by Sandra Martinez, President, Nestlé Confectionery Canada, and Elizabeth Frank, Vice-President, Marketing, Nestlé Confectionery Canada, in 2008.

14   Elizabeth Frank, interview by Heather Fraser, 3 August 2011. All quotations from Elizabeth Frank in this book have been sourced from this interview.

15   Vuka Innovation Readiness Survey is a proprietary diagnostic tool developed at Vuka Innovation by Heather Fraser, Matt Zilli, and Mengze Shi, 2016–18.

16   Canadian Bar Association Re-Think Project, 2014. Project team: Vuka Innovation (Heather Fraser, Stewart Shum, Tyrenny Anderson, and Dayna Griffiths) and Happico (Louise Pauzé, Alicia Pace, Daniel Séguin, and Martin Ouellette). All methodological examples in this book are based on this project.

17   Cathy Cummings, CBA interview by Heather Fraser, 15 September 2017.

18   Based on interviews with Leslee Thompson, CEO of Health Standards Organization (HSO), by Heather Fraser, and the Strategic Transformation Project, 2016–17. Vuka Innovation team members: Heather Fraser, Tyrenny Anderson, Patrick Suen, Matt Zilli, Job Rutgers, and Dayna Griffiths. All quotes and methodological examples related to this project in this book are based on this interview and project work.

19 Ashwini Srikantiah, Fidelity, interview by Heather Fraser, 19 September 2017.

20 For reasons of confidentiality, some details of the project have been omitted. Story based on Rotman DesignWorks Project: Cardiac Patient Pathways Project Plan, 2007. Faculty lead: Heather Fraser. Team members: Jasmin Kwak, Alpesh Mistry, Sandra Ochoa, Rohit Singla.

21 Heart and Stroke Foundation, "Position Statement on CPR," October 2010. https://resuscitation .heartandstroke.ca/guidelines/position/CPR.

22 Dante Morra, MD, correspondence with Heather Fraser, August 2008.

23 Adapted from Vijay Kumar and Patrick Whitney, "Faster, Cheaper, Deeper User Research," *Design Management Journal*, Spring (2003): 50–7.

24 SPICE framework based on an analysis of a multi-project database of need-finding research outcomes conducted by Heather Fraser in collaboration with Eugene Grichko, 2007–8.

25 North Hawaii Community Hospital, "NHCN Celebrates 15th Anniversary," 7 June 2011. www.queens .org/north-hawaii/north-hawaii-community-hospital.

26 Earl Bakken, *One Man's Full Life* (Minneapolis: Medtronic Inc., 1999).

27 Earl Bakken, interview by Heather Fraser, 5 June 2011. All quotations from Earl Bakken in this book are sourced from this interview.

28 Based on Rotman DesignWorks Project: Princess Margaret Hospital-Systemic Therapy Redesign, 2007. Team members and contributors included: Princess Margaret Hospital (Sarah Downey, Dr Mark Minden, Janice Stewart, Sara Urowitz, and Dr David Wiljer), Rotman DesignWorks (Heather Fraser, Eugene Grichko, and Mark Leung), Rotman School of Management (Brian Golden and Rosemary Hannam), and donors Conway Foundation and MDS (John Rogers and Ron Yamada). Additional reference: Brian R. Golden, Rosemary Hannam, Heather Fraser, Mark Leung, Sarah Downey, Janice Stewart, and Eugene Grichko, "Improving the Patient Experience through Design," *Healthcare Quarterly* 14, no. 3 (2011): 32–41.

29 Vijay Kumar and Patrick Whitney, "Faster, Cheaper, Deeper User Research," *Design Management Journal*, Spring (2003): 50–7.

30 Workshop collaboration with David Kelley, December 2005.

31 Website source on Dyson vacuum: https://www.dyson.com.sg/community/about-dyson.aspx.

32 Sir Richard Branson and Virgin Management USA Corporate Communications, interview correspondence with Heather Fraser, March–October 2011.

33 Based on the HSO Strategy Transformation Project with Vuka Innovation, 2016–17.

34 Michael E. Porter, "What Is Strategy?" *Harvard Business Review*, November–December (1996): 61–78.

35 Hans-Joachim Richter and Anna Lundstrom, Nestlé Nespresso S.A. Corporate Communications, correspondence with Heather Fraser, August–October 2011.

36 Inspired by work with Roger Martin, 2005.

37 Guillaume Le Cunff, correspondence with Heather Fraser, August–September 2011.

38 Jeff Ruby, CEO of Newtopia, interview by Heather Fraser, 13 September 2017. All quotations from Jeff Ruby and the Newtopia examples in this book have been sourced from this interview.

39 Maureen O'Neil, President of the Canadian Foundation for Healthcare Improvement, interview by Heather Fraser, 29 September 2017. All quotes and methodological examples related to this project in this book are based on this interview and project work at Vuka Innovation, 2015.

40 Based on Joh Liang Hee, Deputy Principle of Singapore Polytechnic, and Siak Koon Goh, Singapore, correspondence with Heather Fraser, August 2017; also based on Rotman DesignWorks work 2010–11.

41 Meeting between Philip Yeo, CEO of SPRING Singapore, and Heather Fraser, 2006.

42 Tan Hang Cheong, Past Principle of Singapore Polytechnic, discussion with Heather Fraser, 2011.

43 Joh Liang Hee, Deputy Principle of Singapore Polytechnic, correspondence with Heather Fraser, 23 August 2017.

44 Claudia Kotchka, interview by Heather Fraser, 22 July 2011. All quotations from Claudia Kotchka in this book have been sourced from this interview.

45 Vuka Innovation Readiness Survey is a proprietary enterprise diagnostic tool developed at Vuka Innovation by Heather Fraser, Matt Zilli, and Mengze Shi, 2016–18.

46 The Marshmallow Challenge was initially created by Peter Skillman, the former VP of Design at Palm, Inc.

47 Business Design Practicum, 2010. Royal Conservatory of Music course project brief by Heather Fraser.

48 Vuka Innovation Inc. Blueprint, 2016.

49 Peter Schwartz, *The Art of the Long View: Planning for the Future* (New York: Currency Doubleday, 1991).

50 Based on early Rotman DesignWorks work with Procter & Gamble, in collaboration with Stanford and Illinois Institute of Technology Institute of Design, 2005–6.

51 Roger Martin, *The Opposable Mind: How Successful Leaders Win through Integrative Thinking* (Boston: Harvard Business School Press, 2007).

52 Inspired by work with Roger Martin, 2005.

53 Donna Bonde, "Qualitative Interviews: When Enough Is Enough," White Paper, 2013.

54 Vijay Kumar and Patrick Whitney, "Faster, Cheaper, Deeper User Research," *Design Management Journal*, Spring (2003): 50–7.

55 Ibid.

56 Based on Singapore Polytechnic WISH Project, 2010–11. Singapore Polytechnic Team: Keng Hua Chong, Gareth Lai, Kum Yee Lau, Lay Ling Low, Phyllis Peter, and June Tan Teck. All methodological examples related to this project in this book are based on this project work.

57 Ibid.

58 Roger Martin, *The Opposable Mind: How Successful Leaders Win through Integrative Thinking* (Boston: Harvard Business School Press, 2007).

59 Based on Strategy Project for CHFI, 2015. Vuka Innovation team members: Heather Fraser and Tyrenny Anderson.

60 Constantinos Markides and Daniel Oyon, "Changing the Strategy at Nespresso: An Interview with Former CEO Jean-Paul Gaillard," *European Management Journal* 18, no. 3 (2000): 296–301.

INDEX

innovation leadership, 131–3; innovation pipeline, 138–42; innovation readiness, 38–9, 46, 116–17, 141, 153–4 (*See also under* Vuka Innovation); inspiring innovation, 135–8; as nature of business, 1

innovation dashboard, 130, 141–2

interviews, 216–8; with business leaders, 27–8, 41–3, 55–6, 74, 91–2, 119–22, 123–4, 144; data analysis, 227–9; summarizing, 221–2; tips for conducting, 217; transcriptions, 227

intrinsic motivation, 18, 72, 77, 141, 160

Intuit, 140

iterative prototyping, 85, 87, 131, 136; definition, 20, 250–2; at Fidelity labs, 54, 56; in Gear 3, 111; monetizing as, 270; necessity of, 87; at Newtopia, 121; at Princess Margaret Hospital, 78

Jobs, Steve, 83

journals. *See* user journals

Kelley, David, 2, 86

Kotchka, Claudia, 3, 133, 134, 143; interview with, 144

Krups, 13, 104, 269

Lafley, A.G., 3, 134

landscape of players, 47, 49, 102, 180–1, 196, 274

Le Cunff, Guillaume, 115

Lillehei, Dr. C. Walton, 74

LinkedIn, 13

listening and recording, 216–18; conducting an interview, 217; importance of, 19, 62, 67–8, 137; in photo elicitation, 213

Magimix, 13, 104, 269

management systems, 16, 100, 116, 199, 294–6

mapping: of competencies, 160–1; competitors' activity system, 192–5; current activity system, 187–91; experience mapping, 253–4; future activity system, 281–3; motivational mapping, 225–6; project mapping, 171–2; of stakeholder engagement, 175; of stakeholders, 47, 49, 59, 64, 65, 184–6, 273; examples of, 185–6; systems mapping, 20, 54, 111; team mapping, 160–1. *See also* mind mapping

marshmallow prototyping exercise, 162–3

Martin, Roger, 2, 3, 16, 102, 106, 144

Martinez, Sandra, 30

Medtronic, 3, 73, 83, 106

metaphors, 78, 152, 244, 248–9

methods/activities: activity-system modeling, 102, 284–5; applied learning, 141; asking new questions, 135–6; assessing strategic choices, 198–200; collective, 83; contextualizing through storytelling, 237–8; convergent, 19, 33, 50, 64, 81, 90, 100, 112, 159; defining stakeholder personas, 234–6; discovery exchange, 223–4; divergent, 19, 33, 50, 64, 81, 90, 100, 112; experience mapping, 253–4; fear in a hat, 163–4; financial scenarios, 110; financial-sensitivity analysis, 107, 279–80, 288; framing your ambition, 151–2; ideation and concept harvesting, 243–5; identifying friends and foes, 180–1; interviews, 216–18, 221–2; iterative prototyping, 20, 131, 250–2; listening and recording, 216–18; mapping activity systems, 187–95; mapping of, 171; market sizing, 277–8; marshmallow prototyping exercise, 162–3; metaphors, 78, 248–9; mind mapping, 219–20, 221, 224, 225; modifying practices, 137–8; motivational mapping, 225–6; need mining, 227–9; observation, 19, 72, 173, 207–9, 227–8, 259; photo elicitation, 213–15; project blueprints, 32, 36, 171–3; project briefs, 32, 35, 38, 155, 156, 169–70, 204, 210, 213; quantitative, 67–8, 70, 71, 277–8, 295; risk assessment, 288–9; role playing, 202–3, 246–7, 257–8; running numbers, 107; scenario planning, 182–3; small-scale experimentation, 89; soliciting user feedback, 259–60; STEEP analysis, 177–9; storyboarding, 255–6; surveys, 153–4, 232–3; synthesizing value, 265–6; team mapping, 160–1; user journals, 210–12, 216, 220, 224, 231; variety of, 98; video script, 239; virtual feedback, 88, 262–3; visualizing, 59, 78, 85–6, 90, 102; as a way of doing business, 19–21. *See also* experimentation; prototyping

mind mapping, 219–20, 221, 224, 225; example of, 220

mindsets, 17–19; for contextualizing your challenge, 54; in Gear 1, 72–3; in Gear 2, 89–90; in Gear 3, 110–11, 117–18; for preparing for your quest, 39

motivational mapping, 225–6

multiple prototyping. *See* iterative prototyping

need-finding, 39, 65, 66–7, 70, 72, 118; definition, 19; research for, 204–6

needs: as basis for 3 gears, 13–14; as basis for value creation, 66–7; and Gear 1, 24; ideation of, 243–5; multidimensional, 68; need articulation, 230–1; need mining, 227–9; universal, 41, 64, 71, 95, 135, 204, 225, 228, 232–3. *See also* unmet needs

Nespresso. *See under* Nestlé